LEGENDS LIES MYTHS OF FINANCIAL PLANNING

that

Your Financial Advisor may not

explain or be aware of

Over thirty powerful strategies for

Personal

and

Financial Success

by

Lyle Manery, CLU, CH.F.C.

Legends Lies Myths was written to provide accurate informative information. It was not my intent to give legal advice in any way, except that you should consult a lawyer on all legal matters. All advice and information regarding life insurance, annuities and investments was general in nature and it may not apply specifically to any individual. In this regard, neither the author nor the publisher can accept any liability or loss, personal or otherwise, which may be incurred as a consequence directly or indirectly, from the use or application of any of the contents of this book. Throughout the book, the author has consistently advised that everyone should obtain professional advice from competent, qualified advisors.

Published by Lyalta Publishing
Division of Lyalta Management And Realty Ltd.
1403 - 2nd St. S. W.
Calgary, Alberta T2R 0W7

Telephone: (403) 233-2558
Fax: (403) 264-3348
Toll Free: 1–888–322-2558

Canadian Cataloguing in Publication Data

Manery, Lyle. 1935–
Legends lies myths of financial planning that your financial advisor may not explain or be aware of: over thirty powerful strategies for personal and financial success.

Canadian ed.
Includes bibliographical references.
ISBN 0–9699101–4–2

1. Financial, Personal I. Title

HG179.M37 1998 332.024'01 C98-911058-3

Cover Design: Robert Freeman

Printed and bound In Canada
by
Friesens Corporation

TRIBUTE TO CAIFA

O, be some other name!
What's in a name? That which we call a rose
By any other name would smell as sweet.
~ Act II. Scene 2
Romeo & Juliet

The name Canadian Association of Insurance and Financial Advisors, aptly describes the activities of the members of my chosen profession. It modernizes an image that has served us well for many years and me personally throughout my short career.

In 1956, when I began my life as a salesman, the organization was known as the Life Underwriters Association of Canada. In spite of the obvious conclusion that CAIFA is a more appropriate descriptive name for our association today, some of us will always retain a spot in our hearts and in our memories for the old moniker, LUAC. Ah, but what is in a name? Without the dedicated employees, and the volunteers from our membership of more than 18,000, what would we be? It would be nothing special to be sure. Will the modernization of our name make us an even superior organization? Of course not—not by itself, but the staff and volunteers who serve the organization are doing it. They are doing better every day in nearly every way; not by improving in any one area by a thousand percent, but rather, by doing a thousand things just one percent better each time.

Since its early days, LUAC gave salespeople an organized way to intermingle and become acquainted with their peers. It also provided the opportunity to hear qualified speakers explain about developments in the business. In 1957, a pilot course for a new training program was inaugurated in my town, London, Ontario. One of my associates, Murrough (Pat) O'Brien, was part of that trial course. In 1958, I embarked on my educational journey with L.U.A.T.C. and continued through with CLU and CH.F.C., professional designations of which I am proud.

Interestingly, at least to me, I was part of the first established class for L.U.A.T.C. in London, and also of the first for CH.F.C. in Calgary. These courses have been of great value to me and I thank all those who developed them, supported them, and kept them up-to-date. LUAC, by providing current advice and information, has made it so much easier to serve my clients. There were many people, over these forty plus years, who helped me along my way as an insurance and financial advisor. To name them all would be impossible here, but I do remember their deeds. They helped me in my vocation, directly and indirectly, and I do appreciate it. Many of my associates are equally thankful for help received; but they, like me, fail to express their appreciation, other than on rare occasions. When an organization is really good, we just take it for granted.

There are many benefits of membership in CAIFA and every licensed advisor should know about them. If you do not know, you may call 1-800-563-5822 and ask for the most recent information available. What this organization has done and is doing for our members is too complex and important to describe in one short tribute.

That's not all. The public, our clients, have benefited directly over the years in many ways, much of which they will never know about unless we tell them. Nevertheless, the nearly continuous negotiation with governments to maintain the integrity of our product ~ our clients' life, health, and investment policies, has resulted in many good things. Simultaneously, and of equal importance, our associates in CAIFA have been successful in diverting some potentially bad things. It is with great pride that I can tell you that CAIFA works *with* governments at all levels to protect the valuable assets for our clients. The staff at CAIFA is ready at all times to provide the members and our clients with timely information. Another value added service offered is the customer service department at 1-800-307-0206. Also, we have a web site at www.caifa.com. Check them out.

In addition to my sentiments expressed above, I am thankful for the CAIFA staff regarding my *avocation*, as a writer; especially Linda Benoit and her associates. Their enthusiastic, positive attitudes have been most encouraging. Thank you, Linda. Thank you CAIFA.

Acknowledgements

Many of my associates made significant contributions in the preparation of this book. Their support came in many ways. Some of them suggested topics for review. Several people provided newspaper or magazine articles that covered subject matter with inaccurate or incomplete information. Others asked questions which, when answered, provided the basis for one or more of the essays in this book. A number of my associates read and critiqued portions of the manuscript and offered valuable insights and appropriate advice.

Among the many who were helpful, the following individuals are gratefully acknowledged for their special contribution, encouragement and support.

* Dennis Bennett
* Emery Eslinger
* Robert Freeman
* Carole Jeffries
* Allan Johnson
* Rani Lally
* Brian Lee CPS
* Peter Maddocks
* Darryl Manery
* Betty Manery
* Ned Mazur
* Roy Olney
* Nick Perrin
* Frank Rigby
* Regan Stoshnof
* Janet Brigden Strokappe (Dr.)
* Eileen Whyte
* Russ Young

Legends Lies Myths–Financial Planning

Contents /6

ABOUT THE BOOK

This book, *Legends Lies Myths,* evolved from a series of articles that I wrote in order to dispel some of the misinformation which was disturbing some of my clients. As topics occurred to me, from whatever source, I recorded them and filed them for future reference. The subject matter came from conversations with clients and associates; from radio and television programs; and especially from the published material of other authors.

Sometimes when I jotted down something about the topic of my interest or concern, I would write a few lines of explanation. Usually that was enough to cause me to expand it in detail. After writing about ten articles, in this way, I decided to have them typed, for easier review and editing. At first, there was no evidential connection between them other than;

(a) they all pertained to my business;

(b) they were all inspired by some disturbing source or comment;

(c) they have potential value for clients or associates.

At the time these somewhat disjointed essays were written there was no structural design relating to a book. Actually some of the articles never made it to this book. A few of them only managed to get in via the addendum.

As the number of articles grew, I became enthused about writing another book. In truth it was always in the back of my mind—someday. Obviously, I was involved, already, with the basics of a new book. My purpose was to provide information in an entertaining way. My objective was to dispel as many misleading myths about financial matters as possible. These thoughts flowed through my arm to the yellow paper and then to the typed page, thanks to my wife, helpmate, and foremost critic. My associate Allan Johnson read and critiqued every line written. Several clients contributed their valuable insights, and many of my associates offered critical and editorial advice. All of their contributions are truly appreciated. Now I can blame them for any errors. Okay?

In spite of all the developing subject matter, no one phrase described them succinctly. Some of my associates suggested titles such as, *Financial Planning for Dummies* or *Financially Speaking for Dummies*. Actually it has been done.

• *Personal Finance for Dummies for Canadians*
by Eric Tyson and Tony Martin.

Let's see now: Eric Tyson, an American, born in the United States, educated in the United States, living and working in the United States, telling Canadians how to do it. That seems like *par for the course*. Tony Martin, I guess, is along for the Canadian content.

• *The complete IDIOT'S Guide to Personal Finance for Canadians*
by Bruce McDougall and Michael Reardon.

Who are these guys? What are their credentials to write a book on financial matters? There seems to be something missing in this book, such as, the page *about the authors.* The only thing I could find is the following: "Do you feel like an idiot when it comes to finance? So do we. That's why we wrote this book." *Okay!* Now I understand. Enough spoofing!

It was never my intent to write for dummies and a real dummy would not understand it anyway. So this book was written for the normally intelligent; those capable of understanding the terminology and the concepts, but who just do not have the time to find the answers. Some of my clients said, "We enjoyed your book *No Salesman Will Call?*, but couldn't you write a book that makes it easier for us to utilize? Perhaps you could leave out some of the mathematics and calculations." Well okay, I can do that.

Throughout this book, the question of qualifications to write or speak on the various topics will be raised. The matter of credentials and their importance will be examined. How valuable is experience? If you are looking for an advisor, how do you choose one? Whom should you take advice from, journalists, celebrities, authors, scholars or friends and neighbors? Should you get your advice from books, the internet, television and radio, magazines, or newspapers?

Should you follow the recommendations of those with knowledge and experience, or do you prefer to rely on popular opinion? The answer is, hopefully, that you will want advice from those who are qualified to provide it. If so, it may be wise to challenge the knowledge and experience of every advisor. How do you do that? For starters, does she or he have professional designations such as CLU, or CFP, or CH.F.C.

What is a CLU ? One of my brothers used to say that it is proof that I am not clueless. What it really means is that to become a CLU or a Chartered Life Underwriter it was necessary to spend a number of years studying life insurance in all aspects. It was necessary to study some rather technical material while working at the same time in the life insurance business. EXPERIENCE is the best teacher. The official definition of CLU is: *A Chartered Life Underwriter is a financial planner with advanced knowledge in life and health insurance and employee benefits.*

A CFP is a Certified Financial Planner with an emphasis on investment products, especially mutual funds. You must qualify as a CFP before you can obtain a CLU or a CH.F.C.

What's a CH.F.C.? According to one of the shop owners on my beat, it stands for Chairman of the Football Club. It would surprise the president of our club if three hundred or so of us show up brandishing our badges of office. The official definition is: *A Chartered Financial Consultant is a financial planner with advanced knowledge in wealth accumulation and retirement planning.*

"But," some wag commented, "does having one or more of these designations make you smarter than the authors who wrote those other books? Some of them have Ph.D., after their names."

Right. So what? According to another one of my brothers all that means is "Piled higher and deeper." (I would name the brothers who made these observations, but they would expect financial remuneration.)

"But really now, a Ph.D., means something really big doesn't it? Anyone who has a right to use these initials must be super intelligent, don't you agree?"

Of course! If one has a Ph.D., it means that a University has conferred a Doctorate on him or her. We refer to them as Doctor. However, we need to know—Doctor of what? Doctor of Medicine? Doctor of Divinity? Doctor of Philosophy? Doctor of Education?

We need to know the discipline in which the doctorate was obtained and the name of the university that conferred the degree. I know a gentleman who obtained a Ph.D., from my alma mater. He completed his thesis on the study of the strawberry leaf. I do not tell you this to belittle his degree nor his intelligence. He is a very intelligent person and he earned his degree from a highly respectable university. I respect him and his knowledge, but I would not consult him about financial matters. In fact, he is intelligent enough to defer to a Chartered Financial Consultant on matters pertaining to life insurance, estate planning, and estate conservation.

Some people may wonder if I am saying that you should consult only with people who have a CLU or CH.F.C. Let me assure you that is not my point. My advice is to consult only with someone who can demonstrate a reasonable level of professionalism. Having one or more of these designations or studying toward them is an indication that your advisor has gone beyond the basics required to get a license. Unfortunately, a license to sell life insurance or mutual funds does not guarantee that the licensee has the knowledge to be your advisor. Beware of those licensed agents who brag that it only took five hours of study and training to become a *financial planner*.

On the other hand, having one or more of these designations does not automatically guarantee that the bearer is truly knowledgeable. It proves that she could pass the necessary exams, but can she apply her knowledge to help you prepare for your financial future? Probably she can in most cases, but not necessarily always. Usually, evidence of a CLU or CH.F.C. is an indication that the bearer has spent a number of years actually earning a living while studying for the designation. In the past, to become a CH.F.C., you must have acquired the CLU designation first. However, in the future, one may be able to study for either one, because the study program has gone to a modular system. You can now study on a need to know basis.

CLU studies tend to be somewhat technical; while CH.F.C., studies are based on a more practicable approach. Neither course is a breeze. *Both courses require concentrated study.*

How about those who do not have one or more designations? Well, firstly, I believe everyone in our business should be studying to obtain a designation, but there are some highly successful agents who have never obtained any insurance designations. They study about, and learn everything they need to know, regarding the area in which they specialize. It seems to me that some self-taught individuals have to study even more intently to gain the requisite knowledge.

One specialist, known to me, is so knowledgeable in his area of expertise that he is in demand to address CLU Chapters even though he does not have a CLU nor any equivalent designation. He is so successful that CLUs and others frequently consult him on very complicated matters.

There are many fully qualified advisors for your financial program who have not obtained a designation. They have studied and learned as much as is necessary. When they need specialized input, they bring in people with appropriate knowledge and experience. They are willing and able to work with your lawyer, chartered accountant, or tax specialist. These advisors form part of the team and they frequently coordinate the efforts of the individual team members.

However, the majority of the population, those for whom this book was written, do not need all this special knowledge. In the later sections we will give further consideration as to how you should select an agent, or an advisor. Meanwhile, as a generalization, you should require more from agents with less experience. Newer agents should be enrolled in a course of study leading to one of these designations. They should also be working closely with one or more highly qualified people with whom you can consult directly if you so desire. Experience is a great teacher. (See addendum.)

Some say a scholar can study any subject and provide good sound advice. That may be, but there is a double phenomenon involved of which we should be aware. Some people believe that they are authorities, automatically, on any subject on which they wish to comment, even if they have no practical experience. A cerebral approach to the theory may sound extremely erudite and convincing, but in practice without practical knowledge, there may be a serious deficiency.

For example, one of my favorite pastimes is watching children learn to skate. They take a few steps and fall. Soon they learn that it is wise to hold the hands of older more experienced skaters. With this aid the new skater grows in confidence and, as if by magic, the feel of how to balance and push and glide is there. Suddenly the neophyte skater is away all on his own. However, I have to chuckle when I remember the first time the son of one of my best friends tried to skate. Jay, who was four years old, was waiting impatiently to get his skates tied, so he could chase after my sons, who were older and could skate with abandon. The last lace tied; Jay leapt forward only to fall ignominiously on his prat. He tried it again and again with similar results. His dad offered a helping hand, but Jay refused. By now he was not trying to skate. He was crawling. He crawled to a nearby bank of snow (we were outside), and there he sat, hands on his chin, elbows on his knees, staring at the others skating so freely and gracefully. Nearly in tears, he repelled all offers of assistance. Finally, Jay stated with authority, "I'm just going to sit here until I learn to skate." That was funny, perhaps, but not very practicable. *You cannot learn to skate just watching others.*

The second phenomenon, to which we are all prone to err, is the appeal to authority. We often assume that if the writer is a Ph.D., or he is a teacher of business at a college, he must know all about what he is saying. If this academic has authored a book and had it published by a recognizable publishing house, then surely the subject matter must be correct.

Furthermore, we often assume that if libraries have accepted the book on their shelves, it must be accurate. Would well-known book stores carry books in their display that are misleading or misinformative? *You may be sure they do.*

We are all susceptible to this kind of thinking. Nobody is immune. It is a naturally occurring phenomenon. We tend to suffer from a deference to authority. If a person holds a position of some authority, then most people believe that utterances from her, written or verbal, must be right. This attitude gives journalists the license to write on a wide variety of subjects, about which they know little or nothing. Because they can put ideas into words so convincingly, we tend to accept whatever they say or write without a mental challenge. All the better if the writer or speaker makes statements or arguments *with which we can readily agree*. If this pundit makes comments that fit the popular concept, we tend to buy the style and ignore the content, or lack thereof.

As for a publishing house making sure that the content of a book is accurate, who on the staff has the qualifications to make this judgment? Can the editor make knowledgeable decisions based on personal experience? Is that an editor's job? Is it the purpose of the editor of a publishing house to find books that will sell? How does the publishing house make its money? Sales! Sales! Sales! A university press may be more discerning, albeit, and therefore its editors may require a greater degree of accuracy. The subject matter of their concern is more specialized and scholarly, perhaps, but in the final analysis it still must come down to—will someone buy it? Do you believe that a newspaper editor's first concern is the accuracy of the report, or is it rather, *will it sell papers*? How many of us believe every printed word in the newspaper? Why, then, would we believe the printed word just because, *it's in the book?*

Now regarding book stores, do you really believe that some all knowing person reads every book and determines the suitability of the subject matter for the buying public? If you do, send this book back. I will refund your money. An individual book store manager or buyer makes a decision substantially, if not wholly, on the basis of *what will sell*. One book store owner refused one of my books; *No Salesman Will Call?,* on the basis that she did not agree with my point of view. She did not read my book nor study any of the facts. It was enough for her that it criticized the printed thoughts of other authors such as David Chilton's in *The Wealthy Barber* and Charles Givens' in *Wealth Without Risk for Canadians*.

(Another American telling Canadians how to do it.)

These books, after all, were best sellers. I pointed out to her that she carried several other books, that had the same basic premise as those written by Chilton and Givens. On the other hand, there was not even one book that stated an opposing viewpoint. I suggested, that in a progressive store such as hers, her customers should have an opportunity to buy a book that told the *other side of the story*. Unfortunately her mind was frozen solid, like concrete, and she knew my book would not sell. She was right! She owned the store, and in her store, therefore, it would not sell. Fortunately, she was wrong about it selling elsewhere.

Large publishing houses sometimes offer popular books to book store buyers, with a proviso. "We will supply you with this popular proven seller providing you also take some of our dud stock." *Now* these *duds* get on the shelves. You and I are exposed to them and sometimes we buy, because the title is catchy, or perhaps it's because of the cleverly designed cover.

Not all of the popular books are great buys, chock full of accurate information. *Wealth Without Risk for Canadians* had inaccurate information which, if followed blindly, could be hazardous to your financial stability. However, it is still on the shelves of many of the book stores and libraries of the nation. *The Wealthy Barber,* is a novel, by the author's own admission. When I pointed this out to one book store manager, he said, "But it would never sell as a novel." It does sell as a common-sense guide to successful financial planning, and if it inspires some people to save, it will have served a worthwhile purpose. It falls short, however, in the most important part of all. It does not show you how to *keep it saved*.

As evidence of my comments about publishers and book stores, I offer the two books mentioned above for dummies and idiots. These books are clearly trying to capitalize on the popularity of the other books such as *DOS for Dummies* and *Your Computer for Dummies*. Such books may have been very helpful for those who, being *computer illiterate,* were trying to learn the basics.

It is not the purpose of *Legends Lies Myths* to critique the books of various and sundry financial writers. My book, *No Salesman Will Call?,* did that. The purpose of this book is to take the con out of the confusion surrounding the subject of life insurance, mutual funds, retirement income funds, retirement savings plans and annuities. An effort will be made to explain terminology and concepts, in context, so everyone can easily understand them. Mathematical examples are few, but some exist for those who wish to study a mathematical proof of the concept. Beyond that, you should consult a knowledgeable advisor for the mathematical evidence as it applies to your individual situation.

We believe that you could learn whatever you want to know from various sources, but that you would like to have it all available in one clearly stated reference resource. To do so, it is necessary to assume that you have little or no knowledge of the subject material. To help you understand the terminology, there is a chapter at the end of the book which expands on definitions.

About the title; I wanted to call this book MYTHS AMERICA, however my associates convinced me that this was too *broad* in scope. Consequently, I settled on the name Exploding Myths and we actually registered that title. However, as the structure of this book developed, the concept expressed by the title, *Legends Lies Myths,* emerged as a more accurate description of the content.

In this book legend or history is obvious. Myths are clearly indicated. Lies? Well, lies are more subtly disguised. The purpose of a lie, after all, is to mislead others to the advantage of the liar. The difference between a myth and a lie may be a matter of belief. Financial myths obtain a modicum of stature because they seem to provide a plausible explanation of things not so easily understood. It should be an interesting exercise for the reader to discover the lie, the myth, and the truth.

A legend, as you know, is a story or collection of stories about some wonderful event, which has been handed down for generations from person to person. A belief develops that there is an historical basis to these stories, even though it is not verifiable.

A lie is a statement known to be false, that is made with the intent to deceive or give a false impression.

A myth is a traditional narrative, usually involving supernatural or imaginary persons and embodying popular ideas or natural social phenomena. It is often a widely held, but false notion.

In your journey of discovery, you may read each topic or subject myth in any order. It is not necessary to read from front to back. Nearly all topics reviewed, are on a stand alone basis. However, there may be some overlapping of concepts and some repetition.

My intent, in the pages that follow, is to provide information and advice surrounding the topic in an entertaining way. Most of this advice is general in nature; therefore it may not be adequate for any individual. Everyone should review any thoughts developed from these essays with their own advisors for specific application. Likewise, there is no intent to offer any legal advice; rather my advice throughout the book is to check with your legal advisor on all matters pertaining to anything of a legal nature.

Will Rogers spoke to the United States congress on one occasion. There was some concern, at the time, about German U-boats attacking the shipping lanes. Rogers advised them, "Bring the ocean to a boil. Everyone knows that anything in a boiling pot will rise to the top. When the U-boats come up, you can simply shoot them off the water."

There was general laughter, of course, then someone asked;

"Mr. Rogers, how do we bring an ocean to boil?"

Will Rogers' reply was a classic;

"I will give you the ideas—you work out the details."

MORE ABOUT MYTHS

Financial myths are often stories, or attempted explanations, about poorly understood matters that have grown in status in spite of the historical inaccuracies surrounding them. Perhaps at one time, there was some element of truth, or some basis in fact in the tale which provided an acceptable explanation about something that could not be easily understood. In some cases, there may have been a time frame in which there was a degree of accuracy. However, by continually moving the goal posts to make the necessary adjustments, the proponents of the myth could continue to justify the data on which they based their assumptions. In this way the myth becomes a lie.

Many people throughout history have examined the same factual evidence and drawn conclusions that were wildly variant. Cosmologists, biologists, evolutionists, and creationists examined exactly the same data and drew completely different conclusions, reflecting perhaps, the basic beliefs or biases each brought into the investigation. For many generations, one segment of society forced its views on all scientific study. It was heresy, punishable by banishment or death, to advocate that the earth was not flat. To propose that the earth was round and that it revolved around the sun was an unspeakable faux pas. The popular, politically acceptable belief, was that the entire universe revolved around our earth. Now, most of us accept that we, on our tiny planet, are not at the center even in our own solar system. Many beliefs that existed have persisted until the present. What we know, as we have always known it, must be right. Otherwise, why have we always thought so? If it seems to work for us, and if others are advocating the same things that we have always known to be true, it reinforces our viewpoints and concepts.

Facts and figures may need interpretation. If they do not seem to agree with that which we just knew to be true, then we can just ignore them (okay)? We simply accept what we have always known it to be.

This phenomenal tendency to maintain the status quo or to stay with the current popular interpretation without questioning the validity of assumptions and conclusions, is the principle that permits some erroneous reasoning to continue. It allows people form a variety of backgrounds to disseminate inappropriate information. These people assert their views forcefully enough to influence our own basic thinking.

This is the stuff of mythology. Many people find it difficult to accept that certain concepts, if they are inaccurate, are not being challenged by those who supposedly know better. Indeed, why do we not criticize these myth-conceptions? Think about it!

- Some people know the facts but do not want to march against the prevailing winds.
- Some people simply cannot stand against majority opinion.
- Some people have much to gain from advancing the popular theme.
- Some writers and some journalists do not know the facts and they do not understand the basics, but they pontificate authoritatively, nevertheless. Theirs is the ability to record the popular viewpoint in a clear, succinct manner.
- Some report half truths without checking the real story.
- Some may honestly believe that their thinking is correct.
- Some do not know any better.
- Some do not care.

So the myth persists.

Recently, I read the first chapter of a book called *Pay Yourself First* by Timothy W. Cunningham and Clay B. Mansfield. Both of them seem to have backgrounds and experience that would justify a book on the subject of investing with mutual funds and stocks.

However, some red flags ran up the proverbial pole for me when:

- They gave no credit to the author of the phrase "Pay Yourself First," George S. Clason in *The Richest Man in Babylon*. It made me wonder. Do they even know who originated the saying, or is it now so *public domain* that it no longer matters?

• They wrote a section entitled *Beware of Credentialism*. In it they decry the reliance on people with credentials.

The authors define credentialism as *the tendency to judge things not on merit, but on the presumption of merit accorded on the basis of appearance as defined by the supposed significance of the credentials*. Their point of view supports my own and I agree, for the most part, as they continue with the thought that there is no substitute for sound judgment and careful consideration. They say that degrees and titles are just labels. The ability to think is not certifiable. You may ask why I would see a red flag when basically I agree with these statements? Simply, it made me wonder if they were saying these things because they did not have credentials. The authors and I may agree that book learning is not necessarily enough, and that experience over a period of time should accompany formal education. Accountability is even more important than the advisors' credentials. Unless the person or institution providing advice is responsible, and hence accountable for this advice, why would you accept it?

My pet peeve is that so many people have accepted erroneous ideas and concepts, and they continue to believe people who have neither the proper knowledge nor the experience to be addressing the subject. Many people buy books written by these people, and go to sponsored seminars without questioning any credentials. How many people question the biases, at least? That is, from where are the speakers or writers coming? With what basic premises, right or wrong, do they begin? What do they gain from advancing their points of view? If you take a moment to think about it, it's rather obvious in some cases. It may be as simple as a desire to sell a book for profit. It may be a means to a more lucrative end such as speaking engagements. If you attend one of these seminars, you should know at least, who is the sponsor, and what is the sponsor promoting? Knowing these things prepares you to winnow the chaff from the grain.

With this knowledge, you can select between facts and fiction unless of course, you want to be told what you think you already know.

Can you determine my bias? That's easy. I sell life insurance and related products and have done so for over forty years. What is my purpose in writing this book? It is to sell books profitably. That's obvious, but more than that, I hope to simplify the purchase of life insurance and related products by destroying some of the stupid myths that persist, in spite of the evidence to the contrary.

In their book *Pay Yourself First*, the authors gave several examples of myths that, although not supported by facts, still persist.

- They state that Cleopatra was rather plain and had a large hooked nose.
- The Vandals were a mostly respectable group of sea going trading people rather than fearsome marauders.
- Nero did not own a fiddle and he did not set up homeless shelters for the poor after the great fire ravaged Rome.
- Queen Victoria was anything but a prude.
- Niccolo Machiavelli is known for his writings about the darker side of the use of power, but by contemporary accounts he was a mild mannered diplomatic bureaucrat.

How many myths abound which affect the way we think about financial matters and the actions we take toward our financial goals? Are you being buffeted by myths that those on a mission perpetuate? Do popular myths affect your fundamental reasoning and the way you view the world? Do you make some of your financial decisions based on myths disguised as facts?

If you do not think so, you may be in for some surprises.

Concept: Self-Insurance

The modern day concept of insurance evolved from its early beginnings as a relatively simple participatory sharing of a risk by a few involved people to the sophisticated complexity of today's giant corporations. No one knows the exact origin of insurance. Most of the available information comes from insurance text books for various courses of study. Much of the following material, of an historical nature, was taken from a study program provided by *The Insurance Institute of Canada.*

One of the earliest recorded examples of risk sharing, circa 900 B.C., occurred on an island in the Mediterranean. A law was passed which required all ship owners to contribute to a common fund for the purpose of reimbursing any owner who might lose a ship and its cargo.

Another early use of the concept, but without the advanced collection of a premium, was that of some Phoenician merchants shipping their wares on unpredictable seas from country to country. They realized that they could lose the ships and the merchandise they carried in storms or to pirates. Of course, one such loss could ruin a business and its financier.

Trading across the water was a very risky but possibly rewarding business. Similar minded merchants knew that there was wisdom in sharing the risk with each other. The mathematics of such an insurance transaction was simple. If ten merchants participated, each would be risking an amount of money equal to ten percent of the total value of the wares being shipped. No cash changed hands unless a loss occurred. The reward for pledging to share the risk was the knowledge that others would reciprocate when your turn came.

Some sources suggest that Assyria can lay claim to being the birthplace of organized protection against financial disaster from fire and other hazards, such as drought. More than two thousand five hundred years ago, the Governors of some towns and districts were empowered to set up funds, contributed to by individual citizens.

From these funds, certain cases of hardship received a subsidy or a mutual aid payment following a disaster. Later, during the hey day of the Roman Empire, a more advanced scheme was operated by various trade guilds. Their approach was to provide a form of mutual protection against "fire, water, robbery or other calamity." One of these associations, known as *The Guild of St. Thomas*, flourished in the fourteenth century. Its principle was stated as follows: *What man or woman through loss or fire falls into poverty shall be helped by all brethren and sistern of this guild with a portion of their cattle to their power.*

One of the best examples of sharing the risk, without paying a premium, is that of Chinese merchants about six hundred years ago. These merchants shipped their wares on the Yangtze River and, in effect, they practised an early form of cargo insurance. They shared the risk of loss by spreading their cargo among the ships of many merchants. If any one ship was lost, it would not ruin an individual owner.

From the earliest days of commerce, insurance against loss was accepted as a necessary cost of doing business. Even before the beginning of the industrial revolution, risk-takers recognized the benefits of reducing the odds in their favor. There was an obvious need for a readily available source of insurance.

Some of the early attempts at the establishment of insurance programs are listed below:

- In 1574, the British Parliament founded a Chamber of Insurance.
- In 1598, an Insurance Ordinance was issued at Amsterdam.
- In 1601, a Royal Commission was appointed by Queen Elizabeth.
- Until 1666, prior to the "Great Fire of London," fire insurance was provided on a purely mutual basis.
- Shortly after the "Great Fire," Nicholas Barbon set up a business to underwrite fire insurance contracts.
- In 1680, other prominent business men joined Barbon to obtain authority to establish a business known as *The Fire Office*.

- In 1696, the *Amicable Contributionship* was established.
- In 1706, the *Sun Fire Office* was created.
- In 1720, charters were granted to the *London Assurance* and the *Royal Exchange Assurance.*
- In 1777, the *Liverpool Fire Office* was established.
- In 1782, the *Phoenix Fire Office* opened its doors.
- In 1797, the *Norwich Union* began operations.

  Some of our modern day companies are descendants of these pioneers, as may be indicated by a similarity of names.
- By 1799, twenty-two insurance companies existed on the American continent to underwrite marine insurance and fire insurance on buildings and goods.
- In 1804, the *Phoenix Assurance Company Limited* began operations in Montreal, Quebec.
- In 1809, the *Halifax Fire Insurance Company* was organized in Halifax, Nova Scotia.

The chronological order of the above events is really of no great importance other than as an historical reference. The truly notable significance is that each one of the above examples is about business people, in widely variant periods of time and in distant places, who demonstrated a common goal. Although there were three distinctively separate methods used, there was, nevertheless, only one purpose—to *avoid self-insurance.*

Before these remarkable developments, businesses were all *self-insured.* To these merchants, it made sense to risk an affordable percentage of assets against a potentially disastrous loss. Whenever you could find like minded merchants and business people, with whom to exchange and share risks, you could avoid the potentially disastrous results of self-insurance.

It required only a small expansion in thinking to extend this great concept to that of insuring the ship, its cargo, and the life of the captain. The reasoning for including the captain was to recover the cost of finding qualified, experienced, and trustworthy leaders. Training a new ship's captain could be expensive in time and in losses due to incompetency. Similarly to cargo, these merchants covered the predetermined value of the captain for the duration of the trip. As always, the concept was to share the risk so as to avoid *self-insurance*.

Gradually, it dawned on some progressive entrepreneurs that they could insure against the loss of a ship while sitting empty in harbor, due to fire or some other non-preventable occurrence. Similarly, the associates could insure against the loss due to death of the captain in a bar room brawl, or some other unexpected event. A relatively large group of participating individuals could reduce the risk of a ruinous loss, to a reasonably affordable one. It is important to note that these businessmen were attempting to avoid *self-insuring*.

The first recorded life insurance policy was written on the life of William Gybbons in 1583, nearly 2400 years after the initiation of cargo insurance in the Mediterranean. I am not sure who William Gybbons was or why he was important enough to be the first insured, and I could not discover the name of the fledgling insurance company that insured him. However, it must have been dealt a serious blow when Mr. Gybbons died, and his heirs collected £400 sterling after paying a premium of only £32.

In spite of this *one in a thousand* loss, the concept of life insurance persisted. Perhaps some mathematically gifted people, now known as actuaries, realized that if they could insure the remaining 999 people who, according to statistics, would not die in a given year, it would still be a profitable business venture.

Obviously, it took no great stretch of imagination to extend the concept of risk sharing to anything and everything of value. Associates in the venture of pooling funds could extend the concept to cover any risk of loss through the sale of insurance. It seems reasonable that the definition of insurance would be *a means of replacing a financial loss*. In fact, the only reason anyone buys insurance is to provide a way of offsetting a loss if and when an event occurs to cause something potentially disastrous to happen. For example: you can insure against a loss from a car theft, or by an accident, or in a fire, or from a flood, or of residential or business assets. The primary function of any type of insurance is to spread risk among a large number of people so that those who suffer a loss can be indemnified.

Nearly all use of insurance is to insure against an event **if** it should happen. The one exception is life insurance where you insure against the loss caused by death **when** it occurs.

In order to expand this concept beyond the harbor shores of the Chinese merchant marines, the Mediterranean concept of the insurance premium was adopted. Thereafter, you could pay a sum of money for your coverage. The associates, or the syndicate (as they came to be known in England) kept this premium. For your deposit, the members of the syndicate pledged their guarantees to compensate you for your loss to the extent of your agreement or contract.

Through necessity, several things developed in rather short order. One was insurable interest. Obviously, if someone who had no potential for loss could insure anything or anyone, there would be no insurable interest, and the potential for claims against the syndicate would grow exponentially. Clearly, it would encourage murder, arson, and theft, if the company did not require the insurance buyer to demonstrate *an insurable interest*. This was potentially disastrous to the associates.

A second requirement was to limit the amount of insurance to a sum no greater than the value of the item being insured. Obviously overinsurance could lead to bogus claims.

Thirdly, it was necessary to establish a reserve against potential losses. For most losses, there was no way of predetermining the cost with any real accuracy. Thus, the associates pledged their assets to provide for this reserve. They pledged their assets, as opposed to actually depositing a sum of money and, therefore, the size of their estates was the only limit on their risk. For taking this risk, they expected to be rewarded handsomely, of course.

In order to facilitate the calculation of a reasonable premium, as opposed to guessing, the science of statistical analysis based on experience data was combined with the theory of probability. This formula became known as *actuarial science.* Before you paid an insurance premium, someone called an actuary stirred the pot and extracted a magic figure from his mathematical brew. This premium took into account such things as the probability of a loss; the acquisition costs incurred in establishing a contract; and the costs of administration.

Modern day insurance reportedly developed and expanded in the mid 1600s in London England in the popular coffee houses of the day. *Lloyd's of London*, perhaps the largest underwriter of insurance risks in the world today, got its start in this manner in a coffee shop owned by Edward Lloyd. It should be noted that the *Lloyd's of London Association* actually does not write insurance. It simply furnishes a place of doing business, establishes a standard form or policy, arbitrates disputes, sets rules of conduct and operation, and looks after matters of mutual interest to its members.

Merchants who met informally in Lloyd's coffee house, began to collect premiums from ship owners. Initially, each underwriter carried on his business separately. Gradually, syndicates or underwriting groups were formed which allowed them to take on much larger risks. At the end of the agreement, or contract, the syndicate members signed their names and, thereby, became underwriters, making them *liable for a portion of the risk.* Today, apparently there are about 23,000 underwriting members, in various syndicates, from all over the world. This group of underwriters (or syndicates) has accepted an incredibly diverse number of risks. Some people claim that Lloyd's of London will insure anything for a price. At times, it seems so. Some of the more highly publicized undertakings were insuring: Dolly Parton's breasts for $3 million, Betty Grable's legs for $1 million, and a magician's hands for $3 million. The development of this concept of insuring risks has permitted many things to occur which otherwise would not have been possible. For example, without insurance coverage the space program in the USA could not proceed. Indeed, without insurance, the growth of all industry, with its ever increasing demands for capital investment, would have been slowed significantly. Who would have risked investment for buildings, machinery, and raw materials if there was no protection against loss from calamitous events such as fire, floods, or whatever? Surely most investors would have been reluctant to risk large sums of money on any venture without such insurance. Spreading the risk over a large base is the fundamental principle of insurance.

In North America, the earliest record of an insurance company was in South Carolina. It started in 1735, and catastrophe struck in 1740 causing the company to go bankrupt. In Canada, the earliest insurance company, *The Phoenix of London,* started operations in 1804.

The first evidence of life insurance in North America stems from 1759. A fund for the widows and orphans of Presbyterian Ministers was established to provide for them in case of the insured minister's death. This fund, known as the *Presbyterian Ministers Fund,* still exists. It has been pointed out to me by some of my associates that one of the functions of many different churches was to provide funds for widows, children, and other needy members of the congregation. Indeed, one may find examples in the Christian Bible dating back many thousands of years. Some fraternal insurance societies exist even today. However, the first company to offer life insurance to the public in Canada was *Standard Life* from the United Kingdom, in 1833. *Canada Life* came into being in 1847.

With the formation of corporations, as opposed to the underwriting syndicates of Lloyd's, the company became the underwriter. Today, the term underwriter usually refers to the individual or team of people who determines if the risk is acceptable to the company. Of course, the term still applies to the underwriters who make up the syndicates of *Lloyd's of London.*

Sometimes people refer to the sales advisors as field underwriters. The field underwriter presents the company and its product to the individual seeking insurance coverage, and then presents the risk to the company. Usually the only contact that an individual has with the company is via the field underwriter. Field underwriting requires a variety of skills. Knowledge of the product and an ability to demonstrate it to a prospective client, clearly and factually, is paramount. Equally important is the underwriter's ability to provide the facts to the company. This process has become ritualized by the use of an application. If the field underwriter does not present the risk to the company properly, it may decline an otherwise acceptable risk. Some authors like to claim that this relationship creates a conflict of interest. The field underwriter, they say, is the agent of the company and, therefore, does not represent the best interests of the client, but rather those of the company. They claim that this argument is valid, especially if the agent represents only one company. It is true that some sales contracts state that the agent must first offer all risks to the sponsoring company, in spite of the fact that the representative is an independent contractor. All agents must be sponsored by a company in order to become licensed. In my experience, agents can and do represent the interests of both the public and the company fairly.

There would seem to be an advantage if an advisor represents several companies. That is probably correct of general insurance. With life insurance, however, there may be an advantage in representing only one company. For example, the agent becomes well known to the head office underwriting department, and she can better understand the company's style. The underwriting department looks upon gray area cases more favorably when properly presented by a well-known advisor. Nevertheless, ready access to several companies can assist an advisor in some special situations. Some companies may be better at insuring certain risks such as diabetes or heart conditions. Others have developed specialized products or sales concepts. However, few if any advisors can thoroughly understand the subtleties of all products from a large number of companies. Notwithstanding that, a general knowledge of all products is not too difficult to obtain and maintain. In my opinion, the promotion of the idea of a conflict of interest, is definitely overworked by authors who do not understand insurance sales people, nor the companies we represent.

Head Office–Walk-About

By now, you are aware of three parts of an insurance company: the field underwriter, the head office underwriter, and the actuary. To round out your general knowledge, let's review some of the other departments. Depending on the size of the company, it may employ a few hundred people or several thousand. However, most companies have very similar departments regardless of size. Since I am most familiar with life insurance companies, let's do a walk-about in one typical life company. When you approach the receptionist she will direct you to the person or the department of your interest, especially if you have a specific request.

Let's start with the agency department.

This department is responsible for the agents or field force. The head honcho in the agency department is the director of agencies. In some larger companies, the title may be something like marketing vice president. The director of agencies is in charge of the staff that visits the sales offices. These people have a multiplicity of duties. They work closely with the branch manager, often referred to as a managing general agent. They may assist individual agents with special problems. Frequently, they present new products, sales ideas and concepts. They provide a general source of specialized knowledge and information. Many of these people have a background in field underwriting. They know the lingo. Even though they do not expect us, you may be sure that we are welcome in this department, but let's get on with it. We may be able to surprise some others.

Promotions Department

There are a number of extensions of the agency department, some of which are nearby. One of these divisions is promotional. This group is responsible for product development and promotion. They provide brochure and presentation material, with plan descriptions and concepts. In some companies, we could refer to them as the department of creativity. They may develop a concept, often stimulated by salespeople who have an idea of what their clients want or need. Blundering in here could be time consuming. They always want to talk about the wonderful new concepts being developed. But in the interest of time we must keep moving.

Actuarial

Once a new concept nears fruition, the actuarial department takes over for pricing. Actuaries determine the premium for all ages and amounts. When we get to this department, there may be genuine surprise as to how and why we found them. If we can get them to loosen up a bit, we may find out that they are involved in many other areas as well as policy pricing. For example, profitability is a major concern of actuarial; company profitability, product profitability, departmental efficiency, and so on, all come under their direct scrutiny.

This department works closely with the accounting department on budgeting and financial controls. If fact, actuaries become involved, directly or indirectly, in nearly every operation of the company. The chief actuary is one of the most influential people in head office. He is responsible for many things including reports to governments and to the board of directors. Did you notice when we got ready to go, they seemed relieved?

Systems Department

Somewhere about here, we should be able to find the systems department. System analysts need to become active in the set up of complicated programs for policy administration. Complex accounting systems are necessary to follow the policy from numbering to claims. Client data such as name, address, and personal information is vitally important to all concerned. Systems create programs for the recording of policy values such as cash values, paid up values, extended term, and other information. (Do not worry too much about the terminology at this point. We will cover it later. At this time, we are walking through a functioning head office). Let's keep moving. The people here were polite enough but they were not too sure about us. Maybe we can find some activity that is a little less routine.

Computerization.

As we do this imaginary walk through in a typical office, you will notice that all departments are fully computerized. (If you are not on the computer, you do not exist.) Computers are in full use in every department—for product development, for pricing, for promotional material design, or for record keeping. I am sure that today's head office people cannot believe that a company ever could have operated without a computer. They would be amused if they could watch the antiquated card sort system of the 1960s in action. Exciting isn't it ~ this walk-about?

Customer Relations

Ah, here we are in the customer relations or policyholder service department. This is one of the most important divisions in any company. In fact, they are vital to the smooth operation of policy service, communications, and publications, both internally and externally. When I worked in head office, I was editor of the company magazine for two years. We kept our field representatives informed about changes, new developments, and sales ideas. Communication is of vital importance to the customer, our policyowner, as well as to the advisor, for regular policy information updates. The information must be provided in a timely and understandable fashion. (Many of my clients would say that these communications need a lot of work.) Frankly, the people involved in this area are constantly striving to improve the quality of this communication. Policyowner **feedback** is constantly sought and welcomed. The people here may want to keep us talking for an hour or so. They do not get many public visitors and they do not want to miss this opportunity.

Advanced Underwriting Department

Right next door, we may find advanced underwriting; a department that is involved in the more complex concepts regarding *taxation and tax saving approaches.* They provide vital technical support to the advisors. We could stay longer and talk to them if you like, but would we understand what they tell us? Let's not risk it.

Legal Department

The legal department is next. We know we have found it because there are stacks of paper and books everywhere. The people here are very knowledgeable about tax laws and their application to life insurance. Of course, the wording of every policy contract is cleared through the legal department, much to the chagrin of many clients and most agents. Usually the complexity of a life insurance contract is the result of a desire to provide full disclosure. It is very important to the company and its representatives that our clients have a contract that explains everything of importance, accurately and, hopefully, simply. Sometimes simplicity must be sacrificed in the interest of accuracy. Did you notice we were intercepted at the entrance to this department? Perhaps they are working on some secret concept that they do not want us to learn about just yet.

Accounting Department

Some other departments, while important, are even less noticeable. For instance, the accounting department, separate from the agency department, is responsible for many things such as premium collection, record-keeping, payroll preparation, commission calculation, and payment. I would like to spend a little more time here, if you don't mind. Maybe I can pick up a cheque.

Investment Department

Everything is *theory* without the investment department. When the money from premium deposits arrives, the staff in this department promptly invests the portion that is not required for operations. Hopefully, wisely invested! Prudence is the byword of the investment department. Their goal is the maximization of returns with the minimization of risk. A careless investment in real estate has caused some companies great difficulty. On the other hand, too much conservatism would be investing only in government bonds and treasury bills. There would be great safety but a poor return. The investment department, therefore, must provide good investment returns while maintaining high levels of safety. Most investment departments have specialists in real estate, stocks, bonds and other investment vehicles. This department's success is vital to the overall success of the company. I wonder why they covered up some papers when we walked in.

Group Department

The group life and group pension departments, in some companies, are so large that they may resemble separate companies. Usually they operate as separate profit centers. They may have their own departments similar to all those visited already, specifically for group products. A visit here would be like going to another company.

Claims Department

Next on our tour, we will visit the claims department. It processes and pays out the proceeds on the death or disability of a policyholder. In some companies, the claims department is entirely in head office; while in others, some of the claims personnel are located in offices throughout the country. It was nice of them to promise to send our cheque out promptly when we die, don't you think?

Audit Department

Finally, the least noticed department is the audit department. They register surprise when they see us. They think that we have lost our bearings. They do not get many visitors. What does the audit department do? I don't know and I hope I never find out. It's been said that an auditor is someone who shows up after a disaster and shoots the wounded. OOPS! That does not apply to insurance company auditors. Most people realize, I am sure, that an auditor is someone who does a regular examination of accounts and financial records.

Others

Well, we have missed a few departments: the print shop, the supplies department, the records section, the archives, the library, and possibly some others; but we are out of time. For those who need more information about a particular department, I suggest that you consult with your life advisor.

Great, here's the cafeteria.
Let's get a coffee before we fall asleep.

The Advisor

In a previous section, we reviewed the basic principle of all insurance: the sharing of risk. The merchants of earlier eras knew the folly of **self-insuring**. Conversely, they understood the advantages and the wisdom of spreading the risk. It is strange, therefore, that while people in the past made a considerable effort to avoid self-insurance, many people are being influenced to go in the opposite direction, today. Authors of most popular books on financial planning actually advocate self-insurance. They advise, "buy term life insurance and invest the difference" to *become self-insured*. Of course, many proponents of the term-only concept would argue that those pioneers were buying insurance that covered the need, as required, only for a period of time. To this point I would answer, "Exactly, that is why term insurance plus a separate investment is usually not sufficient." Also, the argument is that the emphasis was on cargo or marine insurance as opposed to life insurance. Life insurance, as such, came along somewhat later in the process. Agreed, but that in no way changes the importance of avoiding the costs of self-insurance.

In Canada, some people recognized the need for life insurance more than one hundred and fifty years ago. One enterprising entrepreneur did something about it. Hugh Baker, a bank manager in Hamilton, Ontario, decided to buy insurance to protect his new bride, twenty-one year old Emma Wyatt.

Mr. Baker made a round trip of over a thousand miles to New York City, in order to buy a life insurance policy on his own life. That may not be such a great feat today, but in 1843 this pioneer had to travel by steamboat, horseback, and stagecoach. I do not know how many companies Mr. Baker had to choose from when he reached his destination, probably not many. We do know that the *Mutual Life Insurance Company of New York* started in 1843. It was the first, modern day, life insurance company to start in the United States. Logic would suggest that Mr. Baker bought his policy from them, but not so. He actually did buy a $1,000 policy from the *National Life Assurance Society.* It was necessary for Mr. Baker to present himself to the company in person because of his asthma condition. He was required to pay a 1% higher premium, not because of his condition, but rather because the Canadian climate was reputed to be hazardous to one's health.

By my way of thinking, his insurance should have been in effect before he embarked on that journey. Obviously he thought so too. Sometime after his return, Mr. Baker founded his own life insurance company. In 1847, *Canada Life* became the first Canadian life insurance company. Mr. Baker's first concern was to protect families. The company's mission statement was: *a desire to spread the benefits of life assurance, not an anxiety to make unreasonable profits.* Interestingly, when Hugh Baker applied for insurance policy #1 from the company he had founded, his coverage was restricted to £500. The company medical examiner warned that Baker "applies too closely to business."

In those early days, people who wanted insurance coverage had to search for a company and make the effort to go to the company. Whether the journey was a few miles or several hundred miles, it was not a particularly efficient way of getting insurance. It certainly was not a very effective way of offering insurance coverage to those in need of it. Efficiency was of utmost importance. It was necessary for Mr. Baker's new company to establish a significant number of clients, as quickly as possible, for the obvious reason of spreading the risk.

Since the purpose of this book is not to be an historical study of the earliest methods of selling life insurance, my research was kept to company libraries. My efforts did show me that there is a dearth of information on the subject. The obvious reason for this is who really cares? Nevertheless, there is a valid reason for this review. Forty years ago, when I was a young agent, I knew several older agents with long memories. I listened with rapt attention as these *old-timers* told stories of their early experiences. They liked to compare the old styles and techniques with our *modern* methods. History, literally *his story*, is a look at the past through the eyes of another. As a young agent, I enjoyed a view of the past as related in many old-timer's stories.

While we do not know much about the earliest attempts to market insurance, one could surmise that the original companies advertised in whatever media was available to them. Obviously, newspaper advertising and direct mail were not so prevalent nor as effective and efficient as they are today. The advent of a mail box full of flyers is a modern day phenomenon. It may be a surprise for some, but there were no televisions and no radios in those days. In fact, "telephones and electric power were still the stuff of dreams." Mr. Baker, reportedly placed *educational* advertisements in *The Canadian Almanac*, *The Hamilton Spectator*, four Toronto newspapers, and *The Albion* in New York City. Mr. Baker also appointed his brother, George Jr., as a traveling general agent to promote assurance by lobbying local editors and giving free public lectures.

As other life insurance companies entered the market, the need to expand methods of operation also grew. Apparently, in the early days, some store owners sold insurance over the counter. Perhaps that's one reason why banks feel it's a natural for them. They have larger counters, and so many of them. For some companies, one of the oldest professions (not the oldest of course), the traveling sales representative, was an obvious solution. For some of those travelers, it seemed natural to add another product line for the benefit of their customers, and the concept of an agent for a life insurance company was expanded. Clearly the first insurance salesperson sold other products as well. Today, we would refer to these peddlers as part-timers.

The term peddler is still with us today, but not quite so prevalent as it was over forty years ago, when I became an insurance salesman. In my early years, people quite often said things like "Ah, so you are an insurance peddler," even though they did not know the origin of the term. We still have some part-time salespeople, and maybe some of them are not much more professional than the peddlers of yesterday. Rural agents, in some provinces, currently, are allowed to have a license as part-timers. Most rural agents are as professional as their city cousins; thus, they would not qualify as peddlers. In larger cities, salespeople can have licenses to sell general insurance and life insurance, or mutual funds and life insurance. However the complexity of the products, and the knowledge required *to counsel* about life insurance properly, does not allow *part-timers* or *peddlers* to compete favorably with full time, well-trained, knowledgeable advisors.

Currently we are in an era of specialization. Lawyers concentrate on certain areas of law. Doctors may specialize in various disciplines. Accountants often have associates working within specialized disciplines. Likewise, many life insurance agents specialize in certain disciplines, such as: group insurance, pension planning, estate planning, partnership insurance, business insurance, or retirement planning. A family doctor may be a general practitioner who refers his patients to a specialist when the need arises. Similarly, many life advisors operate as general practitioners. Some of them associate with other specialists whose knowledge and experience is available to them and to their clients.

Perhaps the majority of advisors are operating as general practitioners, although that may be changing. Certainly most new agents need to learn the basics before they can compete with the more knowledgeable, more experienced advisors, in situations where there is a requirement of a greater degree of expertise. Just studying the manuals does not provide the necessary skills for specialization anymore than watching others skate will allow you to learn to skate. Some agents do leap in before they are ready, and they take the predictable pratfall caused by their naiveté. The wiser ones recognize the situation and bring in a more experienced colleague to assist them. There is nothing really new in this approach. We did it forty years ago.

The concept of *the peddler* still intrigues me. Do we still have insurance peddlers today? Alas, it seems that we do! There are a number of salespeople who qualify as peddlers. They usually represent only one life insurance company, which offers only one product: term insurance which cannot be converted. Of course, the answer would be, "Well you will not need to convert it because you will have saved enough money to be *self-insured*. If you cancel your cash value policies and your other savings plans, you can invest in mutual funds. If you do that, you will be so well off that you will not need life insurance any more." Does this sound familiar?

The thing that characterizes salespeople as *peddlers,* is that they have basically two products to sell, a series of term plans and a family of mutual funds. They need to make the buyer fit the mold. They need to sell you on a concept that makes their product seem like the answer. They do not try to find out what your needs, goals, and desires may be in order to tailor-make a plan to fit you. Rather, they try to make you fit the program they are offering. They do this with a variety of catch phrases such as: *Buy term and invest the difference; Self-insure; The theory of decreasing responsibility;* and *Be an owner not a loaner.* We will examine these terms elsewhere in this book. For now, let me say that these phrases are as hollow as the trunk of a dead tree, and just as useless—unless you want to hibernate.

Another characteristic of the peddler is an adamant certainty that any policy you now have is not right for you. They frequently comment, "Do you want an insurance company making big profits on your money? Look at all those big buildings around town which those companies build with your money. As for cash values, well, the company says you can borrow it. When you try to do so, however, you find out that you have to pay interest on your own money. That cash value is an overcharge of the premium to provide forced savings. It's *your money* but you have to pay interest to borrow your own money. Dividends are merely partial returns of overpayments on your premium."

This is all nonsense, of course, even though sometimes it does sound logical. In case you find any of these suggestions appealing, let me ask a few questions. Do you think that life companies do not make a profit on term insurance? Do you think that the peddler's company does not invest in large buildings? Do you think that large buildings are not profitable investments? Do you think that the peddler's company does not pay profits to shareholders in the same way as does any other company?

Have you ever tried to borrow money from a mutual fund or a bond? You cannot borrow *from* these financial instruments at any rate of interest. You could, perhaps, borrow from a bank using them as collateral, but interest free? Try it. You could extend this concept to any other asset you own, such as your car, your house, or your jewelry. The money you invested was your money, but you cannot borrow it, and you cannot borrow against it—interest free.

The peddler seems to believe his arguments, but when we examine them more fully, you will see that it's because of an abysmal lack of knowledge. You can recognize peddlers from the fact that they are not trying to become knowledgeable. They are just peddling policies.

Does this mean that all salespeople who advocate buying term and mutual funds are peddlers? That is not necessarily so. Some mutual fund salespeople are very knowledgeable, and they may do an excellent job of analyzing your needs and goals. They may tailor-make an investment program to fit your comfort zone. Many of them have a wide range of mutual fund companies from which to choose. They may do a reasonable job of analyzing your current need for life insurance. However, if they advocate buying term insurance only, so that you can put more money into a mutual fund, they are not much better than the peddler.

Fortunately, most of the people who sell life insurance today are not peddlers nor policy pushers. Nevertheless, we should review a number of myths that surround the people who sell insurance. Many people believe that a typical life insurance agent is pushy and high pressure. Well, okay, but there is no such thing as a typical agent.

Agents come in all sizes, colors, creeds, and sexes. There have been several studies made to find a common thread in order to determine which characteristics are common among successful life insurance salespeople. None have succeeded to date. The nearest anyone has come to such a determination is a questionnaire that predicts that an individual may have a low probability of success in our business. However, some of our top agents failed this test. You cannot typify agents, but the public does tend to stereotype them.

For example, consider the concept of the high pressure salesperson. What exactly does the average person consider high pressure? When I was a Branch Manager I made a telephone survey of fifteen of the most recent clients sold by our representatives. I explained that I was not asking them to report on their own advisor. The question was simply, "When you think of or speak of a high pressure salesperson, what exactly does the phrase mean to you?" Without exception, everyone replied, "A high pressure salesperson is one who keeps calling back and calling back and just will not take no for an answer."

I suggested that a high pressure salesperson was one who presented the story so forcefully that the prospective client just could not refuse. "Oh no," they replied. "That's just good salesmanship." These people had no problem with a powerful presentation. My conclusion was that what people called high pressure selling was really *pushy* salesmanship. Are there *pushy* salespeople out there? Of course, but most of them will not succeed in the life insurance business. I suspect that they will not succeed in sales of any kind for very long.

Another stereotype is the con artist. When I think of a *con man* I get a clear picture of a person selling a product at the county fair. They have a product, a new type of broom, a potato peeler, a set of pots and pans, or a juicer, and a spiel that is entertaining, informative, and gimmicky. The danger in listening to these cons is that you may buy something that you do not really need, that really will not work as well for you, and it ends up collecting dust. I am a ripe tomato for these cons. I buy all kinds of gimmicky items.

The more accurate concept of a con artist is one who swindles someone by first gaining his or her confidence. Hence, the term the confidence man, was coined. I loved the movie, "The Music Man." What a lovable, fast talking, smooth operator, but most cons are not so obvious. Most cons swindle people with a gimmick, such as prepayment for repairs to the house. These repairs, of course, never become completed. The salespeople and the company simply disappear after they get your money. Some people have bought swamp land in Florida. More recently, people are falling for the free-cruise-gimmick. Of course, it's not entirely free, but it's so inexpensive that you just cannot resist it. You have always wanted to go on a cruise, and this is a chance of a lifetime, at 10% of the normal fare. You have to get to Florida at your own expense, but from there on you will enjoy an incredible cruise on a luxury liner. How can they do this? Well, if you qualify, and you do because they have already checked you out, you must promise to attend a two hour session outlining a timeshare or some other wonderful opportunity. It takes only two hours one morning, out of five beautiful days at sea. It's just too good to be true. You send your $500.00 and book your air flight. You arrive in Florida full of expectation and anticipation of a wonderful cruise—an experience of a lifetime. Then you discover, there is no cruise, there is no cruise line, and the company to which you sent your money does not exist. The address of the company is a vacant lot or a burned out building and your wonderful dream goes *poof*. You know the old adage: *if it sounds too good to be true it probably is*. If you get such a call, tell them to put everything about the project and the trip in the mail to you, so you can consider it when you have time. Do not watch your mail box for it. It will never arrive.

Nevertheless, a con man approach to life insurance does not seem too probable—possible but not probable. I have heard of people giving cash to a salesperson or writing a check payable to the individual, and afterwards never hearing from that individual again. No trace; he just disappeared. The policy he was selling did not exist and there was no company by that name. The technique used was to leave nothing in writing: no proposal, no business card, nothing, but this kind of selling involving insurance is rare.

An acquaintance of mine pulled off quite a deal and nearly got away with it. Please understand that this individual was not someone I approved of—ever. When some of my associates, owners of a large general insurance agency, were considering hiring this individual, they asked me to interview him as a prospective employee. I did, and afterwards reported to the owners that he was trouble looking for some place to happen. They did not like my assessment and hired him anyway. That effectively made him an agent for my office and the companies I represented. Some time later, the real-estate division of this agency, sold a piece of property that belonged to one of their clients. When the cheque was available, this life insurance agent delivered it. He convinced the people, who knew the agency and trusted the owners, to endorse it to him. This agent gave them a receipt from one of our companies for $30,000. The company, unfortunately, never saw the money. Two years later the client began to wonder why he had never received anything from the company regarding the deposit. The company wondered why they had never received the deposit. It's a long story with a happy ending. The people did get their money back and the so-called agent got away without being charged. Later we learned that he went to jail on another scam, in another province. Avoiding this problem could have been so easy. The clients should have cashed the real-estate cheque and made their personal cheque payable directly to the insurance company. Over the years there have been other fraudulent attempts on the public, but they are rare and rarely successful. There have been some very clever scams pulled on the companies, usually involving the agent and a cooperative client, but that's not the subject of this book.

The image of the agent takes a beating when the antics of a few dishonest ones become known. Many of the authors exploit these few incidents to tarnish all agents, as dishonest charlatans who will sell you anything to make a fast buck. One author wrote, "The one person you must not trust is the insurance salesman. He is not your agent. He works for, is licensed by, and is under the complete control of his company." He also states, "You are being swindled by the smoothest most respectable con men in existence." This author does not give any proof or even any examples. He just expresses an opinion, but still other authors quote him and add other endearing terms such as *charlatan* and *crook*. Why do they do it? Perhaps the purpose is to sell their books. Perhaps they just dislike us. At least one of these authors tried to sell life insurance and failed. Obviously, his conclusion was that those of us who are successful must be dishonest, or whatever.

Many of these authors are promoting mutual funds. Are they suggesting that mutual fund salespeople are all honest, but life insurance salespeople are not? Many mutual fund salespeople also sell life insurance but, of course, if they only sell term life they must be honest. Right? Right, at least according to *these authors*.

There are salespeople in every industry who are dishonest, but most are totally trustworthy. It is incredibly unfair to paint all salespeople with the same brush, just because some were less than perfect. Who has not heard of the improprieties of some priests? What do you think about the truly incredible adventures of some of the TV evangelists? Does that make them all bad? If you read the newspapers you could pick members of any profession; lawyers, doctors, accountants, engineers or politicians, (yes, even politicians and you elected them) who committed atrocities that ended in jail terms. And sorry ladies, but they were not only men. We are all saddened and appalled by the terrible stories of mothers, or fathers, who harm and even murder their own children.

Salespeople in any discipline merely reflect society. In our society there are honest people and dishonest people, but some authors suggest that the life insurance business attracts the dishonest ones. Even if that were true, I suggest that these types will either change or fail.

Well, enough of that! The question is can you pick an honest, trustworthy advisor, and if so, how do you do it? Certainly you can, but just because you know the person, or because she is a relative, or because the salesperson had a recommendation, there is no guarantee that you can trust her. So how do you choose an advisor? A recommendation from someone you know and trust is a good start.

However, that does not mean you should never talk to a salesperson you do not know. If a new salesperson approaches you at the right time, why would you not proceed with an interview? As I have stated elsewhere, if I were you, I would favor those who have earned certificates such as CFP, CLU, CH.F.C. However, experience could be an offsetting factor for those without certification. Furthermore, if the individual associates with someone who has the certification, that could be sufficient. One highly successful advisor once quipped, "When I need a CLU or a CH.F.C. I'll hire one."

Ideally, you should sense a mutual feeling of respect as you talk. Ask for the new agent's credentials. Find out if she sells for only one company or for many? Which company or companies does she represent? Does she have only one product such as term insurance? Is the agent really a mutual fund representative pretending to be an insurance advisor? If your main interest is mutual funds, the same questions apply. If the salesperson represents only one company you should be wary. If the agent is recommending that you cancel some plans that you already have, ask him to put his recommendation in writing. Advise that salesperson that you intend to review his proposal with your present advisor. Be sure that the agent dates and signs the proposal. If the salesperson rejects this suggestion about his method of procedure, you should conclude the interview at once.

If you are considering a new purchase, with no cancellation is intended, you should get a computer printout that illustrates:

- The type of plan
- Information about the company
- The interest rate used for the projection
- Whether or not the premium can increase
- Whether or not the coverage can decrease

A computer printout should also illustrate at least one lower rate of interest. You do not have to buy anything on the first interview, but if you do, you have plenty of time to reconsider. After issue of the policy you have ten days by law, in most places, to have the policy rescinded. No legitimate advisor wants you to pay premiums for one or two months and then cancel it. Qualified advisors are looking for clients rather than quick sales. Certainly you can interview several agents and then decide which one you want as your advisor. The process should not be painful, but rather it should be very educational. Finally, if you cannot find an advisor you are happy with—call me!

There is no need to agonize about the selection of an advisor. Most of the people who are attracted to our business are honest and trustworthy. Go with your gut feeling.

If it feels right—go for it!

Myth: Financial Planning

"No cards tonight, George, my financial planner is coming over."

"Your *financial planner*? I'm impressed. You must be doing really well."

"Well, you know, George, I just want to get everything straightened out and get my investments set up properly."

"You've got investments? Karl, I am really impressed."

"No, well not really. This guy thinks I should have some investments. That's all."

"Oh, what's he selling?"

"Ah, nothing. He just shows me what I should buy. He's some sort of advisor."

"Some sort, Karl? What sort? Stocks and bonds, mutual funds, life insurance, real estate, GICs, RRSPs, RESPs, self-directed plans?"

"Sure, all of those I guess."

"You guess? What does this guru charge for this service?"

"I don't know, George. Why do you ask?"

"Sounds interesting. Maybe I could use his advice too if he's not too expensive."

"That's great, George. Why don't you stick around and ask him. He's just coming up the walk now."

"That's him?"

"Yeah that's my financial planner."

"No kidding, Karl?"

"No. Why?"

"Because yesterday he cut my hair."

~~~~~~~~~~~~~~~~~~

Who is your financial planner?
What is a financial planner?
What do you expect from a financial planner?
What does a financial planner do?
~~~~~~~~~~~~~~~~~~

In recent years, the phrase *financial planning* has attracted an incredible amount of attention. Surveys indicate that people want financial planning, but there is a serious question about their willingness to pay for it.

Many of the people in the broad field of financial service now refer to themselves as financial planners. They avoid referring to themselves as a stockbroker, or as a mutual fund salesperson, or as a life insurance agent, or whatever. Surveys show that the public respects the image of *financial planner* more than any of the other categories. I say image because changing one's label may change the perception of a practitioner's activity, but it does not change the fact of his or her qualifications. Many people consult someone who refers to himself as a financial planner only to discover that this person does not have the equivalent qualifications of their current advisor. Frequently, in my experience, the real purpose of the consultation is to see if there is some magical way to make a meager savings program do much more. The objective is to make too few dollars do too much. Sometimes people consult other advisors to get confirmation that they are on the right path. It's sort of like visiting a doctor when you feel well just to get confirmation that you are well. Some people are shopping for peace of mind.

Our clients want something called financial planning but there is hardly any agreement as to what financial planning actually is. Many people believe that it is nothing more than a convenient label, or a disguise, for product vendors to hide behind. Unfortunately, there is considerable truth in this thought. Anyone can call herself a financial planner. There are no licensing requirements. There are no educational qualifications nor standards to meet before one can hold out to the public, "I am a financial planner." However, calling oneself a financial planner does not mean it is so, anymore than calling yourself a salesperson makes it so.

Conversely, there are some who have a concept of financial planning as an entirely new professional discipline, with which those who are qualified to provide this service can make a major contribution to the public welfare.

At present, there are no specific regulations for the practice of financial planning. Rather, members of each discipline adhere to the standards of the practitioners' professional association. The legal profession, the accountant profession, stockbrokers, mutual fund agents, life insurance advisors, and so on, each has licensing restrictions and professional standards within which they must work. Beyond that, there are no requirements regarding the advertisement of oneself as a financial planner. Having said that, I do acknowledge that there are some recommendations for the moral and ethical conduct of those claiming the status of financial planner. The Canadian Association of Financial Planners does have a published code of professional ethics. However, membership in this organization is voluntary.

What is Financial Planning?

There is considerable confusion within the professions and among the general public. Many people use the term *financial planning*, I suspect, when what they really mean is *financial advice*. As the world of finance becomes more complex and as more people have more disposable income, the need for competent advice becomes ever more apparent. So what is it that people want, financial planning or financial advice? Obviously nearly everyone can benefit from financial advice of some kind at some time. The majority of the population, in my opinion, wants good sound financial advice rather than financial planning per se.

Financial planning is a process analogous to putting together the pieces of a puzzle so that they are much more meaningful than when viewed separately. Financial planning is not merely estate planning to provide for one's financial concerns after death. Financial planning is not simply budgeting to determine how one is spending one's money, nor is it to determine how one should spend it. Financial planning is not just planning for retirement. It is not about the purchase or sale of stocks, bonds, equities, mutual funds, life insurance or any of the other financial instruments. Financial planning may embrace all of these items, but it is much more than that.

It is not something one can fix at a point in time. It is not something that one can establish and then just forget it. Personal financial planning is not a destination, but rather it is a journey.
Financial planning is a process whereby a *financial analyst*:

- Objectively gathers all the financial and emotional data required
- Analyzes data and prepares a plan
- Delivers the plan and encourages the client to take action
- Offers ongoing review

In other words, it is:

- A review of one's current financial picture
- An identification of problem areas
- A recommendation for appropriate remedies

Who is the financial planner?

In my opinion, there is only one financial planner. There is only one qualified for the job—*you*. Every individual or family unit must assume the full responsibility for their own financial planning. Thereafter, in most cases, before making timely decisions, they may seek out and consult competent advisors based on specific needs and interests.

Obviously the kind of advice sought or needed depends on many factors such as:

- Age
- Income level
- Marital or family status
- Current assets
- Future potential
- And so on

It is sad but true, that a large percentage of the population has not even begun the financial planning process in any comprehensive way. The majority of the people I meet have never prepared a simple budget. They work from pay cheque to pay cheque, hoping that the money on hand will last until the end of the current pay period. If an automatic cheque does not clear their bank accounts as expected, the money disappears. That is why we have to inform clients that our company plans to double up, to catch up. If they do not plan for the extra amount that they should have accounted for last month, this month's automatic withdrawal will fail—because they spent the money. For most people, in order to save any money they must actually "Pay themselves first." In this regard, any forced savings or commitment to a savings program on a regular routine basis qualifies as financial planning.

Pay yourself first is not a new concept. The earliest advocacy of this concept, that I am aware of, came in the little classic *The Richest Man in Babylon* by George S. Clason published in 1926. When that little gem was first published, banks in North America gave copies of it to their clients freely. Life insurance companies made them available to their agents, and they provided sales presentations for their sales forces embracing that basic concept. Were we successful in establishing that message? If you consider the current interest in the modernized version of *The Richest Man in Babylon*, it would appear that we were not successful. Will this more recent book make a lasting and vital impact on the saving and spending habits of the general population? The answer is no. It will not change old habits.

One of my associates, Roy Olney, pointed out that buying gifts at Christmas saves many businesses every year from financial stress. Similarly the RRSP season does it for financial institutions. Every year there is incredible hype surrounding the so-called *RRSP season*.

Advertising hits us from every angle and in so many ways. People feel guilty if they have not been saving on a regular basis, and the tax deadline creates a sense of urgency. It is this anguish that causes a large segment of the population to race to the bank, to beat the deadline at the eleventh hour. To me that proves the myth of financial planning. Why is there an RRSP season? If people planned properly there would be no need to take any special action before the end of February. In many years this is the worst time to make major financial decisions. Some people claim that they do not do any financial planning because they do not know where to start. Are these people saying that they need someone to help them make basic decisions? Apparently so, but surely we have been doing that job on a rudimentary basis. When we help clients start a life insurance program, an equity savings plan (mutual funds or segregated funds), we are creating a financial plan for them.

Forty years ago, the concept was simple. If you saved as little as ten percent of everything you earned; if you bought life insurance in case you died too soon; and if you had disability coverage in case you could not continue working, you had a good financial program. Not only that, if you took care of today, tomorrow, and the future, you were free to spend everything else earned on better living today. That was financial planning and it still is financial planning.

Financial Planners or Financial Advisors?

Admittedly, the diversity of and the complexity of the financial products available, in a rapidly changing financial world, causes considerable confusion. Most people need financial advice.

They may need advice in many of the following areas:

Real estate

Are you buying a home for your family as your principle residence, or are you buying real estate as an investment?

Mutual funds

There are at least 187 families of funds and the number continues to grow. Each fund family may have upwards of twenty funds.

L*ife insurance and segregated funds*

The proliferation of products makes the input of a competent advisor one of the most important concerns for everyone. The different schools of thought, or basic concepts, about the need for life insurance and its proper use in one's financial program, adds considerable confusion to the process. The entire argument about the proper kind of insurance when so-called professionals cannot agree makes this topic vitally important. It has been covered thoroughly in other chapters in this book, so it will not be considered further at this point.

Stocks and bonds

Obviously most of us are not knowledgeable enough to buy and sell these products without the advice of competent advisors.

All the other investments available

Specialized investments require specialists. The choice of a proper advisor, knowledgeable about the specific or unique opportunity, is obvious—surely? Most people need advisors, but which advisors, how many, and at what level, depends on each individual's needs and objectives. For most of us financial planning is very basic and does not require the services of a *financial planner* per se. On the other hand, our needs, goals, and objectives change as we age and accumulate assets. During some stage in the process, we may need a team of advisors.

For example:

- An accountant or someone competent in budgetary planning, tax analysis and tax advice

  Such advice may include a recommendation to buy products from other capable specialists.
- A lawyer specializing in taxation

Obviously a timely consultation with a tax specialist may save many hours of frustration as well as real dollars. Implementation of a program based on advice from these specialists, that is, accountants or lawyers, may involve other professional advisors.

Where and how does one start?

The answer to this question depends on where you are on the continuum. You need to know where you are. Where are you spending your money? How much do you save? Obviously if you have debts, other than a mortgage, debt elimination should have a high priority. Some strategists even consider paying off the mortgage to be of prime importance, depending perhaps on the prime rate of interest.

Secondly, you need to determine your objectives, short term and long term. What good is the best financial advice if it does not help you reach your objectives? Using a generic term such as *financial independence* is not good enough. There must be a definition as to what it means to you personally. For many people financial independence means debt elimination, adequate funds for education of the children, and a sufficient level of savings for a comfortable retirement. For each individual that sum is different and very personal. Illustrations showing that you will need a million dollars or millions of dollars are inaccurate, and they are valuable only as a scare tactic to get people to save more. My own observation is that most people do not need huge sums of money to retire comfortably. The amount varies, of course, with each individual or couple. No *rule of thumb* should be quoted in this regard.

In summation, the majority of the population does not need a *financial planner,* but most people do need financial advisors. Nevertheless, depending on a given situation, there may be a need for one advisor to help assemble and coordinate an advisory team. Call each person on the team a financial planner if you wish. My own terminology would be *financial consultant.* You are the planner. The person you choose as your consultant should be someone able to help you pull it together into a comprehensive program aimed at achieving your objectives.

For those who have accumulated sufficient assets, a personal financial consultant may be a worthwhile investment. How do you choose your consultant? Ideally, he or she should be able to set aside personal biases and look at the broader scope of what accomplishes your goals. Your consultant may be a lawyer, an accountant, a CFP, a CLU or CH.F.C., as discussed elsewhere in this book, or someone with credentials which indicate a certain level of competency. Ideally, this person should demonstrate a willingness to act in this capacity. A consultant assumes a responsibility to establish a system and an ongoing procedure for follow-up with regular updates—in other words the process. This person or firm must have established a program or a system to collect, assemble, analyze, and process your data in a way that leads to the accomplishment of your realistic objectives. Knowledge alone is not necessarily sufficient. As stated before, financial planning is a process not merely a snapshot of your present situation. Everyone should realize that there is an investment in time; by the consultant and by the one seeking this advice. On the part of the public, there should be a recognition that this service has a financial value and there must be a willingness to make adequate compensation for services rendered. Until people realize this, *financial planning* remains more fiction than fact.

As with so many things in life, we need goals and objectives in order to determine a financial goal. When I see some of my acquaintances floundering about, I think of that delightful story in Lewis Carroll's *Alice in Wonderland.*

When Alice sees the Cheshire Cat sitting on a bough of a tree, she approaches him timidly and asks, "Would you tell me, please, which way I ought to walk from here?"

> "That depends a good deal on where you want to get to," said the Cat.
>
> "I don't much care where," said Alice.
>
> "Then it doesn't matter which way you walk," said the Cat.
>
> "—so long as I get *somewhere*," Alice added.
>
> "Oh, you're sure to do that," said the Cat, "if you only walk long enough!"

If you have no financial goals, no advisor is necessary.

Advisors Are Not Professionals

? Writers and
nd it useful to
rance business,
fessionals.
statements to the
Our associations
nduct. They have
provide us with the
hese courses provide
of other groups, such

Canada, now known as
Financial Advisors, has
must commit to follow.
In my opin... e should *always place the interest of a client above ... or that of any company.* Membership in CAIFA requires ongoing education, and each local maintains an ethics and practice committee.

Our industry has an independent police force established by government edict to examine and license agents. This establishment has the authority to revoke a license or levy a civil penalty, without the requirement of following proper legal procedures.

Recently, the Canadian Life and Health Insurance Association issued a set of standards of ethical conduct for their member companies, and the companies passed them on to the field force. They admonished us to acknowledge and to adhere to these proclamations. Naturally, the companies set the standards, and then tell us to live up to them.

In view of all of this, one might expect it to silence the critics, and to still the negative criticism. Not to be! One self appointed critic stated; *whenever I am confronted by people loudly proclaiming their ethics, I always reach uneasily to confirm that my wallet is secure.*

Another one, reading the guidelines from the CLHIA stated emphatically; *this is an admission that they have not been operating ethically*. He pointed out that making more rules and trying to enforce more stringent regulations will not work. According to him, we first got the Ten Commandments and now we have ten thousand laws trying to enforce them. This *gentleman* closed his tirade with a common misquote of The Bard, "Me thinks thee protesteth too much." Of course, everyone knows, no doubt, that the actual quotation reads; *The lady doth protest too much methinks*. Hamlet. Act III, Scene 2.

Still, another critic stated: "The only thing professional about you guys is your ability to sell." He continued: "Banks and the people running them are professional. They ignore the criticism and meet any legal challenges head on, after they get them hushed up. They do not apologize for charging excessive interest rates. They do not apologize for making exorbitant profits. Furthermore, they do not apologize for pushing an inferior, more expensive term insurance on the public. Quite the opposite, *they claim they make insurance rates go down*."

Frankly, I have always been proud of my ability to sell, so it does not bother me when critics make snide remarks about salespeople and salesmanship. Furthermore, the status of *professional* does not concern me, particularly. I am what I am regardless of what you choose to call it. To put it in perspective, I am a salesman who *helps people buy life insurance and other related financial products appropriate to their needs and objectives*.

I help wealthy people sleep better at night. I help provide for families so they can maintain a reasonable standard of living even when they lose the income from a breadwinner. I provide peace of mind for people, men and women, who want to meet their obligations even if they do not live long enough to do so. In the final analysis, the only critics that matter to me are my clients. Thus I resent all those who write and proclaim things to confuse, to mislead, and to cause doubts among my clients. If you have read some other chapters in this book, you know that it astounds me that anyone is willing to accept this dribble.

Most of the critics have no special qualifications, other than the ability to express themselves forcefully. Why do we place so much emphasis on professionalism? Why is it so important to people, both within the industry, and elsewhere? What must we do to attain this vaunted status?

Hockey players, baseball players, basketball players and other *players* of sport are considered professional if they play in the top league, for example, in the majors. Why do we call them professionals? Is it because they make so much money? Is it because of their level of skill in the *games* they play? Do professionals, in a given sport in every country, have the same level of skills, or are the standards lower in some countries than in others?

The dictionary says, “A professional is one who makes some activity, not usually followed for gain, such as a sport; the source of his livelihood.” It also says, “A professional is one who belongs to one of the professions.” Okay perhaps this is the essence of our problem. No one has declared our business a profession. Do we qualify? What is a profession? Again according to the dictionary; “A profession is a vocation, or an occupation, that requires advanced training in some liberal art or science. It usually involves mental rather than manual work, such as teaching, engineering, writing, medicine, law or theology.” So, we can consider *writers* to be professional, even if they have no special training or knowledge in the topics they write about—by definition, right?

Not so, it seems, with life insurance sales people. Many of the agents I know have a university degree. They have a CLU—Chartered Life Underwriter designation which means they are financial advisors with advanced knowledge in life and health insurance and employee benefits. Many of these agents also have a CH.F.C., designation, or Chartered Financial Consultant, which means that they are financial advisors with advanced knowledge in wealth accumulation and retirement planning.

That should do it; should it not? Not so, say our critics. First, as one critic points out, it is not necessary to belong to one of the official associations to get into the life insurance business. Secondly, you do not need any of these designations to get a license. You just learn enough to pass a basic exam and then you get a license. "Provisional license," I advised. "Yeah okay, so what?" He queried.

There are more arguments along this line and we could explore them here, but to serve what purpose? What difference does it make to our clients whether or not we call ourselves professional financial advisors? It does matter, of course, that the salespeople making this claim can back it up with evidence that they have completed, or that they are studying, the appropriate courses. Furthermore, a prospective buyer could and should determine that a would-be-advisor has the experience and knowledge equivalent to the expertise required.

There are many other questions that we need to address. Finding answers for them has been an enigma. Perhaps, it is just that we have never formulated nor expressed the questions openly. In this matter, none of us is innocent; only some who are naive. All of us have contributed to this perplexity; the public, the agents, the companies, and the governments. So let's look openly and squarely at the mystery.

Why have we, in the insurance business, failed to demonstrate the intrinsic value of our product so clearly and so powerfully that no one could ever doubt it?

Why have we failed to achieve a perfect understanding? One so well presented, that when negative writers fire salvos of torpedoes, armed with warheads of ignorance, the public would react with disdain; and become aghast with the temerity of the unrequited hatred displayed?

Why do we encourage writers, authors, journalists and publicists, to believe that they can write with impunity?

Why do we not fight back, collectively, with a massive educational program? Have *they* not pushed us far enough?

Why do we continue to permit this group of detractors to continue displaying our frailties without a challenge?

Is it arrogance or merely a foolish belief that the public knows better?

How long can we trust legislators to react favorably in the face of these constant negative attacks?

How long should we allow the gnats to gnaw at opened wounds without retaliating?

Why do we leave it to individual agents to defend the industry against exposed errors past and present?

Why should we charge agents with the responsibility of preserving a heritage of accomplishment, for the benefit of the public, against this barrage of criticism from every direction?

Why do we allow our competitors from other financial disciplines to make negative claims about our product and to lobby against a perceived *unfair advantage* for our industry?

Why have we not made it abundantly clear, to all and sundry, that this *advantage* is a great benefit to the public?

Why can we not make it understood that the only *unfair advantage* of our product is to those who do not partake of the *advantage*?

Why do our competitors and their promotional, self-serving writers want to destroy this public advantage? Must we lose it before we realize what a great public benefit it is?

Why do these writers and lobbyists feel that you and I must give up wonderful benefits so they can be competitive?

Why do *they* not react and lobby positively to this benefit and work to create something new and innovative with which to become competitive, and to add to the public welfare beneficially?

As I have said before, it's easier to destroy than it is to create. It's easier to promote negative than it is to sell positive. If our detractors could cause all advisors and all buyers of permanent life insurance plans to lose this perceived *unfair advantage, they* believe *they* would benefit *personally.*

What is this *unfair advantage*? Simply stated, it is the tax sheltering of the growth on the cash values inside a life insurance policy. Is this an unfair advantage? If so, to whom is it unfair?

They say it is an unfair advantage to benefit the life insurance companies. But the benefit is yours, that is, all voting citizens of the country who take the *advantage,* by the purchase of our plans.

Do *they* complain that you must pay for this benefit with after tax dollars? No! *They* would point out that you must buy a savings plan at the bank or a mutual fund with tax paid dollars. Do *they* not realize, that in order to get this perceived *unfair advantage;* you must pay an additional tax on your tax paid dollars?

Do *they* not realize that there is a further tax applied regularly to the earnings on this so-called tax-free benefit; if not, why not?

Do they complain that no similar deposit tax exists on a savings account or on any other investment? No, of course not, and I can imagine how the public would react if the government required them to pay 2% on every addition they made to their savings' accounts.

Do *they* complain that you may be required to pay taxes on your cash values when you withdraw them. Do *they* complain that the government taxes you on the deposits, and that they tax you again during the accumulation process?

No, of course not!

They complain that the life insurance companies can and do deliver products with competitive *advantages* to you, in spite of this extra taxation. *They* complain that our beneficiaries, our families, receive a tax free benefit when we die.

The benefit of this perceived *unfair advantage* is not free. We, the buyers of the product, paid for it. We have earned it! We have a right to it!

Treasure it and protect it. Don't let *them* destroy something that benefits you and your loved ones regardless of *their* greedy attempts to benefit at your loss. It is truly a *fair* advantage to all who take the advantage.

The benefit is yours, not the insurance industry's. The benefactors are your loved ones—*your family*. This totally *fair* advantage allows us to provide better paid-up benefits, that is, paid in full life insurance for your family at your death, whenever you die.

Why must we, the agents, the sales people, be responsible for this important message? Why has the industry charged us with this awesome responsibility?

Why must we be the guardians of what is good and right for our clients?

Why?

Because:

- We are qualified to do it
- We have the training, the knowledge and the ability to do it
- We have the opportunity each day and every day to affect the thinking and the understanding of at least one other person
- We have experienced the power of our product to save families and businesses and the dreams of both from that terrible destruction when death occurs prematurely, or inevitably
- We are witnesses to the tragedy for families and the devastation to estates when a proper permanent program of life insurance is not maintained
- We know the facts—our detractors do not or they could not write nor promulgate so much negative nonsense
- We are not merely salespeople looking for a commission; we are educators
- We do not need the approval of those with specialized or biased agendas; for what do they know
- We do not need to look to those, cloistered in the marbled halls of our head offices, for guidance

It is our duty—our special challenge to succeed in this struggle for the minds of the public. Ours is not the task of selling to greedy natures; for our product is designed to benefit others rather than the self. It is our responsibility—alone—because no one else can do it. If companies could have made the greater public understand it, they would have done so already. If our companies could achieve this impossible dream, salespeople would no longer be necessary. If the population at large ever fully understood the magnificent power of the product we sell, we would be redundant because people would line up, pick a number, and buy without any prompting. Throughout the history of insurance, salespeople have been the very essence of the business. Without our unshakable faith in the value of the products offered, there would be no products to offer.

Duty, responsibility, and opportunity are all within the realm of our domain and ours alone because the salespeople understand this "miracle of paper and ink." (Woody Woodson)

It does not matter whether or not they look upon us as professionals. What is of concern to us, is that the buying public supports us. They can do so by listening to those who have earned the right to be financial advisors while ignoring those who assume authority without earning it. We do not ask for the public's trust. We know we must earn it. Nevertheless, surely it is fair for our industry to ask the public to ignore and to reject the detractors who have never earned the right to ask for their trust.

We are professionals. We have earned the right to be referred to as professionals.

I am a professional.
There, that's not so hard.
Just say it!

Myth: Unbiased Fee Based Advice

A relatively large number of those posing as experts on financial matters advocate getting a fee based advisor. Authors of books or articles and speakers on radio and TV frequently claim that you can get unbiased advice only from advisors on a fee for service basis. Obviously, according to *them*, a commissioned salesperson is biased toward the sale of his company's products, especially those on which she can make the greatest return. According to *them* a commissioned salesperson cannot put his clients' interests above his own or her own. Consider the following carefully:

• *There is no such thing as unbiased advice.*

Such a concept is not possible. A fee for service advisor is, broadly speaking, either highly knowledgeable about the available products and services, or he operates on a system that identifies the problem areas but does not provide specific solutions. The advisor who knows products well enough to give advice as to which product is best to solve a client's problems, will have—must have—a preference of one product over another. It's human nature. Without this bias, the advice from the advisor would not be of much value. At best, it would be wishy-washy. Advisors in the second group, while not having specific in depth knowledge of products, still have personal opinions based on personal experiences. What products do these people own personally? That could be a key to their specific biases. Some people are specialists in the area of diagnosis. They may be knowledgeable in special areas of trusts, wills, estate freezes, budgeting, and life style planning. They have an ability to isolate problems and help people design a comprehensive program. Advice from them is general in nature rather than product specific. Their advice would be to see a product specialist for implementation of the program.

Do you need this much planning?

Can you afford it?

• *Very few financial advisors can afford to work on a fee basis.* Most need to maintain their basic profession on a full time basis and provide their expertise as consultants for a fee. Tax accountants and tax lawyers come readily to mind. In my experience, many commissioned sales people refer their clients to a specialist if they recognize the need for special advice.

• *Some commissioned sales people wear two hats.*

It seems that more advisors are offering their financial knowledge for a fee. They may help you analyze the problem and propose a number of possible solutions. You may take a proposed solution to your choice of sales specialists for implementation. You may decide to buy product from the advisor who prepared the program. You may decide to do nothing or implement only certain parts of it. In any case, the advisor will have earned her fee. Ethical advisors must advise you up front as to their method of operation. They must inform you about their fee rate and how they charge it. It could be a fixed amount for the task, or the fee could be an hourly rate. They should estimate the number of hours required. They must advise you when the clock will start running. Usually the first hour or two for initial consultation is free. During this time you and the advisor may explore what you require. The advisor explains how she works. When there is specific agreement as to what you expect for the fee being charged, you have a contract. The contract should always be in written form. If the advisor charges an hourly fee the clock stops when she finishes the task. Reportedly, some advisors will reduce their fees if you proceed with product purchase from them. In practice, I suspect most advisors do not offer any such incentive. You would be free to purchase product or implement the program wherever you desire. If you decide to purchase product from the fee based advisor, he must now change hats. If they did not earn the consultation fee, surely you would not consider any additional involvement. Now the compensation for your advisor's advice and time comes from commissions, if you buy product.

• *A common practice is for a commissioned sales person to work with one or more specialists such as an accountant or a lawyer.*

There may be a partnership arrangement of some sort. Perhaps they jointly own a financial planning company. In some larger firms the accountant or lawyer may be a full time salaried staff member. Your advisor may refer you to the specialist for her part of the program. Then it is back to the product specialist when you are ready. In effect, you hire the firm and they provide the necessary expertise in all areas, including working directly with your own accountant or lawyer. The important thing here is that your advisor clarifies everything right up front.

• *You do not need to look for an unbiased advisor.*

It's much more important to understand your advisor's bias. Does she always advocate term life insurance only, with a separate investment in mutual funds or stocks and bonds? Does she prefer a permanent life insurance plan; with the investment program as a separate issue? Is she flexible, always being considerate of your special needs, wants, and personal preferences? Frankly none of this matters providing you know it right from the start. In the final analysis you will buy what is right for you and your family providing you have been able to review all of the options.

***Unbiased advice, if it existed,
is not nearly as important as good advice.***

Myth: Pay Yourself First

In 1926, George S. Clason wrote his classic book entitled *The Richest Man in Babylon.* It is still a very popular book, quoted frequently by various authors, but without proper credit to the originator of these insightful concepts. George S. Clason wrote phrases that have become *household* common. Many people use them without knowing or caring from whence they came. Some of these phrases are: "A part of everything you earn should be yours to keep." "Pay yourself first."

Today, as never before, people are advocating that you should follow this precept. The key point that most people remember about *The Wealthy Barber* is that you should start to save young and *pay yourself first.* Chilton popularized this concept, but his was not the original version. In fact, the life insurance business has been using that approach for a very long time, perhaps even before Clason; but certainly long before all of the others who are currently writing on the subject.

The purpose of the concept was, and it still is, to get young people to save a percentage of everything they earn. *In theory, it is an incredible concept. In practice, it is an incredible failure.*

One mathematical theory, advocated by both life insurance and mutual fund companies is as follows. If you save $1,000 each year from age 25 to age 35, you will accumulate more by age 65, than you would by saving $1,000 from age 35 to age 65.

Mathematically that is correct; because of *the magic of compound interest.* Pragmatically it is incorrect. In real life it does not work quite so well.

The late John Savage of Toledo, Ohio illustrated dramatically why the use of the concept is about as effective as the theory of hit the golf ball down the middle of the fairway. It's an obvious truism except for one problem. Thinking it and knowing it is just the first part of the program. Execution is the second and more complex part.

John demonstrated that you could save:
(a) $50.00 each month in an investment of your choice and at any reasonable interest rate you want to assume, plus
(b) $50.00 each month in the bank at 3% (or less), plus
(c) $50.00 each month in a life insurance policy at 2.5% (guaranteed minimum) and
(d) $50.00 in a milk can.
You must do this for 20 years. After a poignant pause, John would ask, "At the end of twenty years which of these investments would have accumulated the most money?" When the guessing subsided, John would point out that there was one piece of vital information missing. *The money deposited to the milk can must remain in the can until the end of the twentieth year. Invariably the milk can wins.*

Why? It is the better solution for most people because they cannot get at it. Very few people have the discipline to save it and to keep it saved. When the bills start to mount up, it is not possible for most of us to maintain a savings program. Young people starting out have many demands on their earnings. Rent, food, clothing, mortgages, car repairs, furniture, and the whole gambit of expenses for children. What happens to the savings account when the refrigerator breaks down or you wear out your stove? How about when you need braces for the kids' teeth, equipment for sports activities, music lessons, and so on and on and on?

For most young people, between the ages of 25 and 40, the demands on income are enormous, and at the same time income levels are at their lowest. During this period of time, the best advice we could give is to stay out of debt if possible. Conversely, if you go into debt, apply all of your resources to repay it.

Saving for retirement is not of prime importance during the child rearing years. The years from age 40 to age 65 are adequate for retirement purposes. Nevertheless having said that, some forced savings can be valuable. Locked-in pension plans have served a vital function in the financial affairs of many people. The most prominent example of a pay yourself first program is the company pension plan. The best thing about a pension plan is that your contribution comes off the top. Secondly you cannot get at the cash too easily. You have to solve your financial problems without this money. That's good, although some people will not agree with me.

However, *pay yourself first* is sometimes an unworkable concept when you are young. We tend to miss the point, that in order to save it and keep it saved, *you need to spend less than you earn*. Sometimes, for those who are just starting out, the ability to earn money is barely equal to the need to spend it. That's why the failure rate of many registered savings plans is so high. Some people borrow to buy registered savings plans in order to reduce taxes. Then the burden of paying the borrowed money back, in addition to the unexpected bills that suddenly materialize, may be just too much. After cancellation charges and taxes, caused by cashing in, many people wonder if it was worth it.

Conversely, if you fail to try to save for your retirement during the years, from age 25 to age 40, should you feel guilty? Some authors have made it sound so simple and so easy, but then some of them are writing novels. With myths and in fantasies everything is achievable, but in the world of reality it does not always work out so idealistically.

Charles Givens may have been a bit of a con man, but he did hit upon something that is more important than what many of the other financial commentators managed. He tried to find and demonstrate ways of saving money, by spending less. Givens advocated buying less expensive insurance; life, auto, and home. Unfortunately, he did not understand insurance. His advice about life insurance was, in a nutshell, don't buy any until you *need* it and then buy only *term life insurance*. Nevertheless, he was closer to the truth than many of the others. None of them seemed to have understood the fundamental principal behind the pay yourself first concept.

Many people read a popularized book and react as though they have just experienced a great revelation. They rush out to the bank or to a broker and buy an RRSP; perhaps a mutual fund, with borrowed money. Two months later, after tax returns, some of them discover that they have other bills to pay, and they need to cash in their *pay yourself first* programs.

This approach provides temporary relief by reducing taxes in some cases. However, cashing these plans to pay bills can be expensive because of withholding taxes and fees. One year later a new problem arises; the remainder of the tax is due. No problem! We can do it all over again. Buy a larger RRSP, save even more on taxes, then cash it in again to pay the bills. It works! Well, not for long! Eventually the question becomes; *do you know a good bankruptcy accountant?*

Many advisors say the right words, but some of them, it seems, never grasp the basic concept. Spend less than you earn and have something to invest. To modernize a classic from the playwright, John Locke: *Earn $4,000 per month; spend $3,900; result: happiness. Earn $4,000 per month; spend $4,100 per month; result: disaster.*

Spend less! Save it! Invest it!

George S. Clason did not advocate that people should save 10% for themselves while ignoring the bills. Rather, Clason was saying live on 90% of your earnings; then *keep* the remainder for yourself. Before you can *save* you must be able to spend less than you earn. Perhaps authors and writers selling this advice *do not tell it as it is* because people do not want to hear it. When you think about it, the thought is a self-evident truth, and nobody wants to pay for advice everybody already knows. What sells well, of course, is the fiction that everyone can do it. Okay then, let me tell you that *you can do it*, but let's temper this enthusiasm with a dash of realism.

If you were the parents of my grandchildren, I would tell you that these precious wards stay young for such a short time. They grow up so fast. One of the most rewarding investments you can ever make is what you spend on your children. Trying to save money for retirement when they are young is for most people a futile exercise leading to frustration and disappointment. Relax. Buy the things young people need. Travel, do the things young people want to do. From age 30 to age 45 spend it on your family. Do your heavy saving from age 45 to age 70.

Be generous on living today.
Let tomorrow take care of tomorrow.

Myth: IF

If you had invested $10,000 in the Templeton fund, when it began in 1954, your investment would have grown to $2 million dollars by 1990; according to Dr. Riley Moynes.

In *No Salesman Will Call?,* this pointless example was answered; (see page 210). Even so, there are other important considerations that Dr. Moynes appears to have ignored. For example, he did not consider inflation nor the devaluation of the dollar. Nevertheless, it would have been a good investment **IF**...

The following are some other examples that are even more impressive:

IF you had bought $10,000 in common shares of Xerox in 1960, those shares would have been worth $16.5 million in 1970.

IF you had bought $10,000 worth of Price Company shares in 1982, they would have increased to $180,000 by 1986.

IF you had purchased only $1,000 worth of Microsoft shares in 1986, the value today would be over $290,000.

IF you had bought $10,000 worth of common shares of Bre-X (gold mining scam), in 1995, it would be worthless today.

There are many ***IFs*** in buying stocks or mutual funds or real estate or exotic art. Investing in matters not clearly understood can be a very dangerous strategy. Buying into the reasoning of "IF you had...," as a reason for making a decision, is like walking on a path of loose marbles.

Assuming that you can pick the next Templeton Fund or the next *gee-whiz* stock, such as Xerox or Price Company, while avoiding Bre-X type stocks is extremely presumptuous. There are many non-exploded *duds* in the market place for one to avoid.

Let's assume that you were twenty-two years old in 1954—forty-three years ago. (You would be about 65 years old today.) You were a precocious youth recently graduated from University at age 22. Your grandmother's estate just settled and your entitlement was $10,000. Your brothers and sisters each bought a new home and a new car—paid for in full. You, however, being the youngest and still single, decided to invest this endowment rather than spend it on fast cars and exotic world trips.

Your market research leads you to a new kind of investment—a mutual fund called the Templeton Fund. You recognize the name from your business administration course 201, and it piques your interest. Naturally, you acquire all available literature and study it assiduously. It looks good! However, being a prudent young educated person, you decide to discuss it with your father. He was born in 1912 and was just seventeen when the market crashed in 1929. He could not afford to continue his education, but was required to work full-time on his father's farm just to survive. He remembers the recovery in 1930 and everyone with any money bought back into the market as it began its ascent. Then, in 1931, an even more devastating crash occurred. He remembers! All too well, he remembers the slow painful recovery. He remembers that there was no money available to buy things. He remembers 1939 and the start of the Second World War. He remembers the young people going away to war and he remembers some of them coming home. He remembers that jobs got really scarce, because of the numbers returning to the work force in 1945. These young people had demands for new cars, new homes and new families. Soon there was a scarcity of product. Second hand or used cars cost more than new ones, because if you paid enough you could get a car immediately rather than go on a waiting list of up to six months. These young people were in a hurry to catch up on the years missed during the war and they went into debt readily in order to get it *now*.

Your father remembers that the stock market had finally recovered fully only now, in 1954 and he observes:

IF you had invested $10,000 in the market in 1929, it would have taken twenty-five years to get it back. Of course, during those twenty-five years, you may have needed the money so badly that you may have sold your shares when they recovered to the $5,000 level. You would not want to suffer through another crash similar to 1929 and lose it all. On the other hand, there may not have been any buyers at your price so you would have to sell for less—perhaps $4,000. "You must understand," states your father, "you can only sell your shares ***IF*** there is a buyer." Liquid investments require the presence of buyers.

You reply, "Thank you father. I came to you for advice and you gave me a history lesson. Times are different now. We are a lot more sophisticated and more knowledgeable too. The government has established programs so that the 1929–1931 event can never happen again."

Your slightly shocked father retorts, "Is that what they taught you in college? Didn't they teach you about dollar cost averaging and diversification as a means of asset protection?"

"Yes, Dad, they did teach us those things and this new fund is very well diversified. It's not like buying one stock and hoping it will grow. They invest in a whole lot of stocks."

"Okay, your desire to save your inheritance and invest it, rather than spend it is admirable, so why don't you buy five different types of funds from five different companies? Wouldn't that be wiser? Better yet, why don't you buy land?"

Nevertheless, you prevail and in 1954 you invest $10,000 in one basket, the Templeton fund. Now, in 1990 when you are 58 years old, you probably would have over two million dollars; **IF**.

IF you never needed to spend any of the earnings on your money.

IF you never used some of it to buy a home or a new car.

IF you did not dip into it to take a well-deserved holiday with your family.

IF you did not need some of this money for your kids' education.

IF you did not sell some or all of it when the signs appeared to forecast another market crash.

IF a myriad of other pressures did not creep up on you.

Unquestionably, the Templeton fund would have been a wise choice, in 1954, in which to invest $10,000; **IF** you had $10,000 to spare. However, the example is worthless when you are considering the realities of yesterday and of today unless you need practice working mathematical equations.

Trying to find the best performing stock or fund, that is, the one in a million to take you from pauper to prince, is like panning for gold in a mountain stream. Besides freezing your fingers, you may end up with a bucket of *fool's gold*. You may say "Ah, but some people do very well in the stock market without any advice from you." Of course, and some golfers do rather well without my advice. I would never presume to advise Jack Nicholas nor Tiger Woods on any aspect of golfing. Likewise, I would never advise those who know what they are doing, on any aspect of investing in the market. However, I do provide advice for those who have made it, on how to keep it and use it wisely, to achieve the maximum benefit for their personal and family goals.

For some people, investing in the market is a process and they have theories, philosophies, and concepts that turn investing in the securities market into a system. For others, the securities market can become a slippery slope, known as the insecurity's market. I never understood the concept of, "**IF** you can stand to risk it all on just one throw (of the dice), you'll be a man." Intelligent risk, based on knowledge, experience, and perspicacity, is a different matter.

Even so, **IF** remains involved and if you listen to your friends in conversation about their investments, you may hear some fascinating statements:

"**IF** the price of my XYZ shares continue to go up, one month from now I'll sell enough to pay off the mortgage on my home and put a million dollars in the bank." I asked a dumb question of the acquaintance who made this precise statement to me.

"Why don't you sell enough right now to pay off your mortgage and put a hundred thousand in the bank?"

Perhaps you can imagine the reaction of my friend and client. He didn't say anything. He didn't have to say it aloud. The look he gave me was similar to the one you may get for giving unsolicited advice on the golf course.

Two weeks later, the banks cut off the company's line of credit, called some of the loans and within days forced them into receivership. Neither my client nor any of the other shareholders could sell any of their shares—because there *were no buyers.* There was no market for shares of a company that was about to be destroyed by its creditors. My client lost his home, and he barely escaped personal bankruptcy. If the bank had not forgiven $250,000 of his loan, he would have been totaled.

Consider the following If statements?

IF I had listened to my broker…

IF I had not listened to my broker…

IF I had sold earlier…

IF I had not sold so soon…

IF I had not missed that putt on #9…

Value Investing

The securities market has been likened to a senior-level Las Vegas—you can make it big or you can lose it all. If you telephone to the New York Stock Exchange, you may get a recorded message that states, "Investment objectives have changed from quick-dollar schemes to savings oriented vehicles concerned with long-term security." This recording suggested that there was an emphasis on ownership without speculation.

But, at the same time;

Of the 51 billion shares listed on the New York Stock Exchange, 31 billion changed hands, that is, the investors traded them. While this recording played, 28 billion more stocks traded in over-the-counter markets and in various other stock exchanges. For further information read *Value Investing Today* by Charles H. Brandes. Mr. Brandes states that you must earn worthwhile results. His book is about *value investing* rather than market cycle guessing and sector evaluation. He states that switching in and out of stocks is just feeding the brokers.

Are you investing or speculating? Investing is when you buy a security, pay for it in full, place it in a specific place for safe keeping, and hold it for the income it produces.

Speculation is when you buy a security on margin and you keep it ready for sale if the price advances. Many advisors state that anything held for less than three to five years is speculation. Any purchase based on anticipated market improvements or forecasting is speculation. Investing is buying based on knowledge, correct action, and patience, according to Warren Buffett. Speculation is dancing with the lightning pace of financial change and setting your sails to the money winds which vary on average three times each year.

Okay, but what is Value Investing? It's really not that difficult. It is merely paying attention to investment fundamentals and taking advantage of under valuation and mis-pricing of individual securities.

That should be easy, right? Maybe so, but for most people it is too painstaking, too boring, and much too disciplined. Value investing is a philosophy. It is not a get rich quick concept. A value investor is not prone to listen to advisors with fancy complicated strategies, such as market timing and asset allocation or as sector investing.

Value investing is a method of capital preservation. As you know, the first rule of investing is never lose your capital, and the second rule of investing is refer back to number one.

Growth investors may do extremely well at times but they are subject to large permanent declines. Value investing, on the other hand, is buying part ownership in the business. Conversely, speculation occurs whenever there is a higher than average possibility of a loss while anticipating a higher than average return.

There seems to be an obsession with total return based on a philosophy of offense without defense. That is; **IF** you pile up enough offensive points you will not need a good defense. Whatever happened to the concept of safety of principal and a satisfactory return? For some that thought is out of date. But consider this if: **IF** professionals cannot retain control over what they are doing through study and experienced analysis, why should the average investor feel confident that she can speculate with impunity?

Clearly there are different kinds of investing, different styles, different goals, and different purposes. Perhaps it is appropriate for some people to take speculation risks. My comments and thoughts do not apply to them. That whole area is outside my comfort zone. Those of my clients who are involved in such activities fascinate me, and I listen to them in awe, but they rarely tempt me to join them. Once, I did consider buying into a pen of feeder cattle, with a rancher client of mine. He and his brother had just made one million dollars in one week. I was ready to write a cheque, but my client advised me to think about it. He showed me a few examples of what could happen. "**IF** you had purchased a number of cattle being fed and fattened for market, at the right time, you could have made a very good return." "However", he cautioned, "look at some other examples before you decide." He then showed me several files where they had invested $120,000 and sold them for $80,000 or $90,000. "You see when those steers are ready for market, they must be sold, even if the investor must lose." My client told me to be cautious. "Ask yourself if you can afford to lose $30,000 to $40,000. Sometimes you get lucky and catch the market when it is high, but not always. Usually you can expect to make a reasonable profit. Sometimes you lose."

"What happened last week when you made so much?" I asked.

"Well, it was sheer luck. You see, just as our cattle were ready for market two weeks earlier, there was a strike and we were unable to ship them. That put a strain on us, the space, extra feed, and special care to keep those critters healthy and ready for market. The extra costs under most circumstances would have guaranteed a loss on each of those pens. Furthermore, in order to sell more than our usual volume, we might have had to sell at an even lower price per pound, thereby compounding our loss, and extending it to the other pens. What happened? Prices went up substantially just as we got to market. The demand was up and supply was low. We got lucky, but don't count on it happening again. That would be sheer speculation. Can you afford to be wrong?"

Will Rogers said, "I am more interested in the return of my money than the return on it." That homespun philosophy works for me. My main activity involves *retirement planning* and there is no room for speculation when you are dealing with sacred dollars. **IF** you can get a satisfactory return why take unnecessary risks? The term satisfactory, of course, has a different meaning for each investor. In the broad concept, satisfactory literally means that which gives satisfaction. The basic concept of satisfaction is the fulfillment of a need or a want.

There are no rules of thumb to guide the investor nor the advisor, except that each individual must determine her own level of risk tolerance. Value investing is a way of minimizing the risk while maximizing returns over time, but it is not exciting enough for some investors. This is not a get rich quick scheme. It requires time and discipline. IF you can follow the advice of value investors like Brandis and Buffett, your retirement planning will carry you successfully into and through your journey on the senior circuit.

With enough insider information and a million dollars, you could go broke in a year.

~Warren Buffett

Myth: The Old Principles of Investing Do Not Apply Today

One of the earliest recorded lessons on investing can be found in the St. James version of the Bible; St. Matthew, chapter 25; verses 14 through 30.

The parable related is regarding an individual about to travel into distant lands. He called his servants together and entrusted each of them with *talents* or units of some value. (You may substitute any amount in any currency.)

Unto the first the master gave five *talents*. The second he endowed with two and to the third he entrusted but one such talent. Then the master left on his vacation. The story goes that the first servant took his five talents, invested them in trade and made an additional five talents. He doubled the money entrusted to him. The second servant, the one with two talents, also invested wisely and doubled the value. The third one, however, took his one talent and buried it in the ground.

Eventually the traveler returned home and called his *servants* together and expected an accounting, or a *reckoning*. The first proudly displayed ten talents. The master, being properly impressed, gave this loyal servant a promotion. The second servant stepped forward with his four *talents*, previously two, and received a similar and equal reward.

The third servant came to the master, sheepishly, bearing the one talent with which he was entrusted. He spoke to his master saying, "I was concerned that I might lose your talent. I know that you reap where thou hast not sown and gather where thou hast not strawed." The servant confessed that knowing this he was fearful of losing this one talent so he buried it. His master, the traveler, was distraught and called him names, "Slothful" and "Wicked" (even). The master continued his harangue—<paraphrased>. You could have deposited this talent in a bank, at least, so that I could have received my talent plus the customary *usury*.

This servant received no reward but was cast out (into darkness?)

The one talent that he had was taken from him.

Then there follows an often quoted saying—verse 29. "For unto every one that hath shall be given, and he shall have abundance: but from him that hath not shall be taken even that which he hath."

Biblical scholars may read different things into these verses; and from a psychological approach, I could draw some irreverent analogies. However, I see a simple principle in this paraphrased parable. There are two sources of income:

1. People at work
2. Dollars at work

When the traveler went on his journey, he left eight talents with his brokers. The first seven entrusted units were returned in manifold fashion. When one talent returned with no improvement, *the master* in anger fired his servant ignominiously. The master wanted his money to be at work. He expected a satisfactory return. You must take some risk if you would improve the value of the investment.

First Taxation ~ First Savings

The earliest recorded demographer, prognosticator, interpreter of dreams, was Joseph; whose story was told in Genesis: Chapter 41, verses 15 through 57.

The Egyptian Pharaoh brought Joseph in for questioning, since he was a well-known, talented interpreter of dreams and thoughtful person. The Pharaoh related his dreams and Joseph explained them as follows: There would be seven good years in the land of Egypt followed by seven years of famine. <Feast or famine>

And Joseph advised the Pharaoh to collect a fifth part of the produce in the land during the seven *plenteous* years. <The first recorded taxation> Joseph advised, moreover, that the collections of corn and grain be stored and saved. <Save for a rainy day> In this legend there appears to be a recording of several basic investment lessons. The principle of saving was demonstrated. Joseph advised the pharaoh to collect one fifth or 20% of each crop. Gradually, this amount has reduced to a tenth or 10%, which continues as a guide even now. Unfortunately, the principle of taxation was born at the same time and a system of socialism was effected. In this early example, the purity of the Pharaoh's intention was evident. This Pharaoh was obviously a benevolent dictator, at least at this stage in history. His taxation was unquestionably for the benefit of his people. Thus, the originator of taxation was noble in deed. (Don't you wish our government would agree to a fifth today?)

Recently I saw a movie entitled *The Day the Bubble Burst.* I had never seen it before but I certainly knew the story. As a kid I listened to dozens of stories about the depression years. You see it was a ritual at our place on the farm, every Sunday after church, to host a group of relatives and friends for lunch ~ chicken ~ always chicken. Every Sunday, we had CHICKEN. However, for supper on Sunday mother served either roast beef or pork chops. That made up for the chicken at lunch time—especially pork chops.

After lunch, the men and boys would go for a walk that ended about a half-hour later on our front porch. There, the men sat smoking their pipes, waving to neighbors going by in spiffy Model A Fords (you could get any color so long as it was black). There were roadsters and coupes with rumble seats. (That's a two seater at the back and outside.) The roads were not paved and these cars usually threw up clouds of dust that, depending on the wind, could easily drown out the aroma of the pipes. Everybody knew everybody, and sometimes these passersby stopped, joined the men on the verandah, pulled up a chair, lit up their pipes and took up the conversation.

While the men walked and talked, the women washed the lunch dishes, prepared the oven for dinner, and reset the table. Thereafter, on occasion, they joined the group on the front porch. In any case, the stories reminisced and related often started out about calving and other farm events of the week just past. THE FARM REPORT. Or perhaps, the discussion would be about hockey or baseball, local or professional. Each visitor reveled in his turn at story telling, while the rest of us—the audience, listened with rapt attention. No one interrupted except to ask a question, or perhaps to remind the story teller of an event apparently being overlooked. We had all heard these stories many times, but we all listened respectfully because the historian was telling or retelling a personal experience. It may have been about Ty Cobb, Babe Ruth, Mackenzie King or Theodore Roosevelt, or any of the other *greats* from that era. We kids sat there with the adults in silent fascination. Silent because *kids were to be seen but not heard*; and fascinated because the stories were incredibly good, and the story tellers were riveting. (Why not, as they practiced every Sunday.)

Eventually, about the time the women left to finish preparations for supper, the subject changed to the depression years. We were still in them but we did not know it. Actually, I was twelve years old before I realized that we were not rich. After all, we had a large number of chickens, all laying eggs or waiting to be next Sunday's lunch. We raised thirty or so pigs. We had a large flock of sheep for wool—not for eating. We owned a stable of seven horses for pulling the plows, discs and land leveling boats; plus between two and five colts at any given time. There were about twenty milking cows, for what else, milk, cream and butter. There was a flock of domesticated ducks (we clipped their wings so they could not fly away). Also my dad's pride and joy was his apiary with the ten or more bee hives that he nurtured for honey. We sold eggs, cream, butter, wool, honey and vegetables. We had two cars in the garage (only one working). And wild game was readily available; geese, rabbits, squirrel, pheasant, and quail. We had dogs and cats, tame raccoons, ferrets and pet turtles. If that's not rich, what is? Ah yes *rich or poor, it's nice to have money*. We had everything that one could want except money. We had no debt but we had no money. (Never poor—never rich.)

No matter, sooner or later, the talk turned to the depression years and the audience sat in quiet concentration while the speaker related a story from that era 1929, 1930, 1931. A period of silence followed each story before someone else remembered another sad tale.

During the earlier story telling sessions, there was a certain amount of jocular bravado. When the stories from the depression or the dirty thirties started, the mood changed and everyone sat pondering the recent past, with long sad faces. When the call came for the evening meal, we left the story telling and quietly filed in to the table. There a sumptuous setting of soups, meats, fresh vegetables, fruits from our orchard, honey from our apiary, homemade bread and pies (fit for a sovereign), awaited them. The contrast between the earlier conversation and this fine meal was notable. Everyone sat down to this veritable feast in quiet contemplation; thankful that they had not succumbed to the ravages of that era; thankful that they had survived to enjoy a better day.

It was not necessary, therefore, for me to have seen this marvelous movie in order to understand it and know its plot intimately. For me it was, as Yogi Berra would say, *déjà vu all over again*. The plot of the stories was not new to me. Nevertheless, one part of the movie fascinated me. A brief scene unfolded between a postman and a young homemaker. Their conversation took place at a time just before the crash, while the average earner was risking everything right there beside the wealthy people. It went something like this, as he handed some mail to the youthful woman:

"What are those other letters?"

"Oh," the postman replied, "they are about the stock market—about buying stocks."

"Really? How does that work?"

The postman beamed enthusiastically to be able to show his knowledge. "Well, that's easy, you just call your broker, and place an order to buy some stock."

"No kidding, what if you don't have any money?"

"You can borrow from your broker—you get credit. It's called on margin."

"Is that a good idea?"

"Yeah, for sure, if the market goes up."

"What happens if the market goes down?"

"Well, the broker calls your margin and makes you pay up."

"What if you can't pay?"

The postman chuckled wryly, "Then he sells your stock and demands whatever is left owing. If you can't meet his demands, he takes everything you own—house, car, etc."

"Oh, that's terrible. How horrible! Does the broker lose too?"

"No, no, he collects his commission and comes out fine—just fine."

It may have happened in 1929 you say, *but it can't happen today*. Wanna bet?

When the advice is rendered, the rendition leaves the old principles of investing intact, as the best ones for most people.

> *If a graduating MBA were to ask me, 'How do I get rich in a hurry?'*
> *I would not respond with quotations from Ben Franklin or Horatio Alger, but would instead hold my nose with one hand and point with the other toward Wall Street.*
>
> ~ Warren Buffett

Myth: Mutual Funds Take All The Guessing Out of Investing

Mutual funds should make investing easier by allowing ordinary investors to acquire professional management, and a degree of diversification that only very rich individuals could otherwise experience. However, it seems there are too many choices now: stocks, bonds, derivatives, small cap and large cap companies are prevalent to name a few. Among the funds available, some classifications are: Technological, Unity, Global, Emerging Country, Pacific Basin, European, Asian, South American, Indexed, Single Manager, Multiple Manager et cetera. Each one has some advocates making claims of its being the best. Who knows, maybe some of them will be better than a guaranteed income certificate, at least. That has not always been the case.

Investors need a way to make sense of all these choices. Frequently, they turn to books written by people who are not selling any of them, and who, in some cases, have never sold any of these products. Of course, there are some common-sense guidelines one can follow, such as:

• *Define the problem before you try to solve it.*

Is your need or desire for wealth accumulation, or is it for a safe return of your investment after a reasonable return on it? Everyone advises that you must know your tolerance level for taking financial risk. We even have questionnaires to help determine your tolerance level and computer software programs to help develop a strategy. However, in my experience, this ephemeral level varies depending on the fortunes of the market. What many perceive as a risky venture tends to lose significance in periods of rapid growth, for some people. They become caught up in the excitement of making exceptional returns and their concept of risk seems to change. Perhaps it vacillates with the amount of confidence each one has in continued growth and market expansion.

• *Beware the expert who cannot explain it clearly and concisely.*

One should always try to determine the advisor's biases. Does she represent several families of funds or is he on the payroll of a specific fund? Some of the quotable experts speak to audiences as independents, but sometimes we discover that they are on the board of directors of a sponsoring company. You may find that a corporation with a vested interest has sponsored the meeting. It may not matter, but you should know the facts before you make decisions based on advice given at the seminar by a supposedly unbiased presenter. One well-known speaker's sponsor, at various events, is a large bank. Whose concepts do you think he supports?

• *Investing is what you do with what you have left after you have paid your bills.*

Sometimes, people who spend everything they earn, try to follow the popularized advice of; "pay yourself first." Investing money that you will need eventually to pay bills can be very costly. Investing always involves some risk. Risk is about loss of income, loss of principal, or loss of purchasing power. Investing money that you may need for something else may be foolhardy.

• *Investing should serve a purpose.*

Are you investing for retirement? Are you saving to provide an income to replace employment earnings? There are only two sources of income, men or women at work, and dollars at work. Are you saving for the education of your children, or to provide money for vacations, new furniture, new cars, etc.? The ability to save is conditional on things over which you do have some control, as well as for matters over which you have little or no control.

There are some basic expenditures that we all have such as food, clothing, and shelter. Others such as entertainment and nonessential or luxury items are somewhat more controllable. In all of these things there is some level of discretionary spending. You can eat T-bone steaks or you could eat chuck roasts without any serious loss of benefit. However, young people may have a somewhat lower ability to earn.

Young parents may have expenses that are relatively high. If you are attempting to survive ten more days until your next pay cheque, it may be foolish to try saving money for future use, or to try investing in exotic stocks.

- *The time frame, or period of years, during which you can save and invest is a very important consideration.*

If you are age 25, you may have 40 to 45 years to actively save and invest before retirement. Clearly you can afford a higher risk on fewer dollars. You have time to recover from temporary reversals or market corrections. If you are approaching retirement, however, things may be very different. People in this group can invest larger sums of money but they cannot afford to suffer major set backs. Stated differently, if you have made it already, why would you risk it? Investing at this point becomes a matter of making a reasonable return after taxes and after inflation. Buying a mutual fund in today's complex financial world seems to make sense for most people. It allows one to buy a piece of a large number of stocks. However, the complexity of funds available today requires a considerable amount of study or the assistance of a knowledgeable advisor.

A mutual fund or a segregated fund provides an added benefit of professional management. Whereas, if you buy stocks separately, even with the advice of a stockbroker, you in effect, become the fund manager. Not everyone has the expertise, nor wishes to acquire it, in order to be a good fund manager. Consequently, your broker may acquire too much importance and the question becomes, "Where does he get his advice and are there any special reasons behind his recommendations?"

When choosing a mutual fund, one should pay attention to the fund manager's philosophy and management style. If the proposed fund is speculative in nature, you should weigh the risk of loss against the potential for gain. Knowing and understanding your level of risk tolerance is important. In the final analysis you still must manage it, because *a mutual fund does not take all the guessing out of investing.*

One aspect that many people overlook when registering a mutual fund, that is, in an RRSP, is the capital gains factor. There is always a risk of loss when buying equities, even using a mutual fund vehicle. The reward for taking that risk, is being able to benefit from capital gains taxation. Capital gains taxes apply only on 75% of the gain; whereas with an RRSP, taxation applies to 100% of any withdrawal.

It would seem prudent to hold riskier investments outside your RRSP and keep the safer ones inside your plan. It does not follow automatically that safer plans return a lower profit. Most people realize that some funds result in losses, even in bullish conditions. Consequently, it may be beneficial to write-off capital losses against capital gains. *Within an RRSP this advantage is lost.*

That's one reason I like segregated funds for RRSPs. Your principal, or the amount deposited, is 100% guaranteed at maturity, in most situations, but in all cases no less than 75%. The return on your money, is no more guaranteed than it would be in a mutual fund, but the return *of* your investment is fully guaranteed, at maturity. Maturity is a date that the buyer specifies. It must be at least ten years from the date of purchase. The purchaser may change this date as she wishes. Furthermore, setting a maturity date does not restrict one's right to withdraw funds prior to that date, in part or in full.

Several segregated funds also guarantee 100% of any gain made, up to ten years prior to your maturity date. For example, assume you deposit $50,000 at age 45 and your fund grows to $150,000 by age 55. If you had set your maturity date as age 65, there is a guarantee that the amount will not be less than $150,000 at age 65, regardless of what happens in the marketplace. Naturally, all gains between age 55 and age 65 are yours, but the fund cannot be below $150,000 at maturity (less any withdrawals). Again, there is no restriction on the withdrawal of your funds during this period.

Another aspect with some segregated funds, which appeals to me, is the *multiple manager* approach. Within the family, you may have fifteen funds to choose from. Each fund may have from two to six managers typically. There is no specific number of managers required, but rather it depends on the make up and philosophy of the fund. The selected manager has an expertise in his or her area of specialization. Each manager may have a specific requirement that restricts her to operating within defined parameters. This approach provides a diversification within the fund and, therefore, an additional degree of safety.

In some mutual funds, a fund manager may exhibit considerable expertise and skill over a period of time. However, what happens if he leaves the fund, for any reason, including death? Some segregated funds retain the best managers from several mutual funds. With the multiple manager approach no one manager is apt to overwhelm the fund, other than for relatively short periods of time. Alternatively, one manager may *save* the fund during a downturn period.

Myth of the no-load fund

No load, no fee, no service and no advice

Frequently, you hear advice or read advertisements proclaiming the advantages of a no-load fund. Of course, there is no such thing. There is always a fee for managing a fund. The phrase no-load most often means no front-end load. A front-end load may have taken up to 10% off the deposit; meaning that if you deposit $1,000 to the fund, it credits you with only $900.00. Frankly, most front-end load plans, currently, are more apt to be in the 4% to 6% range. Sometimes no-load refers to a back-end load. In other words, some funds may not charge a front-end load, but there would be a penalty for withdrawing funds during the first 4 or 5 years, or up to as many as 10 years. This applied charge is, usually, on a declining basis (first year 5% reducing by 1% per annum). However, one should keep in mind that most of these funds have investment administration fees and most of them also have a management fee. The prospectus must specify these fees. Accordingly, some *no-load* funds may charge higher administration fees. The net result could be that the front-end charge is the better choice over time.

Don’t be misled by clever advertising. On April 22,1998, an advertisement for a Canadian trust company appeared in *The Financial Post,* on page 11. It was entitled:

A FINANCIAL SERVICES COMPANY THAT OFFERS LEADING MUTUAL FUNDS, with zero commissions.

Under that, the advertisement showed a genie bottle with the genie emerging. Under the magic lamp the capsulation read, *and now, what would your next two wishes be?*

The advertisement continued with the following: *You may not realize it, but every time you buy or sell a load mutual fund, you are most likely paying a commission, perhaps as much as 5%.*
There followed several other statements, in bullet style, which caught my attention.

- Receive timely, unbiased information from our mutual fund professionals
- Best of all, pay nothing in fees when you buy, sell, or switch mutual funds
- Through (a dynamic mutual fund company), (a Canadian trust company), is the first major financial institution to make available so many funds commission-free

However, before proceeding, you should read the small print at the bottom of the advertisement very carefully. There is a double asterisk reference to the statement; *you will never pay a commission.* It then states: *Minimum $15,000 in account equity to qualify. No front or back load charges on lump sum purchases of $2,500 or more* ***per fund****. Fees will be imposed by (name) Securities and/or the fund companies for early redemption.*

Isn't that incredible? The main advertisement states *you will never pay a commission*. The small print says there is a back-end load for early redemption. You must know that my pen was poised to provide poignant answers to the insinuations in this advertisement. However, two pages later, page 13 in the same edition, there was another advertisement, made and paid for by a leading mutual fund company, answering the previous company's points.

It read:

THERE IS NO GENIE
THERE IS NO FREE LUNCH
ZERO COMMISSIONS?

"...no-load mutual fund investors, inevitably mess up. They buy high and sell low at precisely the wrong times, whipsawed by unpredictable things like interest rates, the Asian flu and everything else that makes a market."

~ Jonathan Chevreau,
The Financial Post

This advertisement proceeds to name the company and to quote directly from that company's ad; especially in reference to the 5% commission charges, compared to their no-load funds with zero commissions. They answer this gibberish with,

We feel it's important for you to know that...

Approximately 75 to 80% of all load mutual funds are already sold by fully qualified, independent advice-giving financial planners and brokers with no front-end commissions. With help and counsel from a knowledgeable advisor, you can make a long term mutual fund investment decision and never have to pay a commission.

They go on, in this advertisement, to say that the other company is a discount broker subsidiary with limited service. "**Yet it still expects to receive full-service commissions from the manager of the mutual fund**."

In other words, this trust company gets a full-service commission from the funds it represents, while offering the public a substantially lower service. Can you believe it? They denigrate the commission system, and infer some things that are generally not correct about the industry as a whole, while at the same time accepting dealer commissions. *Is this hypocrisy?*

As a commissioned salesman, I am disgusted with this continuing attack on commissions. The sales person or service representative expects compensation somehow, either by salary or via commissions.

Generally, as pointed out above, most funds do not have front-end loads. I prefer a plan with a no front-end load; however, a back-end load is of no consequence unless you withdraw funds before the end of the specified charge period. There is at least one back-end load (segregated plan) which pays a 10% bonus beginning in the 15th year and every 5th year thereafter. For someone starting between ages 25 and 35 and keeping the plan until age 65, this extra 10% bonus could be very significant. All else being equal, this bonus plan matures substantially ahead of similar plans. The phrase *all else,* in this instance, refers to the rate of interest earned, and to the expense charges, made by other plans.

It is important to understand exactly what administration and management charges apply as a percentage against your plan. The prospectus, or the contract, or both, should outline all fees and charges. Your contract should specify, also, that these charges cannot be increased beyond a specified amount. For example, one plan I sell has a 1.80% charge with a maximum of 3%, as stated in the contract.

Some people do not understand the application of these charges. Again, the prospectus must outline the procedure. Generally, the applied charge is against the total fund. For example; a rate of .007%, applied per business day, is equivalent to 1.75% per annum.

It surprises some people that the charge is a percentage of the entire fund, not just on gains. Thus, regardless of whether the fund is increasing or decreasing the charge applies. Naturally there is an advantage to the manager when the fund is growing.

Myth: Segregated Funds–the Country Bumpkins

Finally, people frequently ask what is the difference between a mutual fund and a segregated fund. You may have noticed that some fund managers manage funds for both mutual and segregated funds. Obviously, both fund types are active in the same stock markets. Both have funds listed under one of four broad categories; (a) growth, (b) balanced, (c) money market and (d) bond funds. Both mutual and segregated funds have similar expenses and charges.

It is not true that all mutual funds out perform all segregated funds. Some do some of the time, and some do not do so at all. One problem, in any direct comparison between the two, is in making sure that there is a true comparison made between two growth funds, or between two balanced funds. The make up of a true balance fund is one part in equities or growth stocks, *and* one part in bonds. The percentage of each may vary from time to time, but both must always be present. *Some equity funds masquerade as balanced funds*. The tip off is that no portion, or a very small portion, of the fund is in bonds. The purpose of a balanced fund is to provide for less volatility and, consequently, for a greater degree of safety. Many of the funds, pretending to be balanced funds, justify themselves on the basis that they have a balance between blue chip stocks and a generous smattering of slightly riskier stocks. In this case, any comparison should be made to a conservative growth fund, rather than to an actual balanced fund.

Another rather significant difference between mutual funds and segregated funds is the benefit of *creditor-proofing*. What is creditor-proofing? The term *creditor-proof* refers to the protection against creditors, afforded to life insurance products.

Subsection 196 (1) of the bankruptcy act provides that:

"Where a beneficiary is designated, the insurance money, from the time of the happening of the event upon which the insurance money becomes payable, is not part of the estate of the insured and is not subject to claims of the creditors of the insured."

Subsection 196 (2) provides that:

"While a designation in favor of a spouse, child, grandchild, or parent of a person whose life is insured, or any of them, is in effect, the rights and interests of the insured in the insurance money and in the contract are exempt from execution or seizure."

Section 1 of the insurance act defines life insurance to include an annuity contract. A segregated fund is an annuity contract and one of the options is to annuitize the payments. A more accurate way to explain a segregated fund is as a variable annuity with options that permit it to look like, and perform like, a mutual fund.

In effect, the above clauses state that a life insurance contract, including an annuity, is sheltered from creditors' claims providing there is a named beneficiary from within the family group. Such protection applies until maturity, as in the case of an endowment. Prior death, or maturity caused by death, permits the proceeds to pass outside the estate without liability from creditors. Some segregated funds guarantee that a minimum return of 75% of the deposits remains in case of premature death. Most plans start with a 75% guarantee that increases annually, by 5% to 100%, over a five year period. Others start at 100%. This could be extremely beneficial if you were unfortunate enough to die during a serious market correction.

Gordon Pape was quoted in the January 1998 issue of *The Insurance Journal* as saying, "These products (segregated funds) offer some advantages over mutual funds, especially for older people looking for estate protection." He does not think much of the money-back guarantee feature. "Frankly, I don't put much stock in it. If you go down the equity list you will find very few mutual funds that have cut a loss over 10 years."

With this observation, Mr. Pape has missed the point entirely. There are many periods of ten year intervals wherein, at a given point, the market has dipped below the high from ten years earlier.

If we look at the TSE300 as of 1972, you will note that the market went down and stayed down until well after 1975; well below the 1965 high. If you had died, inappropriately, at the wrong time during the 1972 to 1975 period, your funds may have suffered a significant loss. In that case, the segregated fund death benefit would have been of considerable value. If you wanted to use your funds for retirement or if you must do so because you reached age 69, the segregated fund guarantee would be extremely beneficial.

Perhaps Mr. Pape considers only the relatively few companies that out performed the TSE300 during these periods of down turn. Perhaps, too, Mr. Pape would point out that most declines have lasted for less than four years. However, the crashes of 1929 and 1931 sent the market down so far that it took twenty-five years to recover.

Perhaps Mr. Pape adheres to the school of thought that believes that this unfathomable occurrence can never be repeated. I might even agree, since I am realistically optimistic about the future. Nevertheless, why take a chance when the guarantee against loss, in such an event, is so readily available, at no additional cost. The financial welfare of my clients is too important for me to ignore this possibility. Demographically our population is somewhat behind Japan in the aging process. How far behind are we—two years, five years or, who knows? Why is this significant? Well, if you recall, just a few short years ago, the Japanese market was a roaring bull because significant numbers of older people were nearing retirement. As they invested, the market rose. On the other hand as this group began the retirement process, the market came down as they sold stocks.

Admittedly, this is an over simplification as there were many other factors at work, no doubt. However, those same factors may be gathering just off our port side and possibly we could experience a similar market decline. The Japan example warrants some concern. How long has Japan's market been down—three to four years? Do you suppose they would like our guarantees?

You should note the generality of the above comments, and you should realize also, that there may be exceptions where creditor-proofing may not apply. Some of your transactions would not be acceptable, if you purchase an insurance company contract for certain reasons.

For example:

- If you transfer funds from a nonexempt source, such as a bank, or a mutual fund
- If you do this in contemplation of bankruptcy
- If you do so in order to defraud a creditor

The most important thing to remember is that with a life insurance product, including an annuity, you may have a certain amount of protection from creditors. You could have this protection, in some circumstances, where no similar protection exists with any non-life insurance product. There is one exception; company pension plans.

Also, it is a common misconception that registration of a GIC. or mutual fund, as an RRSP provides creditor protection. Definitely, it does not, unless the investment is with a life insurance company.

A somewhat lesser consideration perhaps, but still important, is that the proceeds from a segregated fund are not subject to the costs and delays of probate. These proceeds, with a named beneficiary, pass outside the estate and, consequently, they avoid probate fees. When you add up the many advantages of segregated funds, over mutual funds; it would justify my enthusiasm for them. Nothing I have said negates the value of, and the uses of, some mutual funds to build an estate and accumulate wealth. However, no one should overlook the benefits and values afforded by a segregated fund.

The ability to credit-proof one's assets, designated for retirement, should not be taken lightly, especially in these days of litigation. One lawsuit could wipe out a life time of savings. It is generally accepted that your financial status, at the time of purchasing a plan, or of transferring funds from a nonexpert plan, is the key determinant. If you are solvent for a period, of from one to five years, prior to an event causing bankruptcy, or a substantial loss of assets, segregated funds are not available to creditors' claims. If there is any doubt or any possibility that you are not eligible for this protection, you should consult an accountant, or a lawyer, knowledgeable of bankruptcy procedures.

As the value of segregated fund guarantees becomes more widely recognized, more mutual fund companies are trying to get into the act.

Joanne Thomas Yocatto, a financial analyst for CTV's *Pocketbook,* Saturday segment, did a report involving segregated funds, July 4,1998. She made several statements that were not precisely accurate. Some of the things she said, as recorded by tape, were as follows:

- Segregated funds have been available for over thirty years. That's partially correct, but it is somewhat like saying that the airplane has been available for one hundred and fifty years. [Stringfellow's airplane, 1848] Insurance companies may have had segregated funds for internal use, but very few were offered to the public until recently. The resemblance of the earlier versions offered, to those of today, would be analogous to a comparison of the Wright Brothers Kitty Hawk flight in 1903, with a trans-sonic jet.

- Ms.Yocatto stated, quite correctly, that a segregated fund is a life insurance product. She then made the statement that BPI Mutual Funds was now offering a segregated fund. She did not try to explain how a mutual fund company could do this and, in fact, it cannot. It turns out that Transamerica Life sponsors the segregated fund. BPI Mutual Funds manages the fund but Transamerica markets it. Ms.Yocatto's information is misleading.
- Another, slightly off statement made by Ms.Yocatto, was that a segregated fund guaranteed a 100% return at maturity less withdrawals and less *fees*. To the best of my knowledge, no life company includes fees in this net guarantee. However, any mutual fund in which you have not satisfied the charges, would be an example of what she said; but the implication was that it was a feature of segregated funds. Not so!
- Furthermore, she stated that with a segregated fund; *fees can be higher*. Generally, that is not true if it is a fund created by and owned by the life insurance company. However, if you buy a mutual fund with a life insurance segregated fund guarantee, the fees may be about 30 to 40 basis points higher. In other words, if the regular fee for the mutual fund was 3%, it may now be 3.3% or 3.4%. That extra fee represents the insurance cost for the guarantee provided to the mutual fund. In spite of this cost, life insurance company segregated fund fees are usually slightly less than comparable mutual fund company fees. The cost of the insurance guarantee is absorbed by the life company. It is only when a life company extends the guarantee to a mutual fund company that the extra fees apply. Apparently, mutual fund companies are not prepared to absorb this cost, but rather they pass it on to the client. If the public

buys into this approach, that is, accepts it without much concern, *you can expect life company segregated funds to start charging for it as well.*

- Ms.Yocatto also stated that there could be consumer protection in certain circumstances. The implication appeared to be that there could be creditor protection in case of bankruptcy. Such would not be the case unless the fund qualified as a life insurance product. Therefore, it could not be a *BPI Mutual Fund* product. Her remarks would be correct only because of the involvement of *Transamerica Life.*
- Finally, this financial analyst, Ms.Yocatto, stated that the maturity and death benefits were covered and guaranteed, *within certain limits*, by CompCorp.

CompCorp is a private company. No government owns it nor sponsors it, and this corporate body insures only the products of its member companies. Membership in CompCorp is restricted to insurance companies that are licensed to sell life and/or health insurance. Mutual fund companies definitely do not qualify.

Furthermore, by definition, segregated funds remain outside the company's other assets. If a life insurance company became insolvent, the separate funds would still be there, invested in equities or in bond funds. They are not part of the company assets because segregation means they remain separate therefrom. CompCorp exists to meet the obligations of a life insurance company, *within certain limits*. How then could this apply to a segregated fund?

Three things would have to occur simultaneously:

(1) The market must have declined below the level of the initial deposit.

(2) A claim must be made against the maturity or death benefit guarantee.

(3) The life insurance company involved must be in receivership and unable to meet its commitment.

The coordination of these three events would be a magnificent rarity. It is not an impossibility, but the word improbability is not nearly strong enough. However, in the unlikely event of these things occurring as described above, CompCorp would ride to the rescue. In other words, they would assist, as Ms. Yocatto put it, *within certain limits*. Those limits would be up to $60,000 against the life insurance company guarantees.

Ms. Yocatto's explanation is proof that a little bit of knowledge can be dangerous. Dangerous to whom? Well obviously there is no threat to Ms. Yocatto. It is improbable that anyone complained to the station about this misleading information and, even if they did so, no one would have taken Ms. Yocatto to task for it.

The danger exists for the people hearing her words. They could easily believe things about mutual funds that apply only to segregated funds. They could make decisions based on the implication of her words.

Diane Francis, editor of the *Financial Post,* addresses a similar problem of misconception. In an article, (The Calgary Sun, Thursday, July 2, 1998), entitled *Dissension splits mutual fund biz*, she writes the following. "Sales of mutual funds by banks make some investors think funds are as safe as guaranteed investment certificates, insured by Ottawa. That concern led the Canada Deposit Insurance Corp. to undertake an advertising campaign recently to tell the public funds are not insured."

Insurance companies and most mutual fund companies, make considerable efforts to provide complete information, and full disclosure, to the public. It is unfortunate when the media promotes inaccurate information. It is equally disconcerting when the people employed by banks allow the public to believe things that are not completely accurate. The mutual fund industry is complex enough without the necessity of guessing about what media information to believe, or which newspaper, radio or TV advertisements are accurate.

If you want to take the guessing out of it all, consult a qualified advisor.

Myth: The Stock Market Always Acts Efficiently

The efficiency market theory is one based upon concepts of weak, semi-strong and strong. *Weak* is a theory concerned with linking the past with a projection into the future. *Semi-strong* is a concept that assumes the incorporation of all public information into the price of a share. *Strong* assumes that a given security's price fully reflects all knowable public and private information. Consult *The Midas Touch* by John Train if you want to learn more about this theory.

The more you investigate the various market theories, the more you become fascinated with them, even to the point of mesmerization. The jargon of the trade never ceases to amaze me.

For example, markets can be:

"Long in the tooth."

"Overstepping their bounds" or

"Climbing a wall of worry." (That's my kind of stock—always on a slippery slope.)

What do you think about the media? Does the media have an effect on market efficiency? If you listen to the TV or radio or read the papers, the information you get about market activities gets reported from different slants and then is *rehashed* on the evening news. Reacting to these news reports on market activity could be hazardous to your wealth.

While I am not the expert, my experience is that listening to the gurus is like getting a tip on a horse race and that can have serious consequences. One day a friend of mine, who knows a trainer, called to advise me to bet the house on number six in the seventh. I called another friend to tell him about my tip. I bet $20.00. He bet $2,000. We lost. That's the last tip I ever accepted or shared.

The day before the earth shattering news about Bre-X, a broker advised me to buy. He told me that the *find* was even richer than reported. Fortunately, for me, I did not have any money to invest.

However, one of my clients had some spare cash—a slush fund for speculation. When Bre-X crashed, he tossed in $2,000 on the belief that the negative aspect of the story was over stated. Two days later, he sold his shares for $4,000, a 100% gain. I am happy for him, but whoever paid $4,000 for those shares, at that time, lost his investment and probably fired his broker.

Should you use a broker for advice? Of course! However, do your own research. Don't rely on the advice of so-called experts. Listening to them will get you in near the top and out near the bottom, more often than not.

As already covered, there are many factors that can and do affect the stock market and its efficiency. Predictions or assumptions based on this theory belong to the professionals.

> ***I'd be a bum on the street with a tin cup if markets were always efficient. Investing in a market where people believe in efficiency is like playing bridge with someone who has been told it doesn't do any good to look at the cards.***
>
> *It's been helpful to me to have tens of thousands (of students) turned out of business schools taught that it didn't do any good to think.*
>
> *Current finance classes can help you do average.*
>
> ~ Warren Buffett

Myth: Wall Street Has All The Answers

While there is very little humility on Wall Street, and the New York Stock Exchange is the largest in the world, populated by gnomes and gurus, the fact is that they are not omniscient. Whenever things are going well in the stock markets of the world, there is a tendency for some to pretend knowledge about the unknowable. Salespeople, known as brokers, agents, financial planners, financial consultants, certified financial planners, funds sales people, etc., etc., and so on and on, begin to talk glibly and all-knowingly. Amazingly, people who could not even spell some of the terms being bandied about can now, suddenly, converse with the learned scholars of academia.

One might ask simply, "So what?" Theorists and prognosticators from the world of mortar caps and black gowns have always attempted to define and explain the unknowable. "What's wrong," you may ask, "with practitioners plying the trade of forecasting and prediction for the purposes of crass remuneration?" The fact that it is your money they are messing with is of little consequence; that is, until the market turns—excuse me—in the vernacular, *experiences a major correction* and your portfolio looses all its gains from the past two years. At this point, as you look at your financial account, you may begin to wonder why more stockbrokers than clients own yachts. David Chilton explained it this way, (page 43 of the *Wealthy Barber*). "A stockbroker is one who invests all of your money until it is all his." He should know—he was one, that is, a stockbroker.

Among the cognoscente, the insider, the privileged and the chosen, a jargon develops that could stymie the uninitiated. Or, as by design, it may impress the rest of us so much that we bow at the altar of the great financial Kahuna. Thereafter, we surrender or sacrifice, as the case may be, all of our financial reserves, and perhaps even some of our non-liquid assets; especially if we submit to the concept of leveraging. By mastering a few key words and phrases, anyone can take on a mystical and mysterious (nearly occult) quality as a carrier of forbidden knowledge.

Phrases such as:

"Only two of the fund managers had meaningful positions in the stock."

Meaning: They missed the window of opportunity when everyone else was jumping on the wagon.

"An under-weighting of gold stocks and an over-weighting to oil and gas provided the most significant positive contributions from an industry perspective."

Meaning: Since we were unable to sell our oil and gas stocks in significant amounts, we were unable to buy gold before we realized that gold was declining and the oil and gas sector was up for the thirteenth straight time.

Phew. We were lucky, but do not be concerned; we will make the necessary adjustments to accommodate corrections during the next fiscal period.

"Oil and gas was the only sector to buck the negative trend, gaining 1.2% for the month. In spite of the month's performance, the TSE was down only 0.8% in the first quarter while the Dow gained marginally to finish off only 2% behind the Nikkei."

Meaning: I wish I was a weather forecaster because they are the only ones who can be wrong seven days in a row and still not be fired.

And how about this one, "Weaknesses in all major asset classes caused the Dividend Income Fund to lose ground during the month. However, in down markets, higher dividend paying stocks usually fare better than stocks that pay lower dividends. The reason is that many stock investors believe that high dividend stocks are safer due to their higher levels of income."

Meaning: Higher dividend paying stocks are usually better than lower dividend paying stocks in a poor market, but it is not necessarily so in a hot market, such as during the past month. In other words, if everything and everyone else had not done so well during the past month, we would probably have done much better at least compared to everyone else.

You do not need to be a guru, nor even a student of the game, to know the words and concepts surrounding bull markets and bear markets. Most people know you must ride the bear during the down trends, and expand your participation when the bull breaks from the low lands and begins its trek up the mountain. At some point during this climb one could take full advantage of the bull's journey by a process of leveraging. Well, there is even more complex language and diabolical didactic available to command attention, to communicate information, and to give the appearance of erudition which may provide, *they* hope, a basis for trust and confidence.

Using an obscure language, however glibly, is no guarantee that the speaker is all-knowing. Having a seat on the New York Stock Exchange and an office on Wall Street is no guarantee of success. Even if we accept that they, the gnomes of Wall Street, are more knowledgeable, wiser and richer than you and me, it does not follow logically that they will be more successful than anyone else. *They* sometimes make serious mistakes, inexplicable mistakes, and if you refer to their credentials, you may wonder why.

Some people have drawn an analogy between*playing the stock market* and *betting on horse races*. But you say, the stock market is not a game; most people take it very seriously. Ditto for horse racing. People involved in the racing *game* take it very seriously. Game? Hardly. Business! Big Business! Both, horse racing and the stock market are *Big Business*. The players are deadly serious and the winners make big bucks.

There is even some similarity of terminology. For example, when we use the term *track record* in referrence to a stock's performance, everyone understands. But surely only a horse has a *track* record. Conversely, I have heard people at the track refer to a horse and its performance in such terms as bullish or bearish. The event of horse racing, once the sport of monarchs, and the adventure of investing in the stock market, still the sport of the gentry, has a comparable, analogous side. Both are big businesses. The players approach both with a fervent intensity. Both can make the adventurer wealthy or, conversely, either can create a condition of relative impecuniosity.

No one individual nor group can legally control the outcome of a race, nor the long term performance of the market, or even a single stock for that matter. Any suggestion that there may have been tampering in any way is made in whispered tones, especially if there is a paucity of evidence. Insider trading or insider betting can be serious offenses, and if proven can carry stiff penalties of heavy fines or jail sentences.

Still, most people suspect that the market can be manipulated sometimes for the benefit of a few; to the detriment of the many. Similarly the race results, not infrequently, are inexplicable in terms of track records, causing us to be suspicious that some unusual occurrence may be exerting an influence outside the state of naturally unfolding events.

In either horse racing or the stock market there are many outside influences that can affect results. How many of these can you anticipate or recognize in time to react? Investors are very sensitive to changes in the bank interest rate. Some announcements from the responsible government agencies can cause near panic selling. We say the market is sensitive to world events and properly interpreting them can determine a correct course of action. Should one be proactive or reactive to natural or supra-natural occurrences? At what point does one become paranoid?

While the betting continues at the track, one can get some valuable clues from the changes in the odds' board. It's like watching a stock's ascent or descent on the market's ticker tapes. You can check the prospectus on your selected stocks and the race sheet on your favorite horses. You may listen to touts and tipsters and weigh the advice provided based on the knowledge of the advisors, the amount of their financial involvement and the degree of their accountability. No matter how hard we try, or how carefully we do *due diligence,* how conscientiously we apply the data to the making of informed decisions, there are factors affecting the results of which we cannot have any real knowledge.

When the pari-mutuel window closes there is nothing left to do but hope, while watching helplessly from the bleachers as the race unfolds. Some spectators find it helpful to scream at the horse or jockey. Upon reflection, however, they must realize that neither can hear anything, other than a collective chaotic din that will have little if any effect on the results. What events occurred before the race that may affect the outcome? Perhaps your selected horse did not feel well. Is this an up day or a bad hair day? What does the owner want to achieve in this race? Has he whispered two words to the trainer, "Hold him." Do these words translate to the jockey as "Don't give him his head until the last hundred—no whip." They pay the jockey to follow instructions. Ridden as per instructions, the horse may close with electrifying speed, just failing to win. It makes for an exciting race, but ah shucks, your choice should have won. How does the weather affect the race? Do we have a dry fast track or a slow wet muddy one? How does your favorite run in these conditions? What if the other jockeys just box in your horse? He cannot win if he cannot get through the box. Does this happen by accident? There are many factors that can affect the outcome, which no one could possibly comprehend, understand or correctly evaluate. Gut feelings may be more successful here than scientific analysis.

On one occasion, I accompanied a beauty queen to our local horse race event. We were guests of the race committee. We met jockeys, owners, and trainers at a luncheon given in their honor. We met people who followed the races very closely, who knew the history of each horse. They were very capable of handicapping each race. Everyone gave us their best advice and I recorded it meticulously. With all this *insider* information this could be, should be, would be, my best ever day at the track. I asked innumerable questions about each race. Which horse was the best pick? Which one was the best long shot? Amazingly, these experts seldom agreed. When they did agree the odds were 6/5, meaning that it was a lousy bet. You could break even or even lose with a winning ticket. Why would you risk your $2.00, when winning means you get your wager back, but still you have a chance of losing? That kind of gambling is pointless.

Meanwhile, I noticed that the lovely lady with me asked different kinds of questions. When we met a jockey, Miss Beauty Pageant asked, "How many races have you ridden? How many races have you won?" When she met an owner, she wanted to know where his ranch was located. How large was his ranch? How many horses did he have in his stables? How much money did he win last year? Which of his horses were running today? When she met a trainer she asked: "What does a trainer do? Can you tell a good horse from looking at it? Why do you look at a horses teeth before buying it?"

After the luncheon, we proceeded to the grandstand with our newly found friends from the racing world. We were there rubbing shoulders with aficionados of the sport. When the races were about to start, to add to my escortee's entertainment, I proposed that I would wager $2.00 per race on the horses according to what we had learned at the luncheon. Additionally, I would wager $2.00 per race on a horse of her choice and she could keep the proceeds from any win, without risking her own money. She liked that idea and entered into the spirit of the event with considerable alacrity. Interestingly, she never consulted the race sheet on which I had made copious notes nor did she review the odds' board. Rather, she watched the pre-race parade and made her choice instinctively. In the first three races, she chose one of the favorites each time and we managed to win a few dollars for her. In the fourth race, her choice had odds of 15 to 1. Checking my crib sheet, I felt that 15 to 1 was rather generous, so I suggested that we get a "show" ticket rather than a win or place. She agreed that, considering the odds, it might be wise. *The horse won*. Nobody from our group of experts could explain it, but the horse won at 15 to 1 odds. When I asked this lovely lady how she was making her choices, she replied, "That's easy. I just choose the best looking horse in the parade." On that day, her system worked for her. She won close to $100 while my wins barely returned my investment.

Undoubtedly, some people will say that an analogy to horse racing cannot have any relevance to the choosing of a stock from the market. In a bull market where nearly every stock keeps going up, it would seem that any choice is a sure bet. But even at the best of times there are *dogs* that fail to leave the starting gate.

There are *salted* mines and false assay reports. There are some situations where the players manipulate the price of the stock with timely buying or selling, even to the point of being illegal. Media hype can affect the stocks perceived value. A word from a public figure can boost the price substantially. Frankly, there are so many factors and events that have a bearing on a stock's perceived value, and therefore its price, that not even the experts can be right all of the time.

William Wardsworth might have said, "Oh wad the giftee gie us a crystal ball that we might see." Perhaps, if we could foresee the future we could act as advised by Shakespeare, "There is a tide in the affairs of men which taken at the flood leads on to fortune." (Julius Caesar; Act IV, Scene 3.)

Poetic or pragmatic, no matter, the facts are these; the best we can do is an educated guess.

If you feel you can dance in and out of securities in
a way that defeats the inflation tax,
I would like to be your broker—but not your partner.

~ Warren Buffett

Myth: The Rule of Thumb

It's not uncommon to hear the phrases; *Well as a rule of thumb~* or *A good rule of thumb to follow….* Usually the professor of these phrases is advocating a specific line of action, perhaps to get you to buy a certain product, or a specific type of a given service.

People are often curious about what other people are buying or doing. There has always been a group of trend setters, who appear to be on the cutting edge, while the large majority waits and watches for their leadership. However, does the avant-garde really set trends, or do designers with clever variations, and salespeople with glib observances, actually determine the way it will be?

Sales presentations and promotional advertising often use this particular approach to get people to take action. The presentation may use phrases like:

- Well most people in your age group save about 10% of their gross earnings.
- The really clever people in your social circle are investing in mutual funds.
- People in your income bracket generally use brokers and brokerage houses to make investments.
- Most of the other young people in your company own about $250,000 worth of life insurance.

These causal statements make you want to jump on the band wagon right? You must buy a suede jacket if everyone else is doing it—right?

Frequently, financial advisors field questions like:

- What are other people buying?
- How much life insurance does the average person own?
- What percentage of your income should you save?
- How much money is enough when you are ready to retire?

The answer may come back, *Well as a rule of thumb….*

To me, a *rule of thumb* statement is a cop out answer for a lack of knowledge, or a lazy attempt to avoid taking the necessary steps to determine a proper and correct solution. Each individual person, couple, or family, is unique. Thus, it should be obvious that no one solution can be applied across the board. In over forty years of practice, I have not learned any rules of thumb nor developed any universal formulas that can be prescribed, like aspirin, as a panacea to each and every situation or even as useful broad band generalizations. The challenge and the allure or the fascination of financial planning, at all levels, is the fact that every solution or recommendation, to be effective, must be unique and personalized.

In my experience, so-called experts tend to advocate packaged concepts and vague generalizations that can be interpreted in different ways or denied completely. If the occasion warrants it or if some future development proves the advice to be erroneous, they are not responsible. Consider for a moment the definition of an expert, facetiously given, but more valid than rules of thumb. *An expert is someone who knows more and more about less and less until he knows absolutely everything about nothing at all.*

A rule of thumb followed arduously by some people is: *If you cannot understand what he is talking about, he must be an expert.* Recently, I listened to a radio show where the announcer was practically gushing over the importance of the guest *expert* and the value of the financial advice being given. By listening carefully you could have learned that the guest was not in the studio, but rather he was lounging pool-side at his Florida home. What's wrong with that? Nothing, except that there was a pretense of his presence in the studio. Does that really matter? Not at all! What really matters is that the guest *expert* is not an *expert* at all. What really matters is that the advice given was so nonspecific and so general that you could never hold the speaker responsible for his advice. What really matters is that this *expert,* and others like him, has no experience *one on one* with real people—individuals, couples, and families. He speaks to individuals about general solutions to a supposedly common problem. He makes a very nice income with this amazing technique. What really matters is that this expert is a master illusionist. He is erudite, glib and smooth. So smooth, in fact, that he can reply to questions, to which he does not know the correct answers, by changing the **callers question** to something for which he does know the answer. An admirable technique, you say? That's true, if you are giving marks for clever dialogue and the art of sophistry. That's true, if you are watching a chameleon moving from green to brown and back to green. To admire the artistry and ability of camouflage is natural. What flabbergasts me is that some people seem to revere these *experts because of it,* in spite of their lack of practicable knowledge.

Do beware of the expert who plays word games with your financial welfare. Be skeptical of the one who advertises that he has made a fortune in real estate, or the stock market, or mutual funds, or derivatives, or whatever. And now get this, he is going to show you how you can do it yourself, for a small fee of course. A fee which is small in relation to how much you will make in just a few weeks (or a few months at most). Why? The reason is—are you ready?— he wants to do something for you and all humanity. For all humanity, you may ask? Well, not *all humanity*. It is just for those enlightened enough to take advantage of this incredulous offer. Call 1-800 now or miss out on this unbelievable opportunity. Other people in your community are doing it right now. Do have your credit card ready; our operators are standing by for your call.

This approach is so obvious, but still some people are caught in the web over and over again. Why? Some authors refer to it as *financial pornography*. It includes material that titillates your ego and fuels your greed. Some examples are statements about mutual funds and other investment products that appeal to greed.

Phrases such as:

- Number one performer
- Best fund in its class
- Returned 600% in seven years

This kind of sensationalism sells books and magazines. But this, too, is somewhat obvious to most people, compared to the approaches taken by the gurus who speak to you on radio or TV.

These people are not so obvious. They are more dangerous because they are not selling anything, are they? One such expert, referred to above for his radio show, is more disturbing than the charlatans just described, because he is more circumspect and evasive than the legendary chameleon. He wrote the following words in his book: *Beware of the salesman because he must be paid and it's usually from your pocket.*

Let me ask you this:

Do you think this so-called expert is disseminating his supposedly vast knowledge to you free of charge? Perhaps the radio station is paying him very well for his gems of clever erudition? Perhaps a company is sponsoring his appearance because he is promoting the right stuff—slyly? Does his sophistication as an elucidating speaker, spouting generalizations and rules of thumb, make him more trustworthy than a *commissioned salesperson?*

Just answer one question, okay? Which one should you trust; the clever smooth, glib noncommissioned radio evangelist type, with his free generalizations; or the fully commissioned salesperson, who has considerable certification and accreditation of her knowledge; and who, above all else, *is accountable for her advice*?

Why do you accept advice from non accredited pontiffs, who may be good writers, or smooth talkers, but who have neither basic training nor practical experience in the financial services business? Did it ever occur to you that these people are saying and advocating the things required of them by their sponsors? Why do we not know, *that is*, demand to know who is sponsoring a particular speech or seminar?

Do you not agree that advice from someone who is responsible for his advice is much more valuable, useful, and trustworthy, than any and all of the advice from those who belch popular concepts as though they are newly discovered truisms.

It is nauseating to listen to these lecturers with no accreditation, dumping on people who have years of experience and several degrees and certificates and who are *licensed* to provide advice. This is too important to leave to the experts. Again just answer the one question.

Shouldn't you get advice from someone who can be held responsible for that advice? Let's ask it another way:

How valuable and trustworthy is advice from someone who cannot be held accountable by you?

As a rule of thumb, it's not your best interest that concerns them. Generalizations are sometimes confused with rules of thumb. For example; "The sun appears in the east in the morning and sets, or disappears, in the west each evening." Another one; "after exhaling it is a good idea to take a breath." These are not rules of thumb; both are observations.

A rule of thumb is presented, usually, as an observation. But in actuality it is merely a generalization with no real significance.

Myth: The Written Word

There once was a song—a spoof on the fallacious reasoning of those who accepted things without thinking because…

It's in the Book!

Well, there are many myths expounded upon as fact, both orally and in writing. If it's "In the book," it must be right—right?

"Aha," you say, "as an author you expect us to accept and believe what you say, but not the others."

"Ah no," I say. This book admonishes you to challenge the written word. It demonstrates a procedural technique, hopefully, which allows you to look beyond the spoken or written verbiage. You can look to the essence of the commentary. From it you and I may pull an infrequent gem of insight, while discarding the *filler* or nonsense syllables, which the writer includes to make himself appear more learned.

My favorite nonsense pronouncement follows:

The theory of disappearing responsibility

That's a nice catchy phrase that means nothing. It is a generalization with no basis in fact. Ask the advocate of this dumb concept to explain it. Then watch him squirm.

"Well, it's simply that your responsibility declines when they get older."

"Oh, what do you mean older?"

She replies, "You know when they are older you will not be responsible for them."

"Them?"

"You know—your children."

"Oh, okay. When will my responsibility cease?"

"Well, let's say age 18?"

"Really, age 18? That's interesting. How about college or university?"

"Well with my program you will save enough money for your children's education."

"Really? You can do that with the difference in premiums between my whole life policy and your company's term policy?"

"Yeah sorta."

"Sorta? Let's be specific. What exactly will it cost to provide life insurance and sufficient savings to provide for four children's education? How will the difference in premiums accomplish this objective?" I would like to hear the answer to this question myself. Feel free to mail an answer to me.

Finally, what is disappearing responsibility? Where did that foolhardy concept come from? (In case you don't know I will tell you—A. L. Williams—former owner of Primerica Life Insurance.) When he first wrote that phrase, he was a part-time life insurance agent, and he was trying to augment his football coaching income. Furthermore, he was not yet a grandparent.

My challenge to you is this. Ask any grandmother at what point she no longer feels any responsibility for her children and her grandchildren. Williams assumed that phrase as his theme song because it sounded glib and it suited his purpose. He wanted to sell disappearing life insurance, that is, reducing term, because it appeared inexpensive compared to plans with cash values and there was less competition. The scary thought is: at one point, he may have actually believed it. It's not surprising that he would think this way; after all, his children were young. He had not yet experienced the wonders of being a grandparent.

Perhaps you and I might like to think that way at times, when our children are growing into adulthood. We may have hopes that our children will soon become independent. Recently, I read a neat poster card stating, "To My Son. We have no problem with your not liking the rules of this home. As for your threat about moving out, we think that would be a good idea. You should move out, get a job, earn some money, and pay all your own expenses. Furthermore, your mom and I think you should do it *real quick*, while you still know everything."

Perhaps, in some cases, this silly thought catches us doing a little wishful thinking. We may even say something like: *Okay smart-alec-know-it-all, at age 18 you are out of here*. We are not alone.

In many societies around the world the thought is not uncommon. In one society studied by Margaret Mead, a noted sociologist, the fathers moved their sons at age 18, ceremoniously albeit, into their own homes—built by their fathers.

In a way, we did that too. We prepared a room in our basement for one of our sons. For a time, both of us were happy. Our son, emerging into manhood, had his privacy and we did not notice his presence, for significant periods of time. As I recall, he was in no rush to move. Meals were free, although not always on his schedule. It really did not much matter; there was always food in the 'fridge' for snacks. Shelter was almost free. (Supposedly, his mom charged him something; sometimes.) Clothing was washed and pressed regularly. This style of living was too good to leave. For a while, when he was nearly thirty, I thought we would have to move, and leave him behind.

Anyway, concepts proposed as absolute truisms change; but the published work remains. Do you remember Dr. Spock, the guru of child rearing? My grandparents and parents lived by the rule; *Spare the rod and spoil the child*. Dr. Spock, from the learned pedestal of academia, wrote that this was wrong, and his advice to new parents filled volumes while making him rich. Thirty years later, after the actual experience of raising children and grandchildren, Dr. Spock admitted he was wrong. He was wrong, but millions of people disciplined their children according to the power of the written word. **It's in the book.**

Similarly, A. L. Williams wrote his mission statement before he knew better, that is, before he had the experience of rearing children and spoiling grandchildren. Unfortunately, Williams has an army of followers who do not know better, but nevertheless, are able to use this incredibly myopic concept for their own purposes.

If you love your family, as most of us do, you will probably hold yourself responsible for their well-being to the extent of your ability. What grandmother could see a grandchild suffer if she had the ability to prevent it? It may come as a surprise to some that in most provinces in Canada the grandparents can be financially responsible, if their son defaults on the support of his family. Some people have told me that they think that is a terrible law. I think it's a good one. As parents we have an obligation to teach our children the meaning of responsibility. If we fail to do so…

As we grow older, there may be a reduction in parental responsibility. After all you have paid for your children's education, their weddings, helped them to get their first homes, or helped them to set up in business. You certainly have done your share. Perhaps you have met all of your moral obligations, but what about your wants and desires? Many of us want to help our children and our grandchildren. Some say: *You are responsible for your children until they become responsible for you.*

The written word is not the authority, in spite of its power to convince us otherwise. It should not be accorded any more respect than a vocal argument merely because *it is in the book.*

Myth: The Appeal to Authority

William McLeod wrote a book and made seven revisions. He gave speeches on TV and radio shows and wrote numerous articles about life insurance, the companies providing it, and the agents selling it. A number of peddlers used his material to support their view points and to make sales of their product. Many of them handed out flyers, written by McLeod, which expounded upon arguments against the products of other companies.

Mr. McLeod was a self-appointed authority and the gullible agents who used his material became willing dupes in the spreading of his misleading information. Beyond the attempt to dress it up to appear learned and scholarly, it was little more than hate literature. However, it did serve a purpose for those who needed an outside source to make up for a lack of knowledge.

McLeod, after all, was an instructor of business administration at a small college. Thereby, with the authority vested in him by an accredited college, his verbal diarrhea took on an aura of importance that it did not deserve. He was exceptionally biased and his material was incredibly flawed. The examples in his book and his articles were cleverly written, but they were not merely misleading; they were downright wrong. Mr. McLeod and his railings are perfect examples of the danger of listening to arguments based on an *appeal to authority*. Perhaps Mr. McLeod was knowledgeable in his own field of study. However, when he expanded his authority beyond the carefully structured material for his classroom, he proved that his powers of reason were, to quote his own words, *terribly flawed*.

It would be folly to focus on one author, or any one individual, as an all encompassing example of the dangers of listening to the arguments made by the appeal to authority. Often people quote newspaper articles to prove a point, but how often does the journalist report all sides of the argument without a bias? Where did the writer get her special knowledge to write with such authority? Frequently, I am reminded of the saying, *the consensus of opinion of the person with whom I spoke*.... The *power of one* is a source of amazing enlightenment when combined with the appeal of the popular version. There is no question, that an appeal to the popular version has within its structure the ability to mislead. However, we should question the reason(s) behind such a forgery. Does its author really believe what she says or writes? If not, what is the real reason or purpose for the utterance?

Mr. McLeod wrote and spoke with such fervor that many people accepted his views outright. The fact that these thoughts and denouncements were not challenged, on any level, was all the encouragement that he needed. From what I heard, McLeod is very good at debating, and very few knowing people welcomed a skirmish with him in an open forum. Good speakers, skilled in the art of debating, can take either side of the issue with equal facility. Such a debate, in which the knowledgeable speaker must stick to mundane facts while the skilled debater could rail against supposed evils without the burden of proof, would not be fruitful. The knowledgeable one would be constantly on the defensive, and the debate would serve only to dignify the ridiculous position taken by the opposition.

Consequently, our industry, at an official level, has chosen to ignore the critics while providing answers to the field force, the salespeople. Frankly, leaving it to us is a good strategy, to a point, because we can handle it when given the opportunity. On the flip side, however, some people have become so encumbered with erroneous concepts that we may not get our chance to counteract them.

It amazes me when some people consult accountants or lawyers or even engineers for financial advice and pay for it, in fact, because these people have a position of authority. Perhaps people perceive professionals in other fields as unbiased. To some extent there may be reasonable justification in such an assumption, especially with accountants or lawyers.

Nevertheless, why do we give some people the authority to speak out on any subject of their choosing just because they are experts in an unrelated area?

Are actors more knowledgeable about political issues? Are politicians good actors?

Are physicians, per se, better investors and, therefore, better qualified to advise other people on their financial programs? I ask this with tongue in cheek because most doctors are not known for their ability to invest.

Even if lawyers are experienced in contract law, are they qualified to evaluate a life insurance policy? Are they qualified to advise people about their needs for coverage?

Do engineers know everything about everything?

Authority in any area is 20% given and 80% assumed.

Myth: Omniscience

One of my associates likes to pronounce this word as two separate words, *omni* and *science.* That's not bad. *Omni* means all, or everywhere, or infinite. *Science* refers to knowledge. Therefore, omniscience means; all knowing or infinite knowledge.

David Chilton, in *The Wealthy Barber*, wrote about an individual, a barber, who knows it all. In all honesty, do you think that if the barber knew so much about financial planning he would continue to cut hair and disseminate his wisdom free of charge? David should be forgiven for this illusion, because after all; he got the concept from George S. Clason, who wrote *The Richest Man In Babylon* in 1926. He used the theme of a mythical rich man to make a series of important points. These fundamental thoughts were presented in this novel way to get people to read and study an otherwise drab topic.

I have no objection to Chilton's usage of the same procedure with the exception that he used Clason's basic concepts without credits. Perhaps a so-called modernization of this old classic would have been more tolerable if Mr. Chilton had recognized the originator of the concepts. Maybe he did not know where they came from. The life insurance business has been using the precise expressions from *The Richest Man In Babylon* for the last sixty or seventy years. The first sales presentation that I mastered was called *You Will Earn a Fortune*. It contained all of the basic information provided by George S. Clason.

It is possible that each of the authors, Chilton, Moynes, and White, learned the specific expressions they used from life insurance agents. And maybe, just maybe, none of the above ever heard of the real author of these concepts—George S. Clason. It is curious though how each of these self-appointed advisors came up with the exact phrases used by Clason on page 14 of his book such as:

- Pay yourself first
- A tenth of all you earn
- If you did keep one-tenth of all you earn…
- A part of all you earn is yours to keep

Well, no one knows everything! I suspect that an all knowing deity would have some problems not being confused with some of our current financial concepts and terminology.

Chilton succeeded with his book, in part, because he presented a popular concept in a manner that made it sound feasible and achievable. He appeared to take complex financial concepts and make them sound easy. He made people believe that anyone could do it. He also used a technique popular among authors of criticizing salespeople. They are not trustworthy, obviously, because they make commissions. So sayeth the barber. This technique allows one character to make negative or derogatory statements about salespeople or a group of people, such as, brokers or mutual fund representatives. The all-knowing one, then replies with an ameliorating comment calculated to lesson the degree of defamation. He says something like, "No, no, I didn't say to never trust them about mutual funds. I said don't trust him to buy stocks, but your broker is a good source of information about mutual funds." Is this double talk?

All of the authors critiqued believe in and expound on the popular concept of buy term insurance and invest in mutual funds. They all believe in mutual funds. So do I! But, I do not believe in them as alternatives to a proper life insurance program. Beware of the author who writes about topics where he has no practical experience! Beware of a concept merely because it is a popular one. Look past the facade and get the facts.

Omniscience is not one of the basic characteristics of a good advisor.

Myth: I Plan To Give Nothing To The Kids When I Die

Have you seen the sign on the back of some campers, "We are spending our kids' inheritance." In most cases just the opposite is happening. These parents are traveling and living in a relatively frugal way compared to taking expensive trips to Europe or Hawaii. But we smile at the concept because it has a certain appeal, especially to those under age 55.

Logically, there is no reason to provide for our grown-up children who may be highly successful on their own. After all, we raised them, educated them, and helped them start with homes, furniture, careers and lots of things. Now it's time to spend what we have accumulated on ourselves—right?

Well, it does not necessarily work that way. It has been an observation of mine that sometime between ages 55 and 75 our values begin to undergo a sort of metamorphic change, which affects an emotional change, which overrides our earlier intellectual thoughts.

Beyond providing for the basic requirements of life in retirement why do we want to be frugal, to preserve and conserve anything? Most young people agree with that sentiment, however, as they get older they begin to plan for an orderly transfer of funds to their children or grandchildren or both. [That's where financial advisors come in]. Sometimes, however, we hear people lament, "I wish I had understood this years ago." They are right. A proper selection of life insurance and other financial vehicles would have made the process much more efficient and less expensive.

The reaction of some people amazes me when we look at the options for withdrawal ofRRSP and/or Pension funds. One such option is an annuity, but often people get uptight at the very mention of this word. The reason given by nearly everyone is that, "There would be no money left after I die."

If my clients say that the reason they prefer other financial vehicles is to get a higher interest rate, or to maintain greater flexibility, I could understand the sentiment. However, that's not usually the case, but rather *they want something left at the end for the children.*

The same people who told me that they do not care about leaving money for the kids now suddenly tell me that they do not want to exhaust their funds. Why do people want to live off the interest on their capital? No one believes you can take your capital with you when you die. No one expects to live forever, *but* if you could live past the normal life expectancy, an annuity would be a perfect instrument to provide guaranteed funds.

Why do such authors as Riley Moynes denigrate annuities? It is obviously because very few people understand annuities. Frankly, if the banking industry ever gets the right to sell annuities *they* will advocate them as the greatest discovery of the 21st century. Meanwhile, they must push the only vehicles they can sell RRIFs or LRIFs. Unfortunately, RIFs and LRIFs may not be the best solution, especially since the remainder may be taxable in your estate.

If you do not want to give anything to your children when you die, why don't you spend it all now? Are you saying you want to give it to the government through taxation? Of course, there is another solution—charitable gifting.

If you are among the majority who want to leave an estate to your children, make sure you have a proper insurance program. Whether or not a life insurance policy is a good investment is one question, but let me assure you—*a RRIF is never a good substitute for life insurance.*

The majority of the people with whom I am acquainted make careful calculations to leave part of their estates to their children.

Myth: You Won't Need Life Insurance When You're Older

Who dreamt up that one? Obviously someone who has never been older! The best thing that has happened to me is that I have survived to be older. You see, now I meet lots of people who thought they would not need life insurance when they were older. The premiums on the insurance they did not buy when they were younger are wonderful. I earn more commission now on fifty sales a year than I used to make on three hundred sales, twenty years ago. Those people who refused to listen to me twenty years ago are my favorite people today. *I love 'em.*

Go ahead. Buy term and invest the difference. You will make some insurance agent very happy someday. (I wish I could live forever to serve people like you.)

Do you remember that oil company mechanic advising people on TV to use the correct oil filter? He said, "You can pay me now or you can pay me later. It costs a lot less now!"

About thirty years ago, I sold life insurance to a 30 year old father of two. I showed him the benefits of permanent insurance over term insurance. Still he wanted to buy term insurance, not because that's all he could afford. He could easily afford any plan we offered, but he had read somewhere that term was all you would need, because later in life you would be *self-insured.*

During our discussions I exhausted all of my mental resources trying to explain why he would need life insurance when he was older. I reviewed the net cost of life insurance and the fact that most term plans will actually cost more over the next 20 years anyway. Why pay an equal amount of money, for a term product and get nothing back, when you could have a policy paid for in full?

I gave him every reason I knew why he would need life insurance 30 to 40 years into the future. He gave me every stock objection as to why he would not need it. You know like; "Children will be all *growed up*, therefore no responsibility." "He will have lots of cash and investments, thus he can self-insure."

(It's easy to believe this when you are only thirty years old.)

Finally, I gave up and asked him to call his father to find out why his father, at age *62*, had purchased a relatively large policy earlier that same day. It was a permanent plan that would allow him to maximize his retirement income.

My young client did call his father and afterwards he did buy a permanent plan; less than 50% of the cost of his father's plan. Thirty years later this *young* man has achieved most of his dreams for his family, and his goals in terms of assets and investments. He is not ready to retire just yet, but he could.

Now he tells me that the only thing wrong with the policy I sold him thirty years ago is that it should have been much larger. (He actually said that if I had been a better salesman he would have bought at least double the amount.) Before you ask, yes he did buy other policies along the way and he owns a respectable amount of paid up life insurance. The really good news is that he is still insurable and he is about to buy a large policy to pay estate taxes; and to maximize his retirement income.

There is one really interesting thing happening just now, however. I have had a few interviews with my client's sons, both of whom are nearly thirty years old. They have read a number of books on what type of insurance to buy and which investments were best. To each of the sons, I explained that I could answer every mediocre concept put forth by those authors. I would prefer it, however if they would get the answers from a genuine expert—their father.

Being older does not reduce the cost of dying.

Myth: People Buy Life Insurance Because Someday They Might Die

In my experience, no one ever bought life insurance because she might die. It is not a question of *if* you might die. It is only a matter of *when* you will die.

However, people do not buy life insurance because someday *they will die*. People buy life insurance because *someone will live*. Someone they love will live after they are dead and will need the funds provided by life insurance.

The real reason, and probably the only reason, anyone ever buys any kind of insurance is to replace a loss. Whether it's life insurance, home owner insurance, auto insurance, flood insurance, business insurance, disability income, health care, dental care or whatever, the purpose is always *to replace a loss*.

Of course, some people buy auto insurance because it's against the law to drive without it. Even so, the reason the law requires it is because of the potential loss, if you are the cause of an accident. The basic principle of every type of insurance is to spread the risk among large numbers of people, so that no one suffers an unbearable loss. Without insurance to offset such a loss an individual is self-insured. People in many parts of North America suffered devastating losses through flooding in the last several years. These events are newsworthy and we can empathize with the victims. When people traveling away from home become caught up in some bizarre event, an accident or an illness, in which their insurance coverage is insufficient, we must sympathize with their dilemma. In these situations most of us are happy when the government steps in with aid for the victims.

The government supplies funds from our tax paid dollars to assist the victim and offset the loss caused by the event. In such cases, the government provides the insurance, effectively spreading the loss among the broad base of taxpayers.

When an individual dies, the family suffers an irreplaceable loss. We cannot replace the personal value of a human being, but we can replace the financial value. We can and do replace the loss of income, and the loss of financial security, caused by an individual's death or disability.

One day a few years ago, a client of our agency, who I had never met, came to my office to review his policy. He was what we referred to as an orphan policyholder because he had no active agent. After the introductions, he reached into his brief case, took out an old style policy and tossed it across the desk to me.

He then asked, "Why do I have this policy?"

I reviewed the policy quickly and began to explain it to him.

He interrupted me. "I don't care what the policy is; I want to know why I have it?"

Naturally it puzzled me and I replied, "I don't know. If you're asking me why you bought it originally, I have no way of knowing because I was not present and we have never discussed it before."

"Right!" He replied. "But why would I buy it?"

"Don't you remember?" I queried.

"No, I have no idea."

"Well let's see. You bought it nearly twenty years ago, perhaps for your wife and children."

"I have never been married," he stated.

"Perhaps for your parents," I suggested.

"I never knew my parents. I was raised in an orphanage, and I know nothing about my parents."

"How about brothers and sisters," I questioned.

"So far as I know I have no relatives anywhere on the planet."

"No one? No uncles, aunts, cousins?"

"None." He stated emphatically.

"You've tried to trace your ancestry?" I asked.

"Yes. Dead ends. I gave up." He shrugged.

"Okay, but surely you have some idea of why you bought the policy?" I challenged.

"No. I don't even remember the name of the agent."

I looked it up and told him the agent's name.

"Never heard of him," he commented wryly.

"Is this your signature?"

"Oh yes, and I have been paying premiums all these years. But recently I started to wonder why."

Again I started to review the policy for him. "$35,000 in case of death."

"Payable to whom?" He asked.

"Your estate, according to this."

He started to laugh aloud. "That's funny," he chuckled. "Payable to my estate? That's hilarious."

"Why," I asked.

"Well who will get my estate when I die?"

"That's up to you." I replied. "You can name whoever you wish."

"Yeah, like the government?" he asked somberly.

We sat there in silence for a moment. Everything was somewhat surrealistic during that brief time. I wasn't sure that any of this was legitimate. I sat there waiting for a bombshell to explode.

Quietly and seriously, our client said the following. "If you can tell me why I should have this policy or any life insurance at all, I will buy a policy, today, at least ten times the size of that one."

"Are you serious?"

"Absolutely."

"You're not putting me on?"

"Not at all."

"Okay. You're not married. You've never been married and you don't have any children, right?"

"Right. Not even any illegitimate ones."

"You're sure?"

"Absolutely!"

I did not ask why he could be so sure. Rather, I asked, "Do you have a lady friend?"

"No."

"Not even one?"

"None."

"Ah, how about past tense?"

"No."

"Are you serious?"

"Yes."

"You're not playing games with me, right?"

"Right—I'm not."

"Is there something you're not telling me?"

"No. I am answering all your questions truthfully."

"Well, why are you here? Do you want to cancel your policy?"

"Should I?"

"I don't know. How can I know?"

"Neither do I."

"Well, do you need the cash value?"

That broke him up. "Thirteen thousand dollars?" He nearly choked between his sobs of laughter. "I've got several hundred thousand dollars in term deposits."

When he calmed down from the hilarity of his private joke, he looked at me and said, "Well?"

This was frustrating. "Well what?"

"Well tell me, why should I have this policy?"

"I don't know."

"But it's your job to know. You are trained to know."

"Excuse me, but am I your morning entertainment or what?"

"Oh no. I didn't come here to waste time or anything."

"Okay," I nodded. "What can I do to be of assistance to you?"

"I've told you," he stated. "Tell me why I should have this policy or any policy for that matter."

I sat there wondering why is this happening to me. At that time I was determined to get to the bottom of this matter. My degree was in psychology and I had thousands of interviews with clients—none quite as strange as this one, but this one captivated me.

"Okay," I said. "I'm going to ask you some very personal questions. You may answer them or you may leave as you wish, but I ask you to not take offense, okay?"

"No problem."

"You don't have a girl friend, and you have never had a girl friend, right?"

"That's correct."

"Okay, how about boy friend—male companions?"

"No."

"None?"

"Never."

"Excuse me, but I'm not asking about sexual relationships only."

"That's okay. I don't have any sexual relationships. I have never needed a relationship."

"You are playing games with me."

"No I'm not. Just tell me why I should have this policy."

"All right. My name is not Freud so I'll stop trying to find relationships male or female, okay?"

"No problem."

"Well, there is a problem. You have challenged me to tell you why you should have this policy, but neither of us can figure out why you bought it to begin with."

"That's right, but if you can tell me, I'll buy any size you want."

"I know. You keep telling me that." I was a bit irked.

"Okay, tell me—who do you work for?"

"Myself. I own my own company."

"You do? What kind of a company?"

"Manufacturing. We make wire products for export mainly."

"That must be fascinating."

"Yeah, it is."

"Do you have partners?"

"No."

"How about shareholders?"

"No."

"How many employees do you have?"

"It varies but there are thirty full time permanent employees."

"What volume do you do each year?"

"About three million, but it's growing. Someday it will be over thirty million."

"You're kidding."

"Why would I kid? You can see my books if you want."

"All right. How about key men or key women? You must have some key people, right?"

"No," he stated. "Not so far as I know."

"Okay. Let me explain—a key person is a man or a woman who is so valuable to the business that without them there would be serious consequences or losses."

"I understand."

"How many are there in this category?"

"None."

"Whoa, just a minute. Let me understand something. Of all your employees you don't have at least one that would affect you adversely if you lost him or her?"

"No."

"You're serious."

"Yes." His eyes sparkled with something, perhaps glee.

"What if he or she joined a competitor?"

"Like?"

"Hell, I don't know. Don't you have a competitor?"

"Not that I know of."

"Okay now. Let me ask you this—if you were to become incapacitated or if you were to die, is there someone who could carry on?"

"I don't know."

"You don't know?"

"No."

"Don't you care?"

"No."

"Is there anyone in the company, male or female, that you care about?"

"No."

"Do you care about your company?"

"What do you mean?"

"What do I mean? I mean, you started this company from nothing and now it's very successful, right?"

"Oh yes."

"Aren't you very proud of it?"

"I suppose so."

"Well what will happen to the company when you die?"

"I don't know."

"Don't you care?"

"Why?"

"Hell. It seems to me that if one creates something she or he would want it to survive even after death."

"Why?"

"Well, just because you created it."

"What does that matter when I'm dead?"

"I don't know. But don't you care about your employees?"

"No."

"Don't you like them?"

"Why?"

"Why? It would seem to me that you would get considerable pleasure from creating something for the benefit of other people."

"Why?"

"I don't know why. It just seems logical."

"Logical? Why should it be logical for me to create something for others who can't do it for themselves?"

"I don't know, but don't you want people to think highly of you after you are gone?"

"Why?"

"Why do you keep asking why?"

"I guess I want to know what difference does it make?"

"Wow, if I started something as good as this I would want it to continue even after I'm gone."

"Okay."

"Okay? That's all you can say?"

"No. What you want is of no concern of mine."

"You're exhausting me. I can't understand why you don't care."

"I know. Nobody can. Let me ask you something—okay?"

"Sure."

"If I die, what will happen to my assets?"

"They will pass according to your will."

"But I have no will."

"Well, your assets will pass according to the laws of intestacy."

"Which are?"

"Well, ah… In your case, I don't know. Normally it would pass two-thirds to your spouse and one-third to your issue—that is your legitimate children. Failing this it would pass to your next of kin,that is parents, grandparents, brothers, sisters, cousins, etc."

The uproarious laughter that followed disrupted my entire office. My receptionist, bless her, rushed in to see if we wanted more coffee.

Our client looked over his horned rimmed glasses at me and asked, "If I have none of the above, what happens next?"

"You want the truth?"

"Of course."

"I don't know!"

"Of course."

"I presume the government takes over."

"And?"

"And what?"

"Right!"

"What do you mean, right?"

"Just that! The government takes over because I have no relatives and I have not willed my assets to anyone."

"Obviously you should make a will."

"What for? For whom?"

"Surely you prefer your employees over the government."

"Why?"

"Why, why, why? Why should I know why?"

"Exactly. You ask why I don't care, but you don't ask why our government doesn't care. Consider this. If our government cared why wouldn't they take over at my death and do everything possible to keep the company for the benefit of the employees?"

"That's not the role of government."

"Why not? What is it's role? To provide assistance for the unemployed? Think about it. When I die with no one to inherit my assets, will the government share them with my employees?

"Probably not!"

"Probably not? You know damned well that they will not be concerned about the employees."

"Interesting. I presume they would look for a buyer for your business."

"That would be fascinating wouldn't it? The government inherits, by default as it were, all of my assets and then proceeds to sell them to the highest bidder. Does that seem like they care about the loyal employees?"

"No but…"

"What do you mean—no but?"

"Well, it's just that it's not the role of government to get directly involved in private enterprise."

"I understand. Tax the hell out of private enterprise but don't get involved otherwise."

"This is going nowhere. If you cared about your employees…"

"That's just it, I don't care," he shouted.

Again my entire office became eerily quiet and my receptionist again rushed in to see if we wanted more coffee. I did—that's for sure.

At this point I was ready to give up. I had more important things to do. However, it seemed to me that there was a genuine cry for help and the psychologist in me wanted to respond, even though the businessman in me was saying, "Tell this character to get lost." Politely of course.

After a poignant pause, I said to our client, "I know that you are not here to waste my time nor yours, but I don't understand what you expect of me."

"It's simple, I told you just tell me why I've got this policy."

"You know that I don't know, but let's create a need for it."

"How?"

"Let's get you involved with someone, okay?"

"Male or female," he asked. Again the playful glint returned to his eyes.

"Your choice."

"Not interested."

"I know several eligible ladies who would find you fascinating."

"N*ot interested*," he stated emphatically.

"Okay, let's take a different approach."

"Fine. In what way?"

"Well, mentally, physically, whatever?"

"Such as?"

"Off the top of my head, as an example, a sponsorship of some sort. You could own a football team or a hockey team or whatever. What's your favorite sport?"

"They bore me."

"Did you ever play sports?"

"No."

"How about golf?"

"No. I think it's a stupid waste of time."

"All right, what's your favorite divertissement?"

"My what?" He snapped.

"You know—entertainment or something for relaxation."

"I don't need anything but my work."

"So your business is important to you?"

"Sure that's my—what did you call it—divertissement?"

"Can you think of anything that would challenge you? Something that would make getting up tomorrow more exciting?"

"Like what?"

"I don't know. That's what I'm trying to find out."

"Give me an idea."

"Okay, how would you like to buy some immortality?"

"What are you talking about?"

"Well, Madame Curie discovered radium which lead to a treatment for cancer. Her name will live forever. That's a form of immortality."

"You're joking."

"No I'm not."

"I'm not a scientist. I don't do research."

"That's not the point. You could fund the research. Perhaps your funding could find a cure for cancer."

"Who funded Madame Curie?"

"I don't know."

"Right."

"Okay, okay. You could make a donation to a scholarship at the university for specific research. You could fund a building for a specific discipline to be known forever as your building. Your name would be emblazoned on the front for generations into the future."

"Humph. Who would care?"

"Everyone who knows you and cares about you."

"Like?"

At this point, I felt a shadow or presence of sadness pass through my office. There was an envelopment of gloom. I felt it and the expression on my visitor's face showed that he was saddened.

"Like your employees," I replied hopefully. "They must have great respect for you. Their livelihoods depend on you. They must care about you."

He smiled at me as though I were a mere child.

"Don't you understand? I only know the names of three of my employees—my secretary, my bookkeeper and my foreman. They each have their duties and once each month we meet to review results."

"Once a month?"

"That's right."

There was silence for a period of time that seemed like the passing of a lifetime. Finally I asked, "Do you go to church?"

"No!"

"The ballet?"

"The ballet? Where those guys run around in tight pants? No way!"

"How about the Philharmonic?"

"No. Too serious."

"The opera?"

"You're kidding, right? Those women screaming their lungs out and the men shouting words that no one understands. It's rather pointless isn't it?"

"I don't know. You may be right. However, my next appointment is waiting. Let me introduce you to my office manager. Perhaps we could meet later to continue this discussion, okay?"

You undoubtedly get the point of this entire scenario. *If you have no one and nothing you care about, if you have no one who relies on you, you do not need life insurance.*

To this day, the memory of that interview haunts me. There are lots of unanswered questions. There is only one answer to your questions: **"I don't know!"**

Myth: Buy Term and Invest the Difference

Why?
Why bother?
What difference?

It's difficult to understand where silly myths are started and why they persist in spite of facts and figures to the contrary. Sometimes, we give an author credence because they are knowledgeable in another area; such as, J.J. Brown, Ph.D.— English Professor. He got rich doing it his way. Therefore, according to him, it must be right for everyone else. He had very little knowledge of life insurance, or its related products, but he considered himself qualified to write an authoritative book on the subject.

A.L. Williams wanted to earn more than salary as a high school football coach. He tried to sell life insurance part-time, without much initial success. However, he learned enough to realize that whole life policies that had been in force for several years, developed cash surrender values. Here was a source of money that one could use in other ways to make a higher return. He advocated *buy term and invest the difference*. But that's not exactly what he meant, nor what he practiced. His advice was to take the cash value from older policies, invest it elsewhere at a higher interest rate, buy term insurance and keep on paying an *extra amount* into the savings plan. An extra amount? Yes, you make an extra deposit; not just the difference between a term insurance policy and a whole life policy. It was the lump sum plus the *extra* amount that made his projections look good. When he attempted to demonstrate his system in direct competition to other life insurance programs, he had to revert to a bit of subterfuge and legerdemain. He was not truly knowledgeable; he was not wise; he was not correct; he was not first; but for Williams, it was very good. Many other salespeople and authors wrote and advocated these things before Williams and some still do. He was wrong. They were wrong. *They are wrong.*

William McLeod, a teacher of business administration, wrote a book and revised it seven times. He laced his first book with statements based on an ignorance of factual information. Between the first one and number seven very little in the way of improvement occurred. McLeod started with a bias and he spent his time trying to find examples to justify his assumptions. This amazing display of bias about life insurance, by Mr. McLeod, defies logical analysis. Clearly he had a serious hate for life insurance companies. Proof of this observation is that he used his prodigious powers of reasoning to discredit them. Unfortunately, he tried to take agents down as well, and he ended up damaging the very people he purported to help—*You all.*

Financial Myths Die Hard

Most people do not like to change their minds about something previously accepted as basic truth. Constant re-enforcement from outside sources further justifies the concept we have always known to be so.

Buy term insurance only? What is term insurance?

The term, *term,* refers to a period of time. Therefore, if you buy *term insurance* for the correct period of time everything should be A-okay. Right? Perhaps!

What *term* do most people buy?

The answer to that question probably depends on what salespeople want to sell. Ironically, the companies frequently determine what they want their salespeople to sell. How and why would companies make this determination and how can the companies influence agents?

Complex questions, but let's break them down. The answer to both how and why the companies design a certain plan is simple—profit. What can they get the agents to sell to clients that remains competitive and profitable?

Note: *In this book profit is not a dirty word*. Generally, excessive profit cannot exist in the insurance business because of competition—unlike the banking industry. There is a suggestion that companies use term products as lost leaders, to garner a larger market share.

The theory goes that they hope you will convert your term insurance to a more profitable plan.

As pointed out elsewhere in this book, many companies have no so-called profitable plan; but all companies sell term products. If you hear or read this lost leader argument, just smile, secure in the knowledge that the company making the complaint is really just complaining about its inability to compete.

The second part of this question is, how can companies influence the agents to sell a particular kind of term insurance?
Some of the factors are:

- Basic premium
- Commission
- Qualitative values—value added benefits such as:
- Renewal premiums which are lower
- Waiver of premium
- Dividends
- Extended coverage or convertibility

What are some of these term insurance plans?
Yearly renewable term: Why would anyone buy something called yearly renewable? Well, initially it's inexpensive. Perhaps you expect the need for coverage to last for one year only. You need it for a short term loan, or to assure some limited commitment. What if the need lasts longer? You can renew your plan at an increased premium rate; usually guaranteed in the policy. Some plans are renewable to age 80, others to age 100—at an ever increasing annual premium. Some plans are convertible to level term or to other plans.

Advisors are not really fond of this plan for a number of reasons. It's true they get commissions on the lowest premium with little or no financial recognition for the increasing premiums. Companies do not like yearly renewable term; because with each increase in premium, our clients may review the need for this kind of coverage. Clients are not happy about the annually increasing costs, especially when they understand that over a five year period, a *Five Year Renewable and Convertible* plan would be less expensive.

Five Year Term: Five Year Renewable: **Five Year Renewable & Convertible**:

These are three variations, all of which are less expensive than Yearly Renewable Term—over a five year period. Why would you buy *Five Year Term*? It's important to note that this plan is not renewable after five years without proving insurability.

One partner, in a partnership of four, once told me; "If this business lasts five years, I'll be surprised. Furthermore, if our business does last that long, we will sell it or wrap it up, just give us the cheapest premium." Even so, *Five Year Renewable Term* is only slightly more expensive and it would allow for a change in plans or for renewal at a guaranteed premium. Flexibility is the key reason to pay the little extra.

Similarly the convertibility feature may not seem too significant, especially if you intend to keep it as term insurance. But needs and attitudes change. Over the years my associates sold four policies that were not convertible. One lapsed (i.e., the policy terminated, for whatever reason). The other three insured clients became uninsurable and all three wanted to change their policies before they expired. Since they could not convert their plans, each one of these clients dumped their anger and frustration on me. After this experience, you may be able to buy a non-renewable, non-convertible policy from someone, but I can assure you, you will not be able to buy it from me, nor any of my associates.

Five year renewable and convertible term is still available, but it's not as popular as it used to be. Why is that? Again, there are several reasons:

- Clients tend to review their needs, and the alternative products available, every time the premium increases. Frequently, clients replace these plans at or near the time of renewal. Companies do not like that, especially if the renewal goes to a different company.
- Ten year renewable & convertible term is less expensive, over a ten year period, than either yearly renewable, or a 5 year renewable & convertible plan.

By now you understand, hopefully, that your term premium will remain level for the period of time described in the title. In addition to the above, you could buy 20 Year Level Term (convertible or non-convertible), or 20 Year Renewable & Convertible to age 80. Generally, 20 Year Term would be less expensive over 20 years than any of the other plans described, if you keep any one of them for 20 years.

For those who would like more detail about these plans, or others, such as Level Term to age 65, or Term to 100, please see the section at the end of this book entitled 'Terminology.' The following is a mathematical comparison of the above information:

Annual Premiums for: $100,000

	Yearly R&C	**5 Yr. R&C**	**10 Yr. R&C**	**20 Yr. Term**
Age 47	228	330	332	446
48	321	330	332	446
49	381	330	332	446
50	439	330	332	446
51	481	330	332	446
Total for 5 yrs.	$1,850	$1,650	$1,660	$2,230
Age 52	525	480	332	446
53	576	480	332	446
54	655	480	332	446
55	729	480	332	446
56	811	480	332	446
5 Yr. Sub-total	3,296	$2,400	$1,660	$2,230
Total for 10 yrs.	$5,146	$4,050	$3,320	$4,460
Age 57	900	710	1,042	446
58	1,005	710	1,042	446
59	1,127	710	1,042	446
60	1,264	710	1,042	446
61	1,414	710	1,042	446
62	1,558	1,125	1,042	446
63	1,756	1,125	1,042	446
64	1,953	1,125	1,042	446
65	2,128	1,125	1,042	446
10 Yr. Sub-total	$15,464	$9,175	10,420	$4,460
Total for 20 yrs.	$ 20,610	$13,225	$13,740	**$8,920**

As you can see from these examples, short term plans are less expensive for the short period, but all are more expensive, over the extended period, than 20 year term. *The initial difference is too insignificant for investment and the higher expense in later years destroys the initial savings*. The question thus becomes, how long will you need your coverage. Some of my clients have answered that question with, “Well I don’t really know.” *Good answer!* **Another answer was;** “Well until I die I suppose.” *Better answer*.

If you say you don’t really know, we should consider your plans and goals and we should review the alternatives available. The younger you are the more important it is to maintain flexibility. If you say you may need life insurance until death, you are correct, as you will see in the following paragraphs. However, if we are in agreement, already, that you will need coverage until death, then let’s consider when your death is most apt to occur.

Statistically your chance of death this year is exactly the same as any other individual’s regardless of sex, or age, or health, or habits. Your chance of dying this year is 50/50. Either you will die or you will not. It’s that simple! However, as part of a significantly large group your chances vary depending on many factors.

Basic actuarial tables use a calculation based on the number of people who will die at each age in that year, per one thousand people in a general population. A refinement of these calculations considers the differentiation between men and women. Everyone knows, that according to statistical averages; women are living longer than men. These actuarial tables usually do not take into account the many other factors such as life style and habits. Insurance companies follow the statistical tables when pricing their products, and the underwriting department adds in factors for life style and habits.

One other refinement is between smoker and nonsmoker rates. When companies started to introduce nonsmoker rates, they did it for competitive reasons, but this was a clear break from the basic principle of insurance. *The purpose of an insurance program is to spread every risk over a large segment of the population*. When we differentiate between men and women, the cost for males increases significantly while the cost for females decreases only slightly. Similarly, when we apply the statistical calculations to smoking, the premiums for smokers increase, while the decrease in cost, against an aggregate calculation, is relatively small for nonsmokers. An aggregate policy is one that does not differentiate between smokers and nonsmokers. In effect the nonsmoker saves very little relative to the cost of a product that would include both smokers and nonsmokers, but it forces smokers to pay considerably more. Because of the difference in premium, there is the appearance of a greater saving than would actually exist if we used an aggregate premium.

In a pure situation, with no competition involved, an actuary would start with an aggregate premium. One based on the death rate for the general population with no differentiation for males, females, good health, poor health, or family history. According to some head office underwriters, there are about seventeen significant factors considered. Each one of them results in a plus or a minus against the norm. Adding up the score determines the *rating* each individual receives. If the score falls within an acceptable range, the individual receives a standard offer. If it is negative to the established norm, the applicant receives a special offer. That means she would pay higher than the published rate.

For example, if the underwriter simply added a plus eight for being a woman and a plus ten for a nonsmoker, the simple purity of the science would be preserved. Competition, however, led all companies to offer a lower rate for women—because they do live longer. In fact, there are fewer deaths for women than for men at most ages and perhaps for all ages. It is a logical approach, but it is also a deviation from the basic principal of sharing the risk.

The next step was a somewhat larger leap. Nonsmokers live longer, have fewer illnesses and accidents, and therefore they represent a distinct society, just as definitive as being male or female. Therefore, it seems logical to offer them a lower premium per thousand. Nevertheless this is a deviation from the basic principle or concept of shared risk. An aggregate premium results from spreading the risks, as broadly as possible. Using this basic calculation or aggregate premium, and allowing a significant segment, such as women or nonsmokers, to opt out causes some important and fascinating results. Firstly, as already stated, the saving for the selected group is only marginally better, but the group selected against, i.e., men or smokers, or whatever, receive a disproportionate increase in premiums. That seems fair enough. Right? Well, that depends on which side of the coin you are on.

In my clientele, there are a significantly large number of nondrinkers. They frequently ask for a discount for nondrinkers. The problem is that the studies have indicated that drinking moderately is actually good for your health. It seems logical, nevertheless, to offer a discount for the following:

- Nonsmokers
- Health food practitioners
- A special category for vegetarians
- Those who exercise conscientiously
- People living in certain countries or parts of a country
- Everyone who visits a doctor three to four times a year
- People who attend church regularly
- And so on

The list could become exhausting and pointless. Eventually there would be a discount for everyone other than Mordecai Richler and me. Richler could afford the excessive premium, but I could not. Thus, my family would be deprived of the benefits of a marvelous product, called life insurance.

What has this to do with when you are apt to die? Nothing! So back to the theme—*your death*. Can our statistical tables predict your death? No, absolutely they cannot. However, we do know that at age 35 a certain number of males, per 1000 from the population at large, will die. However, the statistics used to create an actuarial table does not take into account your lifestyle, your habits, your family history, nor your attitude toward living. Actuaries do factor in these things when deciding which clients to *accept*, *rate* or *reject*.

Thus, if you are an acceptable risk for a life insurance company, you may have an even longer life expectancy than predicted by the tables. You should probably expect to live past age 82. *So why would you buy a life insurance product designed to expire before you do?*

Term insurance is cheap but it is not inexpensive. It is relatively inexpensive at any given age, but if you keep it until you die, it becomes very expensive. The reasons term insurance *appears* cheap are twofold:

- Initial premiums increase at regular intervals, as outlined in the contract. Look at the renewal rates in ten or twenty years;
- Your policy will not be in force when you die; statistically you will outlive it.

In spite of overwhelming evidence that term insurance is not the best buy in every situation, there are many who refuse to move from their predetermined positions. Unfortunately, a large number of those entrenched in this rut are salespeople. When two persuasive agents present opposing viewpoints, what does the prospective buyer think? What should he do, other than give up in a state of confusion?

Consider carefully the credentials, qualifications and experience of both the agent and the advisor.

Then it's up to you!
It's your money, your family, your taxes.

Myth: Life Insurance Companies Do Not Like Term Insurance

Frequently, we hear it stated that companies do not like term life insurance because they cannot make money with it. Do you really believe that? How could you believe that any company would sell a product that is not profitable? What do you think about banks? Would any bank sell a product that was not profitable? Why would you want to purchase a product from a company that is losing money?

Ask yourself why there are so many insurance companies selling term insurance? Do you believe that they sell term insurance because it's in your best interest? If they lose money on term insurance where do the profits come from to keep the company going? If it tempts you to answer, that profits would result from conversions to cash value insurance, permanent insurance or whole life, etc., you should consider the following:

- *Some companies do not sell these other types of insurance.*

Ask yourself what ulterior motives do banks and some life insurance companies have to sell term insurance only, especially if they have no related products to sell? Ah yes, some banks and some life insurance companies do have alternative products to sell. They sell GICs at very low interest rates and mutual funds with high administration charges. Beware of those companies advertising low rates. These banks and life companies do not offer inexpensive term insurance compared to the *other* life companies. In fact, they often rank between 20th and 53rd on printouts from LifeGuide, but they do not intend to make a profit at your expense, or *so they imply*. Be especially wary of those companies that advocate *no salesperson will call*. Avoid them like the plague. The reason no salesperson will call is because you can make us responsible for our advice; and we can *always* do better for you than what these companies offer.

Firstly, we can get a better rate, that is, a lower rate per thousand—probably without exception.

Secondly, we would obtain a better quality product—guaranteed without exception.

• *Career life insurance advisors do not like term insurance.*

I have read this and I have heard it said but I do not understand the criticism. If this observation had any factual basis, *why would we sell so much of it*? Furthermore, if we were not selling this product, why would our companies continue to offer it? Why, indeed, would they try so hard to get our attention? Why would they work so diligently jockeying for position?

Some criticism accuses us of not liking term insurance because of the commissions. These critics suggest that we receive a considerably lower commission rate for term insurance. That may be true, but we could get a commission rate that is 50% higher than the rate on *permanent* or *cash value* plans and more than double the rate on most other term plans. Why do we not sell for that company? Its rates are competitive. The company is reputable and very solvent.

The answer(s) to this question would vary from advisor to advisor and I will not conjecture on their thoughts. Personally, I do sell for that company *if it is in the best interest of my client to do so*. However, looking ahead, if and when my client wants to make a change, I want to be able to convert it to a very special plan, one that I work with extensively and understand fully. All else being equal, that consideration justifies taking a lower commission rate.

Frequently, *Primerica's* agents try to cancel our cash value plans in favor of buying their term and investing in their mutual funds. Primerica is a company with an army of agents dedicated to the destruction of all plans with cash returns. These agents ask our clients why their present advisor did not show them this supposedly cheaper term plan. First of all, we did offer it. Most of the advisors I know and have worked with, always demonstrate a term program as one alternative. If it solves the problem then term is fine. However, in many cases term insurance costs as much as or more than our other plans, as I have demonstrated elsewhere. Secondly, term insurance may be a temporary solution to a long range need. This criticism comes from agents who do not understand the larger picture.

It makes me wonder, usually loudly; if your agent truly believed in the philosophy, *why wouldn't he find the lowest possible term rate and the best possible family of funds?*

Elsewhere in this book, and more than once, I have pointed out that you should never buy term insurance in order to buy an investment. It bears repeating. Buy the type of insurance that fits your needs and accomplishes your goals. Invest in products that fit your needs and achieve your goals. But do not confuse one with the other.

It follows logically that you should not buy life insurance based on your desire to be part of a multi-level operation. Too many people dream that they can start their own life insurance business by recruiting agents to sell this expensive product. Their dream is to earn future compensation on the sales of others. It's called multi-level marketing and the very nature of this approach, with so many levels of compensation, requires a life insurance product that is more expensive. Check it out. Get printouts from an advisor with one of the services such as LifeGuide, which demonstrates the products of a large percentage of the companies offering term insurance. Then ask yourself; do I want a group of my associates selling a product to their friends and associates that they could obtain more beneficially and for a lot less? Perhaps you should review your motives if your answer to that question is yes.

Banks in the Business

You may have read recently, as I did, about one of the banks reducing its rates to 25% lower than the nearest competitor. I read the article from two different newspapers (a) *Vancouver Sun*, (b) *Toronto Star.* It was essentially the same article using precisely the same illustration. Two different journalists, one for each paper, took credit for the article. Which one is the real author? Obviously it was neither one of them. These articles should have been entitled ADVERTISEMENT. Clearly they accepted a press release from the bank, as factually correct, without checking it out first.

A simple phone call to one of the quoting services would have confirmed that this press release was not correct. The facts are that the bank's rate ranked tenth among its competitors—not first. The bank's rate was not 25% lower than its lowest competitor. It was 38% higher. However, published as an article under the name of a journalist, the story receives some undeserved credence. This approach is a flagrant endorsement of one competitor over all others.

The article casts aspersions on the other forms of distribution that are different from the bank's system. The bank it seems offers a staff of salaried people. The journalists quoted the president of this company stating that he can offer these lower rates *because he does not employ commissioned sales people.* Apparently he also said, "When you are pricing an insurance product, commissions are a big factor in the overall cost." In this obvious advertisement, this president continued, "When you are selling direct you can maximize the benefit that can be passed on to the consumer in terms of lower premiums." *That would be nice if it were correct but it is not.* In this example, this bank offers lower premiums initially by having an excessively high rate on renewal. We have reviewed this technique elsewhere in this book. It effectively passes the risk on to the buyer at the time of renewal. Where is William MacLeod to complain about this? When challenged about the high renewal rate, the president stated, "Well you should reapply for the initial rate at your attained age." He knows that many people will not reapply and he knows too that some will not qualify next time around.

I would not mind so much if (a) he told the truth about his product, and (b) he did not blame it on commissions. But know this: W*e commissioned sales people are the banks' real competition*—not other life companies. They have seen the enemy and they know we will not disappear quietly.

Okay, let's look at some other aspects:

- Where does the money come from to pay the president's salary?
- Where does the money come from to compensate the staffs of the underwriting and the investment departments, etc.? Undoubtedly, a neophyte company with a mediocre product line would not have all of the expenses of an established life company. Initially, at least, the bank's investment department

can provide the necessary expertise at no cost to its life insurance department. These savings could support lower rates; lower than some companies, that is, but not lower than the lowest now available, as stated in the newspaper articles.

- Blaming commissions is unfair and it's irresponsible. Commissions are a significant part of the cost of the first year's premium when expressed as a percentage of that premium. Why would anyone relate commissions to the first year premium any more than to the other costs of delivering the product to the public? What would happen if we calculated mortality as an expense of the first year only, rather than to spread it over the expected life time of the policy?

There are many costs of doing business, such as administration costs including salaries, which if applied to the first year's premium would cause the cost analysis to skyrocket. Many of these costs would apply directly to the acquisition of new business and if you recorded them as a first year expense they would make commissions appear insignificant. The temptation is to relate the president's salary and the other expenses of operation to the total premium income received in a given year. They may include net investment income in this total as well. *Of course we know that the only significant relational comparison is to profits*. That's why presidents make about ten times more than average sales people. Why then do they, whoever they are, single out the sales advisors' commissions? Taken as a percentage of the total income, or in relation to company profitability, commissions would be insignificant and the argument becomes petty. Remember, advisors brought the business to the company and they keep it on the books. We do the service work for a paltry sum. If we complain about the tiny service fee, known as a renewal commission, they tell us we can make new sales or get new leads while doing this service work—frequently for free. What is the real reason for not providing a higher service fee? *Some of us with a large clientele would be content to service our clients rather than sell new business*. It's a catch 22!

Admittedly it is more convenient to calculate the cost of commissions as they apply to each and every policy in the first year.

However, properly considered as a small annual percentage for the lifetime of the policy the commission factor is rather insignificant.

For example, study commissions over a ten year period.

A $1000 premium paid for 10 years	=	$10,000.00
A first year commission @ 50% of first year premium	=	$500.00
A renewal commission 2 to 5 years @ 5% or $50 x 4 years	=	$200.00
Total payment in commissions		$900.00
As a percentage of total premiums for ten years 900/10,000	=	9%
Of which the first year commission is only		5%

Of course, someone will point out that some policies do not last ten years. To which I would answer that many others survive much longer.

The argument that commissions cause higher premiums is ludicrous and the perpetrators should abandon it. Newspaper writers and authors disparaging commissioned salespeople will be more careful in the future, hopefully. Of course, as already established, it is the purpose of a writer to titillate the readers' minds in order to sell papers. Titillation sells; factual education does not. *I hope I'm wrong!*

Consider the following:

A salaried sales person gets group benefits, Canada Pension plan, unemployment insurance, paid holidays and other benefits. How about providing some perks; a car allowance, parking space and an expense allowance. As you may surmise, a commissioned sales person pays for all expenses and benefits from her earned commissions. If she takes a holiday, it costs her in lost production. That is not so with a salaried representative. One may argue, "Sure but you can write off your legitimate expenses against commissions." All right, but if I take a client or prospective client to lunch, I can write off only 50% of the lunch. If the salaried sales person buys the same lunch, she gets reimbursed 100%. There is more, but you get the idea, no doubt. If we add everything up, the salaried sales agent would cost about the same as a commissioned advisor.

Do you think that other life companies have not considered salaries? At least one company operated on a salary basis for many years, not because it was less expensive, but rather because it fit their style. If the salary approach was less expensive, do you think for one moment, that the traditional companies would offer commissions?

Have you considered raises? If a salaried sales agent does well, will she get a raise? You bet or she will be gone to a competitor. Costs of doing business by a bank may be slightly lower on the start, but that will not last.

What a wonderful basis it is for a *newsworthy* article. Newsworthy because so many people would like to believe it, but it is irresponsible because it's not factual. The journalist should know better. The president of this bank's life company most certainly knows better, *but free advertising is great no matter how you get it.*

Let's look at some facts about commissions compared to salaries:

Policy size. The newspaper printed an example of a $500,000 policy. That's a nice round figure but it's not average. Average would be closer to $100,000.

Let's assume the average term sale is $200,000:

Male age 35

Annual premium	$240.00
Commission rate 30% or	$72.00
Plus an expense override of	$72.00
Total commission & expense allowance	$144.00

- Assume we each make one sale every working day or twenty per month. Our gross commission earnings would be $2,880. Now the fun starts.
- Assume the bank can hire sales staff for $1,800 per month. That would leave $1,080 to pay expenses.
- Space at $45 a square foot; a 10 by 10 cubby hole would cost $4,500 per annum or $375/mo
- Telephone—one line $50/mo
- Long distance charges $50/mo

- Secretarial, telephone answering shared by 5 sales people — $1,500÷5 $300/mo
- Office supplies $25/mo
- Expense allowance $100/mo
- Employee Insurance $68/mo
- Canada Pension Plan $57/mo
- Share of space for secretary $375÷5 $75/mo

Total cost $1,100/mo

You may quibble about any of the amounts shown above; it really would not matter. Costs vary from place to place, but precise and accurate expenditures is not the point of the exercise. The principle remains regardless of how you would vary the numbers. *Distribution systems of every type cost money.* To single out one system is immature.

But that's not all.

There may be cancellations and non-taken policies. Cancellations cost money. Who pays when policies lapse? Commission sales advisors pay. Salaried agents do not.

What does it cost us?

During the first six months, if the policy lapses, the company recaptures 100% of the compensation; thereafter, from the seventh month to the twenty- fourth, the chargeback is calculated on a declining scale. Example: 12th month lapse—12/24 = 50%.

Do policies terminate?

Statistics indicate:

- 45% of all policies terminate or convert in the first year.
- 72% of all policies terminate or convert in the first three years.
- The average duration for term insurance is two years.
- Less than one policy in ten survives for its intended period.
- Only 1% of all term insurance results in death claims.

These statistics are from a study done by Penn State University. The study involved over 20,000 policies with a total or aggregate face value of four billion dollars. The study covered plans for 5, 10, 20 year renewable and convertible term and term to age 65. This study concluded in 1993. What has happened since then? If anything, the figures would be more dramatic.

Beyond the above, there are expenses for servicing. If we were like a regular banking operation, we would charge you for each service.

Change of address	$ 5.00
Change of beneficiary	$25.00 and so on

Perhaps the bank can get agents to sell for less than $1,800 per month or perhaps they can have a higher average than $200,000 per sale. Perhaps the agent will sell two or three new policies each day—or maybe not. Perhaps the bank's insurance company can hide some of the expenses elsewhere. If not, they will discover that the commissioned sales advisor is still the least expensive way. Commissions are paid primarily in the first year, but a president's salary carries on year after year until he is fired or retired. By the way, does the bank include the costs of the telephone solicitors in the comparison? Obviously it does not.

It Pays to Shop Around

How much advice do you want from your life agent? Do you want an advisor who can do more than quote you on a price per thousand? Do you want an advisor with more than one product to offer you, that is, someone who can offer you choices? Do you want someone who knows something about wills planning, estate planning or partnership and keyman coverage, disability income, and critical illness products? If so, you should *shop around*. You should look for and find an advisor with the credentials and the qualifications that come with experience.

Just after the articles referred to above appeared in the papers, another journalist could not resist getting into the act. Two days later he wrote an article entitled, "It pays to shop around."

This journalist, while admitting that the bank's rates were not the lowest, stated. Nevertheless, "The (bank's) (sic) rates are unquestionably at the lower end of the spectrum…" He goes on to admit that if you had been a smoker and you had given it up less than three years ago, a large number of companies would beat the bank's rate. He also admitted that the bank has no product to which you may convert at this time. Even if they had such a product what makes anyone believe that it would be a competitive product. If it is your goal to buy the cheapest term available, you should shop around but not for prices. You should shop for an advisor who has more than one product to offer. Your advisor should have the knowledge and the experience to make a proper comparison between various products. She should be able to help you choose your best approach short term and long term. You should shop around—but not for price. The *initial* cost of a product is probably the least significant factor of all.

Life insurance companies like term insurance and every other type of program they offer; otherwise they would not sell it.

People believe lies
not because they are plausibly presented,
but because they want to believe them.

~ Malcolm Muggridge

Myth: All Term Insurance is Created Equal

A flock of geese fans out across the sky, each one behind the one in front, which is to say, of course, they are in single file. This streamlined bevy of birds appears cloned from the leader. Each one appears to have been stamped in the sky by a single stencil, at a moment in time. In near perfect uniformity they fly with elegant grace and consummate skill. As each one prepares to come to land there is no exhibition of individual uniqueness. Watching the second, third or fourth bird achieve its goal is a motion picture re-run of the leader's style. Here, there is a precise imitation on a grand scale. Here, there is a perfect creation of equals.

In a world of naturally occurring phenomena, you may trust your observation that it is what it appears to be. However, in the world of business it is wise to look beyond the facade. In the business world, term insurance for example, is seldom what it appears to be:

- The lowest initial premium may not be the best choice
- The highest initial premium may be the lowest cost over time

It is important to know your purpose when you buy term insurance. You could buy a no frills plan, at the lowest premium, if you knew that your need for insurance was for a specific number of years. However, if you are not sure about your future requirements you may want to add one option—*Renewability*. Now what should you do? *Check the renewal rate*

Many companies have renewal rates that are higher than their attained age rates. That means you could cancel the old policy and start over with a new one at a lower rate than was offered on renewal; without changing companies. Why?

Because, when you reapply you must re-qualify. Your insurability is in question, and someday you may not be able to qualify for the lower rates. For that matter there is no guarantee that a lower rate will exist ten years from now. *You will have to pay the higher rate.* The *old* name for this approach was *re-entry term,* but that concept fell into disrepute, since it clearly favored the life insurance companies.

However, what we offer now is merely a variation of that old theme without the certainty of lower rate availability. Not only that, with re-entry term, the suicide restriction and incontestable period did not start again. When you consider these differences, re-entry term would be a superior choice—if it were available. The initial premium on this type of policy *should* be lower because the company is not on the risk for your insurability. Re-qualification requires new medical information, with all tests as specified for your attained age. Originally you may have qualified on a nonmedical basis, but now ten years later; you may need a full medical with all the tests. Remember, as pointed out above, if you do get your new plan, suicide and incontestable restrictions apply. (See 'Terminology' for an explanation of these terms.) *This approach is a despicable development, but it was caused by the pressure of competition.*

Here is an example taken from LifeGuide printouts, using the lowest initial premium for a $100,000 death benefit. My client was a 47 year old male nonsmoker at the time of preparing this quotation.

10 Year Renewable & Convertible			**Purchase New**
Age 47	$271.00		
Renewal @ age 57	$1,065.00	age 57	$649.00 (same company)

The *purchase new* rate is significantly lower than the guaranteed renewal rate. The catch is that you would have to qualify *again* at age 57. If you prove insurability you would pay $649.00 for the next 10 years, rather than $1065.00. Many people will not know about this, or they will not think about it. It's great for the insurance company. It receives over $400 a year too much, and it is not refundable. The bad news is that nearly all companies are currently pricing their term products in this way. The initial price is lower *because* our clients must assume part of the risk—insurability.

How can you avoid this type of plan? You will need to find a plan with an initial rate that accepts the liability for your insurability. However, you should know that the premium for such a plan will not be the lowest one available. However, there is a sure way to know if you have found it.

Look for:

- A renewal rate that is the same as the attained age rate
- A renewal rate that is lower, because your initial premium included a cost of acquisition that is not applicable to the renewal rate. However, this benefit may not be available anywhere, at this time.

Here is an example of a plan that is available:

	10 Year Renewable & Convertible		Purchase New
Age 47	$322		
Renews @ age 57	$779	@ age 57	$779

The initial rate is slightly higher, but the guaranteed rate at age 57 requires no additional qualification. Now if you include a second option, *convertibility*, the question is, to what is it convertible?

- If you are certain you will never convert your plan, why do you pay for this feature?
- If you may convert your plan someday, you should find out what plan is available for conversion? Ask your advisor to provide an illustration of a conversion product. Ask her if you can convert to level term to age 100, or to some other product, such as quick pay whole life?

Life insurance companies respond to the demands of the buying public; a public that has become sensitized to the concept that when buying life insurance they should look for the cheapest. *Some myths die hard but this one refuses to die at all.* When I think of the arguments proffered for the concept of buying term and investing the difference, I think of the story about the three accountants. They were applying for a prestigious position in a new company. The interviewer asked the first applicant to provide an answer for 2 + 2 =? He answered truthfully "2 + 2 = 4." The second applicant, sensed that the question could not be as simple as it appeared. He replied, "Well now, usually 2 + 2 = 4, but it is possible in some situations that it could be 3.999, and in other situations it could be 4.001." The third interviewee, when asked the solution to 2 + 2, looked over his horned rimmed glasses and replied, “What would you like it to be?” He got the job.

My apologies to all reputable accountants because that may not be a generally acceptable accounting procedure. However, when it comes to answering the question of *buy term and invest the difference,* it is a highly appropriate analogy. It is surprisingly easy to present a plausible argument to prove your point, regardless of the position you have taken, pro or con. Thus it is important to know the presenter’s biases. By over-weighting one section or under-weighting a different factor, anyone with minuscule ability can provide a mathematical solution to prove a point.

In a comparison of term insurance with whole life or a paid-in-full plan, there are several features to take into account. They are as follows:

- The cost of life insurance
  Is the promoter using current whole life plans compared to current term insurance, or does she use current term rates, against whole life rates from 40 years ago. Is the rate for the term insurance a stripped down version, that is, non-renewable, and non-convertible. If it is renewable, is it renewable at a guaranteed rate? If it is convertible, to what does it convert? Does the company offering this so-called conversion actually have a reasonable plan to which you may convert?
- What permanent plan is being used in the comparison
  Comparing the most expensive whole life plan in the industry, against the lowest term rate in the business, is not a reasonable approach. Furthermore, does this comparison take into account that the whole life plan may include *dividends*. Comparisons on a premium to premium basis are no more effective than comparing the cost of a Cadillac to a Volkswagen.
- Interest rates
  Does the calculation assume that the whole life or permanent plan earns only 4% while the investment supposedly earns 38%?
- Need for insurance
  Most arguments suggest that you will not need life insurance when you are older. Frequently the comparison is between, (a)

life insurance from age 25 to age 45, against (b) an investment from age 25 to age 65. The advocates of this approach state emphatically that following their recommendations will make you independently wealthy, and, therefore, you can *self-insure*. (The admission that you can self-insure is an obvious admission that the need for life insurance continues.)

- The cash value

Using the values from an old life insurance policy for a current day investment in a mutual fund is a common occurrence. For example: If you have a whole life policy of $25,000, purchased 20 years ago; the present cash value may be $9,050. It will grow to $37,275 at age 65 according to the guarantee in the policy. However, using the $9,050 plus an additional deposit of $100/month, *they* demonstrate that *they* can provide you with a $100,000 death benefit. The cash value from a separate investment at age sixty-five will be $120,016.81. That sounds good to me!

Why should you not buy into this argument?

- Well, number one, the $9,050 cash value is an accumulation that you would never have had if you had not purchased your whole life plan 20 years ago.
- Secondly, the separate accumulation in the example assumes tax sheltering.
- Thirdly, it does not take into account the cost of life insurance. It assumes you do not need life insurance after twenty years. However, let's include the cost of life insurance to age 100. The Term 100 premium is $1,087, payable until death. The separate cash accumulation at age 65 is now only $35,447, assuming compound interest earnings of 10%.

Using a *ten year renewable and convertible term plan* to age 65, the separate accumulation plan at age 65 would be $52,160, after factoring in the cost of insurance. Consequently, you would be *self-insured* at this point for only $52,160 unless you continued to pay premiums at the new rate of $2,440 per annum. Even then, you would have no life insurance at age 65.

Furthermore, your cash would accumulate to only $57,497. That's a far cry from the illustrated amount of $120,106.81.

- Fourth, what does the additional $100/month have to do with a fair comparison? If you rolled the cash value into a new plan with your company you may get a valuable benefit, and the results could be an early paid-up policy. Using the extra $100 per month would provide even higher death benefits.

For example: Using the same Term 100 premium plus the $9,050 cash surrender value and adding $100.00 per month, you immediately have a life policy paid in full for $102,196. If you continue to include the total deposit, that is, ($1087 + $1200) or $2,287, to age 65, your death benefit becomes $248,701. The cash value would be $114,272. (Interest assumption 8.5%.)

The following are other actual examples of a change within the original company compared to a separate (*buy term and invest the difference*) plan. First, let's review the variables:

(a) the cost of a whole life policy
(b) the cost of term insurance
(c) the period of time the life insurance is expected to remain in force
(d) the interest rate assumption for
    (1) the life policy projection, and
    (2) the separate investment
(e) the amount of deposit made to each program

(Remember this is a comparison of an investment using the difference in premium between life insurance until death, and term insurance plus a separate non-sheltered investment.)

Example: #1 — Illustration A

Assumptions:

- The insurance plan is universal life plan with several investment options.
- The interest rate assumed; for the life product is 8.5%; for the non-sheltered plan is to 10.5%
- The term insurance will be in effect until age 75. The plan is 10 Year Ren. & Convertible.
- The premium for universal life is $1,212 annually for a male non-smoker age 47.
- The marginal tax rate is 50%.

	Permanent Plan			Term + Investment		
				Premium		Total
Year	Premium	Coverage	Cash Value	T10 R&C	Coverage	Cash
1	1,212	100,076	0	304	100,000	956
5	1,212	100,491	0	304	100,000	5,309
10	1,212	101,776	1,776	304	100,000	12,165
11	1,212	102,170	2,170	944	100,000	13,086
15	1,212	104,422	4,422	944	100,000	17,276
20	1,212	109,357	9,357	944	100,000	23,877
21	1,212	110,712	10,712	2,440	100,000	23,838
25	1,212	117,792	17,792	2,440	100,000	23,709
Age 75	1,212	125,396	25,396	2,440	100,000	23,503
Age 76	0	127,218	27,218	0	* 0	24,737
30	0	129,241	29,241	0	0	26,036
35	0	142,560	42,560	0	0	33,627
Age 82	0	163,362	63,362	0	0	41,264
Age 92	0	195,846	95,846	0	0	56,093
Age 97	0	246,578	146,578	0	0	72,447

* At age 76 if you die the term life insurance death benefit is *0*. Let's assume you die at age 82. The life policy pays your named beneficiary $163,362 whereas your separate investment is only $41,264. OOPS, I can hear an objection. Someone will point out that this example assumes a marginal tax rate of 50% even after you retire. Fair enough. For some people the tax rate will drop after retirement, but for others it will not.

However, let's look at another example that illustrates a tax rate of 35%, after retirement. Otherwise, we are using the same assumptions as in illustration A.

Illustration B

	Permanent Plan			Term Premium	+ Investment	Total
Year	Premium	Coverage	Cash Value	T10 R&C	Coverage	Cash
1	1,212	100,076	0	304	100,000	959
5	1,212	100,491	0	304	100,000	5,309
10	1,212	101,776	1,776	304	100,000	12,165
11	1,212	102,170	2,170	944	100,000	13,086
15	1,212	104,422	4,422	944	100,000	17,276
20	1,212	109,357	9,357	944	100,000	24,592
21	1,212	110,712	10,712	2,440	100,000	24,959
25	1,212	117,792	17,792	2,440	100,000	26,695
Age 75	1,212	125,396	25,396	2,440	100,000	28,332
Age 76	0	127,218	27,218	0	0*	30,266
30	0	129,241	29,241	0	0	32,332
35	0	142,560	42,560	0	0	44,977
Age 82	0	163,362	63,362	0	0	62,569
Age 92	0	195,846	95,846	0	0	87,040
Age 97	0	246,578	146,578	0	0	121,083

Clearly, reducing the tax rate to 35% makes a significant difference for the investment. Even so, if death occurs at age 82, your beneficiary would receive only $62,569 rather than $163,362. Obviously a 35% tax bracket will not provide the significant difference required to make up the difference.

Illustration C

Similar assumptions to those in Illustration A using;

- Same permanent plan
- Same interest rate, but the non-sheltered plan is a mutual fund with the interest earned assumption exactly the same. The universal life investment option is, 50% TSE 300 (Canada), and 50% S&P 500 (U.S.A). This is more than a fair comparison to a mutual fund plan since both indexes out-performed the fund managers, 80% of the time during the past 20 years, according to John Doe.
- The term plan is Term to Age 100. Many people acknowledge that they need life insurance until death, whenever it may occur. The advocates of buy term and invest the difference say you become self-insured with their approach. Interesting point is it not? Being self-insured is a tacit agreement that you will need some form of available cash whenever death occurs. Why should it be your cash, at 100 cents on the dollar?
- The marginal tax rate assumed is 50%.

	Permanent Plan			Term 100 +		Investment
						Total
Year	Premium	Coverage	Cash Value	Premium	Coverage	Cash
1	1,212	100,076	0	1,087	100,000	132
5	1,212	100,491	0	1,087	100,000	732
10	1,212	101,776	1,776	1,087	100,000	1,680
15	1,212	104,422	4,422	1,087	100,000	2,908
20	1,212	107,034	7,034	1,087	100,000	3,813
21	0	106,722	6,722	1,087	100,000	1,879
25	0	106,094	6,094	1,087	100,000	-3,931
30	0	106,026	6,026	1,087	100,000	-11,458
Age 82	0	106,306	6,036	1,087	100,000	-21,207
40	0	106,742	6,742	1,087	100,000	-33,836
50	0	108,490	8,490	1,087	100,000	-71,389
Age 100	0	109,398	9,398	1,087	100,000	-87,001

Obviously, buying Term to 100 is a very expensive approach compared to our permanent plan. If you are still wary, let's compare the same plans with premiums on both plans, payable to age 100.

Illustration D (same assumptions as in illustration C)

	Permanent Plan			Term 100 +	Investment	
						Total
Year	Premium	Coverage	Cash Value	Premium	Coverage	Cash
1	1,212	100,076	0	1,087	100,000	132
10	1,212	101,776	1,776	1,087	100,000	1,680
20	1,212	109,357	9,357	1,087	100,000	4,499
25	1,212	117,792	17,792	1,087	100,000	6,560
30	1,212	131,876	31,876	1,087	100,000	9,230
Age 82	1,212	154,258	54,258	1,087	100,000	12,689
40	1,212	189,211	89,211	1,087	100,000	17,169
45	1,212	243,798	143,798	1,087	100,000	22,972
50	1,212	329,047	229,047	1,087	100,000	28,827
Age 100	1 ,212	401,728	301,728	1,087	100,000	36,028

Continuing to pay premiums in your permanent plan after age 65 results in continuously increasing death values and cash values, that substantially outstrip the separate investment.

Which would you rather have: $154,258 at death, assuming age 82 or $100,000 plus $12,689 ($112,689); and $401,728 or $136,028 at age 100?

Okay, the above examples assume a 50% tax bracket. What happens to our calculations if we change the tax bracket to 35%, at age 66?

Illustration E—same assumptions as Illustrations C & D. Permanent plan premiums payable until age 65; premiums for T100 continue until death; no difference in interest assumptions; 35% tax bracket starting at age 66.

Illustration E

	Permanent Plan			Term + Investment		
Year	Premium	Coverage	Cash Value	Premium	Coverage	Invest. Accum.
1	1,212	100,076	0	1,087	100,000	132
10	1,212	101,776	1,776	1,087	100,000	1,680
age 65	1,212	107,034	7,034	1,087	100,000	3,813
19	0	106,874	6,814	1,087	100,000	2,897
25	0	106,094	6,094	1,087	100,000	-3,940
30	0	106,026	6,026	1,087	100,000	-11,886
35	0	106,306	6,306	1,087	100,000	-22,656
40	0	106,742	6,742	1,087	100,000	- 37,251
50	0	108,490	8,490	1,087	100,000	-83,841
age 100	0	109,398	9,398	1,087	100,000	-104,305

The only way that term insurance, plus a separate investment can match our permanent plan, is if you assume a significantly higher interest rate for the separate non-sheltered investment. Alternatively, you must assume that there will be no need for life insurance past age 65.

Myth: Life Insurance Companies Keep It All

A common criticism of life insurance companies is that they return only a small percentage of premium deposits to the policyholders. If this is a reference to accidental death and dismemberment policies that are masquerading as death insurance, I would agree with that statement. The reason that double indemnity or accidental death policies are inexpensive is because there are so few claims.

We hear of an accident killing 43 people in a bus crash, or of 57 people dying in a train derailment, or of 290 people perishing in a plane crash and it appalls us. When 510 people die in auto accidents on a long holiday weekend, we refer to it as carnage on the highways. These events are tragic and there are hundreds of people affected by them. However, compared to the total number of people *exposed* the number of accidental deaths is very small. For every individual who dies in a bus crash, many thousands of people ride safely. The same may be said of all public transportation.

Naturally, I got quite excited, recently, when one of the oil companies sent me an offer ~One Million Dollars~. Well, that is what my eyes saw. Upon closer inspection I noticed it said up to One Million Dollars accidental death coverage.

Reading on:

- No cost to you for sixty days
- Guaranteed acceptance
- Premiums can never be increased
- Coverage cannot be canceled
- Pays in addition to any other insurance
- Worldwide coverage

Awesome, right? Well maybe not. My next thought was, "How much will it cost after sixty days?" Okay, $7.95 per month or $95.40 per annum. *All right!* $95.40 for 1,000,000 of coverage is great. I can sell it for about $100.00 per $100,000. But wait, the question that popped into my mind was, "What's the catch?"

First of all I realized that I had misread it. *Ah ha!* I assumed that the brochure was advertising for "Accidental Death *and* Dismemberment." This one was for Accidental Death only. Why would I make that mistake? It is probably because I have become accustomed to both coverage's being offered as a package. Even so, a $1,000,000 accidental death benefit for only $95.40 per annum? Well, let's not be too hasty with our assumptions. Let's see what this plan does cover precisely.

Ah ha #2: *$1,000,000 as a fare paying passenger in a plane, ship, train, bus or any licensed common carrier*

Your chances of getting a pay-out from this plan would be lower than for winning a lottery.

Ah ha #3: *$125,000 auto accident if struck by a land motor vehicle*

That's better, but as you may see below, the chance of death by auto accident is very low. There is a far greater chance of a serious injury in an auto accident. What I would really prefer is auto coverage that includes a clause for loss of *use* of; arms, legs, sight, hearing, etc.

Ah ha #4: *$25,000 for all other covered accidents at work, at home, or anywhere in the world, 24 hours a day*

Obviously the real offer amounts to a $25,000 accidental death plan only. Now the premium does not impress me so much. Anyway, let's look farther to see what this plan does not cover.

Any loss, *that is any death*, resulting from;

- Intentional self-infliction, sane or insane
- War or act of war, declared or not
- Taking any narcotic, barbiturate, or any other drug unless prescribed by a physician
- A blood alcohol level of 80 mg per 100 ml of blood or higher
- Being a non-fare-paying passenger or acting as a pilot or crew member in any aircraft
- Commission of a criminal offense
- A disease, body or mental infirmity, or medical or surgical treatment of these

Wow, that is impressive. At least they did not exclude death by poisoning, asphyxiation or drowning, unless it can be attributed to self-infliction, or one of the other above named exclusions. Many other similar plans pointedly exclude these possibilities as well.

On the surface, the exclusions all seem reasonable enough, but *I expect my plan to cover me for all of the above.* If you need the coverage, *if* you die by an accident as qualified above, you need the coverage no matter how you die. A proper plan has none of these exclusions. Buying a plan like this at any price is a waste of money. This type of plan was originally the creation of an actuary who received instructions from the president of his company; "Get us an inexpensive plan that can be sold easily, but with which there would be few, if any, claims."

Some of my acquaintances think these offers are great. There usually are at least three or four of them each year. So they apply to each one for the *no cost period*, such as sixty days. At the end of the free period they simply cancel it. That's a good strategy if you can be bothered with it.

Now let's consider the hype about accidental death. In my home town, with a population of over 800,000 people, 103 people died accidentally on our streets last year. That is serious and we, the citizens of this great city, should do everything reasonably possible to reduce this figure. Taken by itself, the cold stark figure of 103 is disturbing. That's why they always present these figures in isolation from other pertinent information.

For example, let's assume that only 10% of the citizens of this city expose themselves to traffic of any kind, on any day, but a similar number does so on every day of the year. That would mean that 10% of 800,000 or 80,000 for 365 days, or 29,200,000 people experience the risk of dying accidentally in traffic. This is a ridiculously low number, because it means that 720,000 people do not venture outside their homes on any given day. While I have no evidence to support my opinion, I suspect that there may be 80,000 cars on our streets during any one hour and they are all downtown during the rush hours. In spite of that observation, let's examine the example in more detail.

Expressed as a percentage, only 103/29,200,000 = .00035% are endangered. Of the assumed number of people exposed to this danger, only an insignificantly small percentage actually dies.

Looked at in another way, there were 103 deaths per 800,000 people, not including visitors, or only 1 death for each 8000 people in our study. That would be 0.125 per 1000 per annum if all 800,000 citizens of this city were exposed just once during the year. From these calculations it should be obvious that the risk of death by accident is very small. If you travel extensively, your risk of accidental death increases slightly but the difference is barely measurable. It should be obvious that banks, trust companies, air lines, travel agencies, department stores, oil companies and on and on, offer this product because it is nearly pure profit. People apparently are buying it as a cheap replacement for proper life insurance, which will pay on death no matter how or when it occurs. It is unfortunate when people buy this inferior product merely because it's cheap.

I repeat; if you need a specific amount of death benefit if you die by an accident, you surely need that amount ***no matter how you die.***

The return to the public, on the term life series of products is slightly higher than for accidental death plans. While accidental death is the largest cause of death among younger people, a term life policy has *none* of the exclusions listed above. The only exclusion in a life insurance contract is suicide during the first two years. According to my information, the death rate by accident is higher from ages seventeen to twenty-five. Thereafter, it tapers off significantly to age 60, at which time it begins to rise and so does the cost to purchase a proper plan. One company advised me that accidental death is the leading cause of death at all ages between age 20 and age 65. However, that bit of information is not very significant when you look at the total number of deaths per one thousand people, at any given age.

The percentage of premiums paid out as death claims on term plans, excluding term to 100 and all forms of whole life or permanent plans, is still extremely low. Even if we include the amount kept as a reserve against potential future losses or potential disaster losses, the total amount would be significantly less than the premiums collected. Of course, costs of administration such as policyholder service, underwriting expense, and acquisition costs, eat up a large portion of the paid premiums. However, if you look at accidental death or term life from the viewpoint of the percentage returned as a death benefit, then *both are very poor investments*.

It should be fairly clear why some life companies and banks with life insurance programs sell only term life products. It is a profitable product for companies, as illustrated elsewhere in this book. Remember, all life companies sell term insurance, but some of them do not sell competitive products with cash values, and paid up benefits.

Referring back to the original statement that "companies return only a small percentage of the premiums paid to policyholders," there is a modicum of truth if we relate the statement to term life and accidental death products. However, if we expand the sample base to include other forms of life insurance, such as guaranteed whole life or variable interest sensitive products, it becomes much more difficult to measure the relevancy of the above statement, except to say that it is definitely inaccurate.

The percentage return to policyholders from cash reserve plans would change with each passing year. No one would disagree that if you buy any type of life insurance, other than term life, and cancel it in the first five years, you have wasted some of your additional premium deposits. However, as you make more deposits, the growth in cash value causes the percentage of return to change significantly. In most modern policies, the payable death benefit also increases.

To determine the inaccuracy of the opening statement, when applied to variable whole life products, there are many factors to consider and assumptions to be made. An extensive study would prove somewhat boring to those not interested in mathematical examples.

However, some of the factors to be considered are:

- Total deposits made
- Variable interest rate applied
- Amount of death benefit—level or increasing
- Paid up value after a specified number of years
- Release of up to 100% of premiums paid to date

With some of the policies available today, you can withdraw your premium deposits while the policy remains in force. Actually, you may be able to remove most of the cash value while the basic life insurance remains in force. (If you find this difficult to believe, check it out with your advisor.)

Generally, the total amount of cash value from permanent plans is much higher than the premiums paid. No matter how long you live, you never could pay more than about twenty-eight cents on the dollar, even if death occurred at age 100. In other words if you live long enough, you might pay as high as $27,566 for a $100,000 death benefit, on a fully guaranteed whole life plan. Death at any earlier age would result in a lower cost per thousand.

Using interest sensitive products, usually referred to as universal life, the rate per thousand would be much lower and, therefore, the percentage returned would be much higher.

For example;

Male age 23—Initial coverage	$100,000
Annual deposit	$600.00
Fully paid in 11 years at 8% interest.	
Total deposit	$6,600.00
Death benefit at age 34	$102,734.00

This plan requires no further premiums after 11 years, if it earns 8% per annum, but the death benefit and cash surrender values continue to increase. At age 65, the death benefit would have increased to $116,371. Therefore, the growth would be 17.53 times the deposit if death occurs at age 65. You would need to make nearly 10% annually on $6,600 for 31 years, after taxes, in order to match this return.

Another example;

Age 23—Initial coverage	$100,000
Annual deposit	$600.00
Paid for 40 years, (assumed interest rate 8%.)	
Total deposit	$24,000.00
Death benefit @ age 64	$241,634.00
Cash Value	$106,115.00
Withdraw cash at age 65	$24,000.00
Fully paid up net policy	$212,501.00
Remaining cash value	$91,978.00

These calculations are accurate @ 8% interest. The plan quoted does not guarantee the rate assumed for the calculations. A different rate would change the numbers, of course.

It doesn't matter how you calculate it, there would be an excellent return. The myth is, of course, that you do not get a good return on the cash build-up inside a life insurance policy. Keeping in mind that there is always a cost for the life insurance benefit, the argument is not valid. Term to 100 would cost at least $249.00 at age 23. This premium must be paid every year until death or age 100, whichever comes first. If you paid $249.00 for 77 years, your total deposit would be $19,173. The additional amount required to buy a policy with cash values would be $351.00. In other words, if you pay an extra premium of $351.00 per annum for forty years, or $14,040, you could cash surrender the policy for $106,115 at age 65. What is the return on the additional $351.00 deposit in the above example?

Proponents of the poor return argument like to point out that there is very little cash back in the first few years, if you decided to cash it. At the same time, they also advise you that a mutual fund is a long term investment.

Give it a break!

Myth: Death Benefits and Savings Do Not Mix

Clearly this is a variation of the argument made to persuade you to invest the difference between term insurance and a real plan. It's also obvious to me that there are several considerations that invalidate this myth. The savings portion of the premium on conventional whole life policies provides many benefits; some of which are;

• A disciplined means of saving money systematically

In the past, people would have saved much less money, if this feature did not exist. More often than not the choice was between saving a little, by paying a slightly higher premium than required, or not saving anything at all. For a new salesperson to come along ten to twenty years later, and suggest that you could have done better is sheer arrogance and the height of ignorance. Where was this new breed of salesperson when you were making decisions twenty years ago? What do they know about your situation when you were young? Where were the great new products when you started your plan twenty years ago?

• Tax sheltering of interest earnings on a non-registered product

This is one of the few legitimate avenues still available to the average person for investment on a tax advantageous basis.

• A paid in full death benefit

No Salesman Will Call? illustrated several times that the *pure* cost of term insurance, over time, is greater than the premiums in total for a paid-in-full life insurance policy. The question remains, *why would you pay even more for term insurance and forfeit the benefit of cash values?*

• A guarantee that the policy cannot lapse if you miss one or more deposits

The non-forfeiture values of your policy provide guarantees against a loss due to an inadvertent or careless act, such as failing to pay a premium, as long as any cash remains in the policy.

• An increasing death benefit

There are two ways for a policy to experience automatically increasing death benefits. One is to add this feature to the policy; the other is by continuing to pay premiums after the policy is paid-up. Perhaps the most significant benefit that a plan with cash values and paid-up insurance benefits has, is the tax free transfer of assets from one generation to another.

Term insurance can be used to replace the loss of income caused by the premature death of a father or a mother. Term insurance steps in to pay for the costs of raising a family; to pay for the children's education; and to maintain the family's standard of living. What it cannot do is preserve the estate if the insured outlives the life insurance, that is, when the term insurance expires first.

In recent years, some salespeople laud Term to age 100 as the answer. What a wonderful product it is. Except that, if you are under age 60, the difference in cost between Term 100 and a plan with cash values or paid up values is very small. Not even an ignoramus could argue that it is better. With only a handful of extra dollars, you could have a fully paid policy, in ten years or less, compared to *paying premiums until you die or to age 100.*

Of course, as an alternative to a proper plan, if you die without life insurance your heirs could sell assets to pay the taxes. That's definitely one possible solution, but which assets are the most salable just after your death? They will sell your best ones, naturally; the most liquid ones such as your retirement investments. Who will buy that apartment building that is losing money, just because your estate needs it? Would your sons and daughters be required to sell the office building, that provides the income that allows you to keep the other one; that dog of an apartment building. Perhaps they must keep the drain on income in the hopes that it will appreciate and become salable. However, think of this. After your children have sold the income producing building to pay your taxes, they are left with the other one. Selling it at a loss is a possible solution. If you do not care, go ahead; buy term insurance.

The growth of cash values in a life insurance policy is tax sheltered. Withdrawal of cash from the policy is tax free up to the adjusted cost base—an amount determined by a government approved formula.

The features and benefits of a cash value policy provide a variety of advantages to an astute buyer. They offer an increasing death benefit, that could equal or exceed the initial face value of the policy. In addition, the accumulated cash value can be paid as a death benefit.

Another benefit is that you may use the accumulated cash values to augment income from your RRSP. The use of these cash values for extra income has the added feature of flexibility. You are not required to start withdrawals at age 69, as is the case with an RRSP. You may withdraw lump sums periodically, or you may take regular withdrawals monthly or annually or nothing at all. Skip a month, skip a year. The flexibility of choice is yours. Even better, in some situations, is the fact that you may borrow against the cash asset in your policy without triggering a tax liability. Just like any other asset you own, you can pledge it at the bank as collateral. The difference is this; you will not need to pay it back until you die. Then, your loan is paid automatically, with the tax exempt death benefit.

In the July, 1998 issue of *Consumer Reports*, the authors have once again written extensively about term versus whole life. They wrote on this topic at least once before. One thing I must admit—they are consistent. The same biases are persistent; the same examples are prevalent; the same lack of understanding and knowledge is obvious.

This edition was clearly marked *Canada Extra*. However, the examples given and the quotations illustrated are from US companies. I have never heard of ninety percent of them. They started the article with the statement: “There is only one reason you need life insurance.” If that were true, the many following pages of attempted proof would be redundant.

They entitled the article *The Mysteries of Life*, but their first statement proves that they know very little about the subject matter. The unnamed author proceeds to make several inaccurate, misleading statements such as; “$250,000 of protection that cost $600.00 seven years ago, costs only about $275.00 today.” Where is the journalistic integrity in such a stand alone statement? There was no attempt to quote a specific plan with a certain company. Rather one must wonder: did they find a somewhat similar plan, at least in name, with the highest rate from seven years ago, compared to the lowest rate currently available? What is this policy that they claim costs only $275.00 now? What benefits, such as renewability and convertibility, have they stripped away? At what age could one pay only $275.00 for $250,000? Be careful; that premium is approximately equal to the costs of an accidental death and dismemberment policy. They may be quoting a rate for a plan that covers you only in case of an accidental death.

However, we could match the premium with yearly renewable term at age 35. Otherwise we could use a 10 year renewable and convertible term plan at age 30. In any case you may be sure, it did not cost $600.00 per annum seven years ago.

As in the past, these authors attack conventional whole life policies citing high commissions as the reason agents sell *so-called cash value policies*. This stupid argument is wearing very thin with me. The current version does make one new statement that I never read in this rag previously. It is: *The industry has engaged in questionable sales practices that have abused policyholders*. The authors of this article do not quote the source of that statement, which I suggest is, Norman Dacey in, *What's Wrong With Your Life Insurance. They* do not document this statement in any way. *They* merely throw it out as a self-evident truism. Such a statement is incredibly irresponsible. This so-called Canadian edition offers no Canadian content, but they provide it for the consumption of those gullible citizens up north.

Unfortunately, some people reading this article are under the misconception that this is a respectable magazine, operating under the guise of factual reporting. Equally unfortunate is the fact that some agents selling life insurance use this trash as a third party influence or an appeal to authority, in order to sell their own frail concepts and mediocre products. When an author of a magazine, such as Consumer Reports, writes with such an obnoxious bias about one product, how can anyone trust their opinions on any subject?

Recently a client of mine, age 62, sold shares in his company and realized over one half million dollars in cash. His goal was to invest it in such a way as to provide $50,000 per annum for his and his wife's lifetime. Thereafter, he wants at least $500,000 to remain for his children to share. It's not an impossible task. If he can invest the $500,000 at 10%, it would provide the $50,000 from interest only. Of course, if he experiences years where interest rates are lower, he would not receive $50,000. He would have a choice in those years to (a) take less income, or (b) to encroach upon capital.

Another problem with this approach is that the interest earnings are taxable. If his investments are in equities, he may be able to receive them as capital gains. In that case only 75% of the $50,000 or $35,000 would be taxable. However, with income from all sources, my client would pay taxes of roughly 50% on this $35,000. This would provide a net of $17,500 after tax plus the $15,000 tax exempt part, for a net total amount of $32,500. An obvious solution to this taxation problem would be income splitting with his spouse. However, on this specific asset it was not permissible because of the *attribution rules*. In case this is not a household phrase in your home, let me explain. The attribution rules, with respect to spouses, provide that where property is transferred or loaned by you to your spouse, then all income or loss from the property, and any capital gain or loss on the disposition of the property, will be *attributed* back to you for tax purposes.

Now if that did not clarify it, let me try again. If you have a cash asset, you cannot give half of it to your spouse for investment purposes because the resulting benefits will revert to you.

Okay, let me try it again. You cannot split the income from one source into two in order to save taxes. Phew! I think we have it.

Another feasible solution, in this case, was to earn more on the equity investments. For example, a fifteen percent rate of earnings would render a $75,000 income, of which 25% would be tax exempt. On the remaining $56,250, the net amount after tax at 50% would be $28,125. Adding the tax exempt amount of $18,750 to the net after tax amount generates a total of $46,875. Close enough. However, everyone knows that a 15% interest rate requires a riskier investment than does a 10% rate of return. Thus, in turn, this would endanger the principal. During the life expectancy period of about twenty years there could be many changes in the equity market.

Another consideration of some importance is that this type of investment would require regular monitoring. Can you always assume that you will be competent, mentally and emotionally, to cope with these decisions? If not, what happens then?

There was an excellent solution; joint last to die life insurance with his spouse. Even after assuming a significantly lower rate of return, we were able to provide the equivalent income, tax free, and guarantee a considerably larger estate for the children than $500,000, from the proceeds at death.

A corollary benefit to this approach is that the money released via our bank loan program will not increase the tax burden on his other income from his RRSPs. This is not an insignificant consideration. It may even permit this couple to operate in a lower income tax bracket overall.

***Sometimes death benefits and savings do mix superbly*.**

Check it out. Call your advisor.

Myth: Just 10% More

Curiously, nearly everyone feels that if they could earn just ten percent more, after taxes of course, their money problems would vanish. Regardless of whether we earn $2,500 a month or $25,000 each month, we all have a propensity to spend a little more than we earn. It is as though a tiny mechanism in each of our brains forces us to do it. Look at the columns of bankruptcies and you will discover that some of the people, declaring a state of impecuniosity, have assets of $350,000, $750,000, $3,000,000 or even more. Why would any of them declare bankruptcy? It's simply because their liabilities are 10% higher than their assets.

Many people tend to relate financial happiness to the standard of living that they feel they should have. Frequently, they suffer the common malady of a grasp that exceeds the reach. Some say; *money cannot buy happiness*. The debate rages on over the accuracy of that tidbit. Scholars, philosophers and comedians, all find it useful to their purposes. Other people retort, w*ell, money can buy more happiness than lack of money can, and, furthermore, it buys everything that makes me happy*. One of my favorites is; m*oney cannot buy poverty. The poor will always be among us. It's your duty to make sure that you are not one of them*.

Clever commentary and slick bromides aside, it seems that enough money can buy a form of happiness. Conversely, a lack of sufficient income will lead to various degrees of unhappiness. Many marriages, like business partnerships and other financial endeavors, end up insolvent or in bankruptcy because they were under-funded. Very few young couples entering into a matrimonial state have any real understanding of financial matters. Regularly, I hear people say that there should be a course in school to teach people the basics of saving, spending, and investing. It sounds like a great idea to me, but there is a very serious problem with such a course. Certainly it would not be difficult to provide people with a sample budget and some common sense principles to follow. Indeed the basic, yet overriding principle, is simply spend fewer dollars than you earn. It sounds easy doesn't it? Budgeting and dieting are easy concepts to comprehend. *Spend less than you earn and accumulate the difference. Eat no more than you require to maintain good health and reduce the pounds*. Many people have tried budgeting, and even more have tried dieting, but neither budgets nor diets seem to work very well. This is not a book about dieting, so I will end the analogy at this point, except to say, if one could save money dieting it would aid one's budgetary attempts.

Frankly, budgeting and financial planning usually does not work the first time around. I doubt if any course in money management, in high school or university, would make much difference, because successful budgeting and saving require a set of values, and some experience in the real world. It would be improbable, if not impossible, to impart a lasting set of money values through books and classes for some young couples, without involving practical experience. Even the values imprinted from parents, through good or bad examples, seldom have the desired effect on the children before they face a serious crisis, or a series of financial crises.

My father believed that one should never buy anything using credit. He believed and practised a basic concept that you should never go into debt for anything. He always paid cash for whatever he desired. He saved first and then bought. He paid cash for new cars, tractors, and farm equipment. He understood the concept of deferred gratification. From his point of view, there was little difference between a luxury expenditure and a capital investment in equipment. This was so, even though the latter would permit greater earnings and create a better cash flow to pay off the debt. On the other hand, you could fix up an old tractor cheaply, especially if you did your own repair work.

Another completely opposite philosophy is that you should always use other people's money. Borrow it, if you can. Get others to invest in your venture. Moreover, some people seem to need the imposed discipline of borrowing to buy and of meeting monthly commitments. Many advisors believe that it's permissible to borrow to create an increase in assets, but it's unwise to borrow for luxury or lifestyle items. In other words, you could borrow to invest in the stock market or a business or for your savings program. Doing it this way would allow you to spend cash for a newer car, while you borrow money for things for which you can write-off the interest expense against your income. If this procedure reduces taxable income, it makes sense.

Many people attempting to budget for the first time try to follow some type of model based on an average family and a universal expenditure pattern. Trying to follow an arbitrary model or even trying to design your own plan based on generalizations, will lead to dissatisfaction usually because budgeting is such a highly individualized endeavor. There are other obstacles to budgeting that we, as individuals, must overcome before we can hope to find success and happiness with it. Perhaps we will need to overcome some basic attitudes, or in some cases, some deeply entrenched concepts and beliefs in our value systems.

Clients of mine have told me that when they attempted to prepare a family budget, it caused money quarrels that actually could have degenerated into a family feud. My reply is simply—that's good! It is better, surely, to have small quarrels about money matters before they become insurmountable. The process of discussing your family needs, goals, and dreams can be extremely rewarding. Planning a strategy based on facts and establishing goals for your future could be highly beneficial for marital bliss. Obviously, it is better to develop the big picture by setting short term and long term goals, than it is to focus on specific or isolated mistakes. Mistakes are always things that happened in the past. Insofar as possible, I try to avoid the comparison between my wife's profitable investment in 3M stock and my loss in a travel agency. She invested $750.00 for ten shares, which split 3 for one and went up to $96.00 per share after the split. We will never recover my investment of over $200,000. My answer is: "Let's look at the big picture my dear. Let's not sweat the small stuff."

Sometimes clients tell me that budgeting is too limiting. They see the process as too restrictive—a sort of primitive, puritan control mechanism or a punitive constraint that makes living unnecessarily miserable. Any budget that is designed to control the people involved is doomed to failure. The real purpose of designing a budget is to give you control of your money and its use, rather than taking it away. For many people the very concept of a budget is threatening. Some people tell me, "It is too complicated and involves too much dreary bookkeeping."

That's it! Some people see the process of budgeting as accounting for every penny spent. They see it as a system of double entry accounting which records every expenditure down to the minutest detail, one ice cream cone 0.98 cents.

Bookkeeping entry;

debit food	0.98	
credit cash		0.98

What nonsense! If this is what budgeting meant I would agree; it's too complex and counterproductive. Notwithstanding the fact that some people *enjoy* keeping extremely detailed records, most of us do not need it. For those who do need this minutia in their lives, I say this; we have no right to deny them a harmless enjoyment. To their spouses who complain about such marital tightwads, I reply, that this problem is beyond the scope of a mere financial consultant.

Done properly, budgeting is not complex. First of all, budgeting is not bookkeeping. These are two different disciplines. Budgeting is a planning process. Bookkeeping is keeping score. For those who enjoy it—great, that's your demon. For those who do not enjoy the role of *bean counting,* relax. Budgeting is a process of looking at facts. You and your spouse and your children, if they are ready, should look at the situation as it exists. Your family income is either specific or variable.

Basically there are three kinds of expenditures: fixed, discretionary, and irregular.

Fixed expenses are such things as monthly commitments:

(a) mortgage, or rent payment
(b) water and electricity
(c) telephone—basic charges

(d) installment payments—car, clothing
(e) insurance auto, home and life
(f) miscellaneous—licenses, etc.
(g) bank loan payments

Discretionary expenses. These are noncommittal or variable expenses:
(a) food
(b) automobile operation
(c) clothing
(d) fuel—heating and auto
(e) non-accountable spending allowances
(f) charitable donations
(g) household supplies
(h) entertainment, movies, Philharmonic
(I) newspapers, books and magazines
(j) telephone—long distance

Irregular expenses:
(a) vacation
(b) furniture
(c) household repairs
(d) clothing—major items
(e) extra charges for medical and dental

While it is possible to break this outline down into more detail, it is really not necessary. Simpler is better. The most important thing about a budget is *the process of planning it.* The budgeting process should be a device to help you understand the situation as it currently exists, and to help you plan for future events. This process should be a cooperative family analysis of current affairs and future goals. After you have followed the creative process, tear up your notes. Follow the general concept; details are not important.

Another negative thought about the budgeting process is that it really will not change anything. That is, expenditures will not decrease and income will not increase as a result of budgeting. So what is the point? If there ever was a perfect point for the negative debate this would be it. Budgeting does not increase your family income, nor does it decrease your expenditures.

This argument is accurate, if you are merely recording things as they have always been, but if budgeting is used as a creative tool, you can change certain behavioral patterns in your lifestyle. Over a period of time you can reduce some fixed expenditures. Discretionary expenditures are those that you can consider more carefully. By budgeting carefully, you may be able to follow the admonitions of modern day gurus who advocate *pay yourself first*.

Pay yourself first? What a novel concept that is. We should congratulate Chilton and Moynes on the formulation of such a concept. Right? Of course we would, if it was their concept. But it was not! As you know, George S. Clasen presented it in his booklet *The Richest Man in Babylon*. BUY IT! It's a classic.

That concept was correct in 1926 and it is correct today. If you reduce discretionary expenditures by $100.00 per month, you can *pay yourself* that is, save it for your future. Trying to follow the concept of paying yourself first, before you know where the money will come from, is foolish advice and it's doomed to failure.

If you do not have a budget how can you know if you are using free money, or are these funds that you must use for other pending expenses? Perhaps you will need this money for a fixed expense not yet due; such as insurance or any annually billed expenditure. You may be able to reduce your *fixed* expenditures over time. You can assuredly change your discretionary expenditures significantly, if you want to do so. For example: the support of a child in Biafra may be wonderful, but why not support a charitable cause in your hometown?

Some people avoid doing a budget because friends and neighbors claim that they do not have one. Perhaps the others can keep score mentally and, thus, they really do have a budget after a fashion. Nevertheless, just because it works for someone else does not make it right for you. Many people consider the family to be a business partnership. Any business without a budget could be in serious trouble without even knowing it. Without a budget, the partners may not know what is happening. How could any business people make decisions without a balance sheet, and a statement of income and expenses?

If you handle your family affairs as a partnership, many benefits can accrue. The lines of communication between the key partners open up and remain open. Decisions made together about financial matters will reduce arguments and eliminate some serious family stress. Furthermore, as children develop and begin to understand the use of, and the value of money, you can include them in the discussion. Understanding family finances may help them to be less demanding. Knowing that there is a fund for post secondary education may provide incentive for them to do well in school—especially if they know that you expect them to continue their education beyond high school. There could be many other positive reactions as well; but above all else, the example you set for your children could provide one of the best lessons possible. The psychological benefits of involving your children in a periodic family budget conference, similar to an annual corporate board meeting, can be multi-faceted. Involving the family may enhance self-esteem and build a greater appreciation for the major provider(s). Finally, no class on financial matters, at any school, could compete with the practical education you can provide your family. No theory, no artificial model, and no composed example can equal the real thing. If you provide the basics, your family will not need to consult the local financial planning barber.

A constantly expanding income by at least 10% a month would not be a solution. Teaching oneself to manage within current constrains is the happy answer.

It's not that I want money. It's the fun of making money and watching it grow. (I) (sic) enjoy the process more than proceeds, though I have learned to live with those also.

~ Warren Buffett

Myth: The Vanishing Premium

Several authors have had much to say about the coined term *vanishing premium*. It is not merely the volume of their utterances, but rather, it is the implied impropriety that disturbs me because they are not always technically correct. Secondly, by the tone of their expressions, they clearly mean to cast aspersions on all life plans other than term and on all life agents other than termites; those advocating buy term only. This is a window of opportunity for them that is too good to pass.

As frequently displayed, their ignorance of facts is glaring or, perhaps, it is merely their selection of self-serving facts. To ignore that not all so-called vanishing premium plans failed to meet their objectives is callous and irresponsible. Furthermore, to promote the concept that those plans that did not get to the party on time as disastrous, is an exaggeration of real events.

The purpose of a paid-up policy was obvious; no more premiums past age 65. This concept became very popular during the high interest bearing years. Some clients, unfortunately, did not understand that if interest rates went down the policy would not be paid in full as illustrated.

Currently, there are many plans that are even more responsive to the changing money winds. Illustrations show policies paid in full after a certain number of years at a specific interest rate. It may not be clear, however, that this interest rate must continue in order to be certain that the policy will remain paid-up. If earned interest remained lower for an extended period of time it may be necessary to resume payments.

The catchy phrase *vanishing premium* is merely a more expressive way of describing a paid-up policy. You have no more deposits to make on a life insurance contract stamped *paid in full*. The phrases are new, to be sure, but the concept is not. It existed long before I joined the business. Forty years ago, we called these policies *limited pay* plans. We *guaranteed* a fully paid policy in 5 years, or in

10 years, 20 years or at age 55, or at age 60, or at age 65 or at *age 100—your choice.*

The more knowledgeable reader may say, "Wait now, Term 100 is a relatively recent development is it not?" Perhaps in the purest sense, that may be correct. However, I am reminded of the story of a Beaver as it viewed the Hoover Dam somewhat in awe. The Beaver's thoughts reportedly were, "I can't take credit for this one, but it was definitely based on a concept of mine."

The precursor to Term 100 was Whole Life. The similarities are many. When I heard an agent from the USA expounding on the virtues of Term 100 on a Vancouver radio station, I was not amused. He stated, "You Canadians are really lucky, you know, to have a plan like this one. We don't have anything like it Stateside." Was it tongue in cheek or was this guy really that dumb? Of course they have plans like Term 100 in the USA. Term 100 is merely a *stripped down* version of whole life or a pay to age 100 plan. In both Canada and the USA there are low-cost whole life plans. As you remove some of the benefits of whole life you can lower the premiums required.

For example;

A common version of a whole life plan was one guaranteed to endow at age 100. That is, the policy would be cashable by the life insured for the full death benefit. Pre-1982 the cash value was tax free. Alternately, you can pay a few dollars less for Term 100 and at age 100 you would get only the double zero after the one. Nothing! If you pay this lower premium for 65 years you better make sure you do not extend your visit on planet earth for one day too long.

Secondly, conventional whole life has an increasing cash surrender value or a reduced paid-up value as the plan grows. Paid-up values mean that you can stop paying premiums at any age, such as age 60, and have a fully paid, although, reduced death benefit. With our stripped down model called Term 100—you stop paying premiums and the death benefit disappears. Even if you miss paying the premium inadvertently, thirty days after the due date your policy lapses as per the terms of your contract. You may be able to reinstate it by proving you are in good health and by repaying all back premiums with interest. So you can pay a lower premium but you must give up a number of benefits.

A traditional whole life plan is:

- A policy which either endows at age 100 or is paid in full until death
- A policy which has cash surrender values or paid up values increasing regularly
- A policy that cannot lapse inadvertently

The company cannot cancel it, for any reason, until they exhaust all internal cash values. How much is it worth to have these extra benefits? How much can you save with the basic factory model as advertised—no extras, no frills, no special benefits?

Let's look at an actual example:

	Plan	
Amount: $100,000	Whole Life	Term 100
Male, nonsmoker		
@ age 35: annual premium	$488.00	$455.00
*premiums to age 100, both plans		

There are no cash values nor reduced paid-up values in the whole life policy for the first 10 years. However, the illustrated Term 100 plan will not have any cash values nor any paid-up values, until age 100. Both plans become paid in full at age 100. The benefit of paying this additional $33.00 per annum is that your policy will not lapse inadvertently and, secondly, you can get some or all of your premiums refunded if you cancel your plan.

There are many variations of benefits for which a small extra deposit may provide considerable additional values.

For example, a small increase in annual deposit will cause the policy's premiums to vanish at an earlier age.

$100,000 @ age 35

Payable	Annual Premium	Total Deposit
to age 65	$564.00	$16,920
to age 55	$636.00	$12,720
to age 50	$745.80	$11,187

The obvious benefit of these slight increases in annual premium is that the total amount deposited is lower. From the example, the lowest initial premium results in the highest total expenditure over time. In this review of premiums, we have made no attempt to evaluate additional benefits that may be value-added with any given plan. All of the above quotations are from different companies, and they may have additional special features. At this point, we are simply looking at what it takes to make the premium disappear at a specified time. If that is the only consideration, it should be apparent from the above examples that you should buy the 15 pay plan to age 50.

Of course, there are usually other benefits that you should consider, and that fact justifies using a knowledgeable agent to advise you and to assist you in your deliberations. As we add back various benefits to the stripped down model, Term 100, it begins to look more and more like a conventional whole life policy. A number of companies offer alternative Term 100 plans with cash values and/or paid up values. Some companies even offer a return of all premiums paid if you live past a certain age. This entire issue may be somewhat confusing to some people and that's why so much detail is being provided. The proliferation of plans and their variations can be overwhelming. No wonder the authors writing exposés of these concepts are prone to faulty analysis guiding them to make so many erroneous and misleading commentaries. The ignorance displayed is understandable but not forgivable. *They* should not critique on matters about which *they* know so little.

The comparison of interest sensitive plans illustrating vanishing premiums at a chosen interest rate to conventional limited-pay policies is ludicrous. Admittedly some similarities do exist. Some companies offer limited pay policies on a participating basis, that is, by applying dividends. The guaranteed plans illustrated above are on a non-par basis. Including the dividend option, i.e., using a participating policy for which the company declares annual dividends, could cause a policy to be paid-up much sooner. The policy owner could use the declared dividend to reduce premiums or to buy additional coverage, known as paid-up additions. The policy would have an increasing death benefit, until at some point the total paid-up benefit could equal the initial death benefit with no further premium payments. *Hence you have vanishing premiums.*

When the concept of the interest sensitive policy was introduced in the later 1970s, the majority of companies did not react excitedly, that is, they did not create competitive plans of their own. Rather these companies found that they could compete using a combination of a conventional limited-pay plan with a term insurance rider. Each year the declared dividends purchased paid-up additions, thereby, gradually replacing the term insurance. Initially this worked reasonably well. However, as interest rates skyrocketed in the 1980s interest sensitive policies could react quickly to take full advantage of the situation.

This proactive approach gave them a competitive advantage. Dividend declarations by their very nature are reactive. Companies declaring dividends do so after the profit rather than in anticipation of future earnings. Of course, companies do not guarantee dividends and they are indirectly dependent on interest rates.

However, some illustrations in the mid to late 1980s began to use dividend assumptions that allowed them to appear highly competitive. Some of these illustrations did not disclose the basic assumption, nor express the equivalent interest earnings required. In some instances my calculations indicated that an interest sensitive plan would require an assumption of at least 16% to match them. To some people, it may have seemed reasonable at the time; but in retrospect, we now know that it was exceedingly optimistic. Unfortunately some of these plans did not *pop*; that is, they did not become fully paid as projected. One should note, however, that these plans may be excellent if maintained for a few more years. The premium will *still disappear* but it will take a little longer because of lower interest earnings.

Nevertheless, like a pack of ravenous vultures, the attacking authors swooped down with sneak attacks when the wounds became evident. Even so, they cannot seem to get it correct. Without mercy these authors lash out at the industry on two fronts, making statements that: (1) the products were inadequate or inferior; and (2) the agents were greedy dishonest opportunists. *They* are wrong on both counts. What's new? In spite of what the reporters of doom and gloom may say, a significant number of policies have reached fully paid status and the premiums have vanished. Many more are on track to become paid-in-full.

One such author Norman Dacey points out, smugly, that the premium never really vanishes but rather "It continues to rumble on inside the policy." In his narrow minded way, he is correct. Mortality charges do continue to be levied against the earnings on the policy accumulations. So what? This piece of trivia matters not if, in fact, the policy remains fully paid-up. To accomplish this, a reasonable assumption of interest rates and cash accumulation is necessary. It follows that the higher the cash value accumulated the lower the required rate of interest and vice versa.

However, to accomplish their nefarious goals of discrediting the industry, the agents, and the products they offer, these authors focus on plans that failed to meet projections. *They* need these negative examples to justify *their* broad based assumptions that a term plan plus a separate investment is the wiser approach for everyone.

Unfortunately, these *after the fact* authors have the advantage of timing. When all was well, *they* were quiet. When the dam burst, *they* leapt on a surf board to ride the waves of negativity. On the other hand, *they* ignore or belittle the efforts of companies and agents to rectify and/or salvage the situation.

Quite correctly, *they* point out that some agents and some companies have been sued and some settlements have been made. Naturally, *they* ignore the many cases where thc lawsuits were not successful. The generalized attack on the integrity of agents overstates the situation and it is grossly unfair. This is not to say that no agent ever made a mistake or that no client was ever misled. The recent spate of lawsuits and adverse publicity (especially in the USA) about disappearing premiums, shows that things can go wrong.

There are many factors one must consider.

One: You always hear about lawsuits, claims and settlements, whereas you rarely hear about the ones that failed, or about those that were dismissed. Most agents learned about a huge claim in the USA against one of our Canadian companies operating stateside. A large number of Canadian agents assumed this company would lose and, thereby, they began to question the future solvency of the company. To the best of my knowledge, there was little or no information released when the company won. After a reasonable period of time, I contacted someone at the company and was advised, "Oh, haven't you heard; we won. Furthermore, it was never in doubt that we would win." That was not the view on the street. The grapevine for negative news is much more efficient and effective than any positive news release.

Two: After a few months or certainly after a few years, it is common for people to believe something about their policies that is not accurate. One client told me that a competitor's policy for one million dollars would *mature* for the full face amount (death benefit) at the end of ten years. When I questioned him as to what he meant by *mature*, he stated that the cash value would be $1,000,000. What the agent actually said, as proven by the illustration, was that the policy would be paid in full in the tenth year with an actually interest earned rate of 10%. Nowhere was there any indication that the cash value would equal the death benefit.

Three: Some clients may have known that the illustration used an assumed interest rate of 12% or more. At the time, these clients may have agreed that 12% seemed reasonable enough. When interest rates dropped some clients may have forgotten that this would cause it to take longer to achieve paid-up status. Some earlier computer printouts did not illustrate clearly how a lower applied interest rate would affect the policy. Currently all such interest sensitive illustrations must show the effects of at least one lower rate.

Four: In some instances where agents made serious mistakes with illustrations, the real culprit was the company that did not make a proper disclosure to the agent. Increasingly, agents were being held accountable for things over which they had no control. One example is the one given earlier of the illustration that would require a 16% interest rate, according to my calculations. The software for this printout was supplied by the company and the agents could not vary the assumptions. Agents using the supplied illustration software believed, perhaps naively, that the company could and would deliver.

Full disclosure must start with the company. In view of past and current events, agents should use only those illustrations that clearly disclose all variables. Similarly, clients should satisfy themselves that the illustration clearly indicates all pertinent information. When the policy is issued, the purchaser should be certain that the policy and the illustration are consistent. The policy is the legal agreement.

Finally, each prospective buyer should require several printouts based on:

(a) a reasonable, agreed upon, conservative interest assumption; and

(b) at least two illustrations with lower interest assumptions.

These plans do work!

The premiums do vanish,
in spite of negative reports to the contrary.

Check it out!

Myth: Retirement Bliss

When my grandfather was a youngster, he decided to be a farmer. He grew up on a farm. He knew farming. It was a lifestyle he liked. He would never retire. He never even thought about the concept. Perhaps in his seventies he would slow down a little. One of his sons could take over the heavy lifting—but retire? *To what?*

It seems that many people retire from something rather than to something and that's a mistake, especially for those who really enjoyed their work. Many retirees are not prepared to be idle. To be suddenly retired at age 60 or at age 65 is a shock to one's system. It's like diving from the high board into a wet sponge.

Young people today, in their twenties and thirties, are not much different from what we were forty years ago. They are more aware, however. When I started to work in the head office of an insurance company at age 20, the department head described the company pension plan glowingly. I did not even comprehend the concept. My first month on the job and he was talking about retiring? He must have noticed my blank expression because he cut the conversation short with a terse statement. It's mandatory! All it meant to me was less take home pay.

When I left head office to become a salesman, the branch manager's words found their mark. "One of the great things about selling is that no one can tell you when to retire. You can work in this business for the rest of your life if you want to do so." It sounded like farming to me—without the back breaking labor.

When I became a salesman most of my clients were young, that is, under age 30. We never talked about retirement except in terms of if you have to quit, perhaps because of ill health. Most clients agreed that it would be good to have enough saved so that they could quit if they really wanted to, or if they could not continue. At that time young people thought in terms of a long productive life. Very few people gave much thought to living beyond their usefulness. We were born into an *era of the work ethic*. Even so, quite early on, some subtle changes in thinking began to exert an influence on us.

After the second world war, Fords, Chryslers and General Motors, attracted the boys from the farms and small towns with high hourly wages, and a pension plan, if they stayed with it. Most of these young people looked at this pension scheme as merely a reduction in take home pay. They were skeptical about its value. After all, when they tired of the factory, they would return to the farm, or the family grocery or hardware store.

As more people left the safety and the security of rural life to settle near factories in urban settings some people began to recognize the need for more sophisticated planning, for life after retirement. Consequently, many people welcomed a mild form of social engineering, and in 1966 our government decided that this country needed an enforced pension plan above and beyond company programs. They also created a concept of registered retirement savings, which was especially appropriate for those who were not part of a company pension program. Nevertheless, at first, there was not much interest among the majority of the people. One reason for this, perhaps, was that there were very few qualified plans available for RRSPs.

Then we experienced inflation—rampant inflation—and ever increasing taxation. So-called progressive taxation, hidden taxation and sales taxes (including more recently, GST) made savings and investing more difficult except via RRSPs. Simultaneously, tax sheltered programs were falling into disfavor and, one after the other, they disappeared. Incomes were higher because of inflation and progressive taxation made more people top-bracket tax payers. Registered retirement savings plans (RRSPs) emerged as the best way to postpone taxes, the preferred way to avoid taxes for the moment. Registration was doubly rewarding if you used it right. For one thing, you could save on taxes at your top marginal level. Secondly, you could reinvest this savings creating, in effect, an interest free loan from the government.

Trust companies, banks, and mutual fund companies discovered a ready market. Life insurance companies lost their lead position.

The other financial pillars, their competitors, took over and stole the show. Life insurance companies suddenly had a lot of catching up to do.

Since the banks got into the act, there has been a constant advertising campaign with posters in nearly every bank. As everyone knows, this barrage of advertising heats up during the first two months of each year. Direct mail, newspapers, TV, and salespeople extol the virtues of an early start on retirement. The result of this pressure causes a buying spree at the beginning of the year, which does for the financial industry what Christmas buying does for the merchants and manufacturers. With the melding of these various factors, we seem to have developed a sort of obsession about retirement that was not nearly so prevalent just a few years ago.

Another modern day development is mandatory retirement at age 65. Other innovative approaches are early retirement packages—some of them so generous no one can ignore them. More and more people have *retired* at younger and younger ages using one of these packages. It's also significant that people are living longer. Life expectancy now means that many people will live nearly one-third of their lives in retirement. Some people suggest that this is one of the problems with a pay-as-you-go Canada Pension Plan. The government never foresaw the problem of so many people living so long, thereby, causing a significant shift in demographics. An ever increasing number of people over age 65 is beginning to put a strain on the decreasing percentage of people in the work force.

So how can I refer to it as the *myth of retirement*? Everyone, it seems, is talking about it and more than ever before, people are planning for it. It is no myth; it is real. Or is it?

It is a myth to think that everyone *wants* to retire and lead the leisure life. Some people may travel extensively for a while, but some also grow tired of this lifestyle. No doubt we all know people who really enjoy not working and many who throw themselves and their great energy into volunteer programs. Some of my acquaintances tell me they do not know how they ever had time to work.

However, many others have gone back to work on a contract

basis with the same company from which they retired. Still others have started their own businesses from which they have no intention of retiring. They do not want to just sit and look out the window. Warren Buffett, one of the richest people in America, when asked about his retirement plans, summed it up this way. "Retirement plans? About five to ten years after I die." Mr. Buffett plans to live a long time. He states, "We take as our hero Methuselah." Buffett claims that he had to scrap his mandatory retirement at age 100 policy, so Mrs. Rose Blumkin could continue to manage the Nebraska Furniture Mart. She was 94 years old at that time. According to Janet Lowe, author of *Warren Buffett Speaks*, Mr. Buffett commented, "My God, I can't afford the luxury of letting them go just because they've added a year to their age."

It is a myth that older people are no longer as capable as they once were. Many people with high qualifications have acquired valuable skills from years of experience. They want to continue using these skills. For some people, retirement means the loss of a lifestyle they came to enjoy. Several factors make the idea of leaving the work place less than palatable. Some of them are as follows; making important decisions; being part of the team; socializing and meeting new people; enjoying the status of, and the authority of, the position they have attained. Warren Buffett says that, "When I go to my office every morning, I feel like I'm going to the Sistine Chapel to paint."

Many people are not ready emotionally to make the transition from a career of forty or more years to a new and radically different life style. They may not have addressed their personal concerns about how they will spend so much leisure time. They may have doubts about being able to afford an active retirement over the next twenty or thirty years. How much money is enough? For most people it is just a little more than they now have. For some people there is a period of disillusionment after retirement. They may feel isolated and not needed. They may lose the sense of belonging. Just because people reach age 55, 60, or 65, does not mean they no longer need to feel worthwhile and useful. Most, if not all, still want to share their knowledge, skills, and experience. They want the excitement of making decisions. They want to continue to learn and to grow. They need the mental and physical stimulation that their careers provided.

It is a myth to think that the ability to learn new things after age 65 declines rapidly. According to Janet Lowe, Buffett claims, "We find it hard to teach a *new dog old tricks*. But we haven't had lots of problems with people who hit the ball out of the park year after year. Even though they're rich, they love what they do. And nothing ever happens to our managers. We offer them immortality." Older people retain the ability to learn new things and acquire new skills for as long as they remain mentally and physically active. For some people, the myth of retirement bliss caused them to focus on escaping from a job they never enjoyed and perhapsfrom co-workers they did not like. The unfortunate thing was working only for the time when they could make their getaway. Hopefully, when they got there, the rewards justified the years of drudgery.

Myth or reality? It matters little. Thinking so much about retirement has become a modern day phenomenon. It seems that everyone is talking about it. Many are saving thoughtfully for the great day. Some are even planning for the emotional aspects of a life after work, but many are not. Many of the people I know have not given much thought to the vital questions such as:

- When should we retire?
- Where will we live?
- What will we do to stay active?
- Will we need new friends?
- How will we react to a new lifestyle?
- How much money will we need to maintain our standard of living?
- How will inflation affect us?
- What are the sources of income on which we can count?
- What investment strategies should we follow?
- How will taxes affect us?

Chains of habit are too light to be felt
until they are too heavy to be broken.

~~ Warren Buffett

Myth: Social Security

The Government will take care of us~ from the cradle to the grave.

There once was a popular misconception that the government collected our premiums for the Social Security program and placed them in a special fund or a retirement trust. The political promise appeared to be that of a sound underpinning for a firm foundation to a financially secure retirement.

The first miscalculation that we made was due to a lack of understanding of a second level of inflation. The first level we recognize as a fact of life. That is, the cost of goods and materials keeps rising—even though the real value does not change. The cost of eggs, milk, butter, honey, wheat, vegetables, and so on has steadily risen but the products themselves have not changed significantly, at least not for the better. Everyone knows that produce in the stores cannot begin to equal the quality of fresh fruits and vegetables harvested fully ripened on the vine. It's sad, but a whole generation of people has grown to adulthood and, except those who have been growing backyard vegetable gardens, they do not know the difference. It is also true that the basic cost of produce, at the farm, has not increased significantly. Nevertheless, the cost of delivery to the consumers' table has mushroomed. (Check out the cost of mushrooms.) One definition of inflation, therefore, is that the cost of buying a product has increased while the intrinsic value of that item has not improved.

Okay. Let's review another example that does not involve taste buds. What else should we consider? The automobile, of course! Forty years ago, I bought an automobile for $2,200.10. Why was it not an even $2,200.00? I don't know! That ten cents was a special tax, added by the government for road improvement or something. But that's a different story. A comparable automobile today would cost about $22,000. (How much of that is tax?)

What justifies this huge increase? Do the current models look better? No! Do they drive better? No! Are they safer? No! Well, maybe.

I don't know. Does a safety harness really save lives? Do air bags really improve your chances of survival in a head-on collision?

Well, that's not the point. How much would these value-added benefits have cost forty years ago? Would they have cost two hundred dollars more? Cars today are not really safer. They used to make them with steel. Now cars rust just as quickly, maybe more so, and they break down just as frequently. They need oil changes at least as often, and gas mileage has improved marginally, if at all. What do you think about all the computerization in today's automobile? It certainly adds to the basic price and it costs a lot more for repairs. The automobile is another example of the first type of inflation.

There is, however, a second kind of inflation that no one understood when we conceived social security. Social security payments became equivalent to ground level zero! If you do not have social security income, that is, an income from the Canada Pension Plan and from the Old Age Security plan, you start in the basement. If you do receive these payments, you start at ground level.

There are at least two things that most people do not understand about the Canada Pension Plan. One is, the real purpose of the plan. We needed it to provide an infrastructure for the *Medicare program*. Prime Minister Lester B. Pearson announced on national TV that, "In order to have a national Medicare program, we had to create the Canada Pension Plan." Why was that? The answer was that a Canada Pension Plan would fund the horrendous cost of administering a *universal* Medicare program. Pearson's real goal, and possibly his only one, was Medicare.

At that time, the actuarial society approached the government with an outstanding solution for the Canada Pension Plan. Their presentation proved that the government could increase the already-in-place *Old Age Security* program with no increase in administration costs. There would be no need for an expanded civil service. There would be no increased costs of administration in any way. How much new administration expense would we need to add a zero to each cheque? How much would it have cost to add that zero to the Old Age Security payment? Some people claim that the increased expense would have been less than the cost of administration to manage the Canada Pension infrastructure. Why?

As stated already, the cause was the purpose of the Canada Pension Plan, which according to Prime Minister Pearson, was to fund the administration of the *Canadian Medicare program.*

When young people, today, are critical of the Canada Pension Plan, I get slightly annoyed. We read that the youth of today is furious with their elders for squandering the funds in the Canada Pension Plan. This new generation feels that they should not pay for this under-funded program. At the same time, these young people and their maturing parents admonish the federal and provincial governments against any reduction in the benefits of the *Medicare program.* Well young people of Canada, let us understand the facts. The Canada Pension Plan was not under-funded. Our governments misused the funds. The Pearson government bribed the provinces with the promise of very low interest rate loans. In other words, they bribed us with our own money.

If they had invested the premiums collected at modest rates, the Canada Pension Plan would be relatively financially sound. If the administrators had wisely invested the deposits from those of us who have paid since 1966, at a reasonable but safe level of interest, perhaps we could enjoy a larger pension during retirement. Regardless of this conjecture, everyone continues to overlook the fact that the Canada Pension Plan has funded the administration costs of our wondrous universal Medicare program.

What a conundrum! The same tax payers who believe they have a right to Canada Pension Plan payments each month also continue to demand an all encompassing universal Medicare program.

If you could stand back far enough to look at this historical event dispassionately, you would be able to see the dilemma of the ages as rather humorous. If you were closer to the action, you would understand that we, who paid the additional tax for the Canada Pension Plan, intend to collect it. We also expect the guaranteed promise of the best Medicare program to continue as presented by the Liberal government of Lester B. Pearson.

These comments are not made as a criticism of either the CPP or the Medicare program. It is not my intent to do a critical analysis of either one. My point is just this: The Canada Pension Plan raised everyone's expectations and consequently our standards. The Medicare program, similarly, has raised our expectations of a higher quality of life. These expectations have now become basic features to the Canadian value system. That which we would have considered the *lap of luxury* in 1966, we now perceive to be the absolute minimum. The myth of our social security system is that we are somehow better off, today, because of these programs. It's not necessarily better, however; it's merely different. Thirty years ago, and earlier, people saved for the future and there was health care. Health care provision has changed, albeit, but it existed nevertheless, before Medicare. Health care is not something new and not necessarily better. It's just different. Institutions have attempted to replace the *family* as the main source of health care provision, but, and there are many buts:

- The cost of this service is spiraling upwards.
- The quality of care is a constant source of dissatisfaction and consternation for close family members.
- The person requiring this care is rarely happy and seldom satisfied with this state of existence.

If you have experienced it with a loved one, you know what I am saying. If you have never experienced it, I suggest that you prepare yourself for it before it touches your life. There is no substitute for eyewitness experience. If you know of relatives or friends so institutionalized, try to visit with them two or more times. Then, to understand what everyone is going through, read Nancy Millar's book, *I Think I Should Know Those Trees~A true story of Life and Death; and Long Term Care.*

Nancy's book is an incredible tale of distressing situations involving her parents and their lives in institutions. Her story takes us from hospitals, to nursing homes, to health care units. The history of her father's suffering and dying of Alzheimer's is sad but educational. The story of her mother's suffering, while in full command of her mental faculties, but housed with other people who were losing theirs, is disconcerting. These stories are riveting for those of us who have faced similar difficulties with the health of our loved ones.

Alzheimer's disease, strokes, arthritic conditions, early onset senility, heart conditions, and so many other problems that beset our old folks, can create havoc in the orderly daily lives of the people touched by them. It is not my purpose in this space to describe what happens to the people suffering with any of these ailments. Nancy has done that in some detail.

However, if I had read her book before experiencing these things first hand, it would have prepared me better and given me more understanding of the situations with which we would have to deal. Nancy's frustrations and discouragement's were very similar to those faced by my family and by some close friends. One of my best friends was stricken with Alzheimer's. My father suffered a stroke, or more specifically, a series of strokes. My mother has wrestled courageously with crohns disease for many years. It is not their stories that I want to tell. Rather, I would like to add my voice to that of Nancy's in order to alert as many people as possible to the problems of those involved in institutional survival. One could hardly call it living. For many inmates it is merely an existence while waiting to die.

We, like Nancy, experienced both the good and the bad. We discovered the frustrations of dealing with institutional systems of administration that our governments have under funded. Of course, under funding causes under staffing. We learned that the staffs of these health care units really tried to care but their frustrations led to not caring enough. Perhaps these people really do care for their wards, however they cannot afford to become involved.

Qualified personnel costs money. In theory, there is always someone available with the proper qualifications. In practise, however, they are difficult to find. For the most part, the real *care-givers* are the menial task workers. They care, as much as they dare, but they do not know how to cope with illnesses that they do not understand. These people have assigned tasks and a schedule to follow. Any change in routine is an intolerable disruption to the process. Sooner or later, usually sooner, everyone involved with a loved one wants some answers. Questioning the care-giving staff is frustrating.

Perhaps they do not know the answers to our questions. Perhaps there is no reward for offering an opinion. Perhaps it is safer for them to say you must speak to the duty nurse.

You may discover that you need answers and you want them now. Catching up to someone in authority may be frustrating and time consuming. And then when your turn comes, the *authority* may have few if any answers. After a few pertinent questions, followed by some unsatisfactory answers, you may suffer from a common malady—institution frustration. Sometimes this frustration leads to impertinent questioning.

To say that you are being lied to may be somewhat harsh, but you do know that you are not getting at the truth. Always, when you become insistent enough, they refer you to another level of authority. If you experience this stepladder referral, you may discover that at each new level the people involved are more adept at not telling you the truth, while making it sound plausible.

What do we want for our loved ones who are suffering from debilitating ailments? Surely everyone would answer *quality of life*. Assuredly, we want our parents, our uncles and our aunts, good friends and close acquaintances to enjoy *living* rather than merely *existing*. We hope for them an avoidance of humiliation and deprivation. We do not want to see our loved ones drugged to a state of compliability or worse to some level of comotosity.

The myth is that these health care units are golden age homes for the loving care of the elderly. The suggestive names chosen for the units and the mottoes on the walls confirming states of happiness and bliss are belied by the facts.

Very few people care until they become involved with someone they care about. Fewer people yet are willing to take a stand—to demand quality programs. Alone we can accomplish very little. Together, we could make a difference. Let me ask those who have read this section to get involved, now, before you face the grim facts in some personal way. When your turn comes, and I hope it never does, it will be too late.

If you want to help *make a difference*, do it now.

Myth: The Dinosaur Annuity

To some advisors, and with too many of the people who are considering retirement, the word annuity compares favorably with the mighty dinosaur—now extinct.

Why?

The most obvious reason is that many advisors do not understand the basic concepts, and the uses of annuities. Many advisors do not have a life insurance license to sell them, and their companies do not have a product. Banks, trust companies and mutual fund companies have not earned the right to sell annuities. Consequently, they promote alternative concepts such as a retirement income fund (RIF) or a life income fund (LIF). We will review these concepts in more detail as we proceed.

At present, only Life Insurance companies can sell annuities, although some banks erroneously refer to their programs as annuities. Also, some trust companies have a product, term certain to age 90, that resembles a life company annuity. An actual annuity is a life insurance contract and, therefore, it requires the establishment of a reserve. Annuities have significant advantages; some of which will become evident in the following material. Guarantees, safety, and creditor protection, are some of the beneficial advantages. In spite of the hype to the contrary, annuity sales are booming, because some clients need and want the benefits provided by this vehicle.

What *is* an annuity? Simply put, it is a series of payments for either a fixed period of years or for a lifetime, whichever is longer. It can provide a guaranteed income for the annuitant that she cannot outlive. Some people compare an annuity to a mortgage. With a mortgage, an individual borrows a sum of money from a loaning institution and then repays the principal and the interest over a period of time. When an individual buys an annuity, he actually loans the money to an institution. We say that she buys an annuity. There are two ways to purchase an annuity. One is by depositing a lump sum, or a single deposit. This deposit purchases an annuity so that payments may begin immediately; or you may defer them to a future date. If payments start immediately, usually one month after deposit, we call it a single premium immediate annuity (SPIA). If payments are deferred, the annuity is a single premium deferred annuity (SPDA). With the second approach, you make a series of deposits over a period of time, to any of the savings plans offered by a life insurance company; registered or non-registered. These deposits accumulate with interest until the annuity date when payments to the *annuitant* begin. The annuity date is a date set by the purchaser, and she may change it as desired. There is one exception; for registered retirement savings' plans, payments must commence in the year the annuitant reaches age 69, or earlier.

One month after the annuity date, the insurance company begins making payments of principal and interest to the annuitant, and continues payments over the period of time selected. The payment period, and the amount of the annuity, depends on the type of annuity purchased, and it varies depending on the life expectancy of the annuitant. To continue with the analogy of a mortgage, some people use the concept of a reverse mortgage.

Life expectancy, as we know, has been improving. People are retiring earlier and living longer. This longevity makes the annuity a valuable planning tool for one's retirement years. A significantly large number of retirees are trying to live on the earnings from their investments, without encroaching on capital. Many people are afraid to touch any of their principal for fear of using it up before they die. In other words, they are afraid of living too long. Frequently, people die leaving significant sums of money to their heirs. At the same time they do not enjoy as much income as they would like to have, and could have had, if they felt comfortable spending some of the principal. The use of an annuity is a practical way to enjoy both the earnings and the principal without the fear of living too long.

There are a variety of ways to withdraw funds from an annuity:

- *Lump sum payout.* With a registered plan, the full amount withdrawn becomes income and the tax applies at the usual rate. In most situations this is not a viable consideration.

- *Fixed period or term certain annuity* This is a payment made to the annuitant or her estate for a specified number of years. This plan may also be available from some trust companies, but without the advantages of creditor-proofing and the avoidance of probate.
- *A life income* or single life annuity with no years certain would be payable only as long as the annuitant lives. However, an annuitant may specify a minimum payment period, such as 5, 10, or 20 years. If a life insurance policy exists, in order to renew the funds in case of premature death, a no years certain plan may be a better choice. This way the monthly payment would be somewhat higher.
- *A joint and last survivor plans* are payable as long as either the annuitant or a spouse remains alive. In most plans of this type no further payments occur after the second death.

For all annuities there are a variety of options available such as:

- A guaranteed term
- Indexing for inflation
- Reduction of payment amounts on death of a spouse
- Reduction of payment amounts when old age pension begins and so on

When interest rates are low, RRIFs or LIFs appear to be a better choice. However, if you buy your plan from a life insurance company, you have the added advantage of moving the remaining amount to an annuity, at any time, with no charge or fee.

A RRIF or registered retirement income fund is attractive to many people because they can invest in equities. However, this requires some degree of active management of the investment options. The potential for a loss exists. The real advantage of a RRIF is its flexibility. The recipient may vary the amounts withdrawn. He may take the minimum withdrawal required by the government, or he may withdraw as much as is needed, up to the entire amount in the fund. The benefit of this is that one can take larger amounts in the earlier years and lower payments later in life. This approach effectively encroaches on capital and, therefore, it may result in the annuitant outliving her funds.

An LRIF, or a life registered income fund, is basically the same as a RRIF, except that we use it with locked-in pension plans, as an alternative to an annuity. An LRIF, however, has a minimum required withdrawal and a maximum amount that an annuitant may withdraw until age 80. Some funds governed by federal pension regulations may not be eligible for an LRIF, in which case the recipient would buy an annuity.

It is not uncommon for people to tell me that they do not like annuities because all of the capital disappears at death, following the guarantee period. That would mean that there is nothing left for the heirs. This is one result of *self-insuring*. Also, it is strange that younger people who claimed that they did not want anything left for their families look for methods of estate preservation as they near retirement. That is the function of a life insurance program and using annuities or RRIFs to accomplish that end is not very effective. It defeats the purpose of having retirement funds. If a proper life insurance program exists, or can be purchased, the annuitant is free to maximize her pension payment. With sufficient life insurance, there is no concern about providing for a spouse or other loved ones at death. Using RRIFs, LRIFs or MIFFs {Miffs?? Misinformation from fops}, for this purpose is inefficient. That's the business of life insurance.

Before we developed RRIFs and LRIFs, one of the most popular plans in use was a joint and survivor annuity. Advisors sometimes referred to it as a good alternative to a life insurance policy. However, the cost to the annuitants was often greater than the premium on a life policy. For example: The difference in payout between a no years certain annuity and a joint and survivor annuity could be higher than the cost of life insurance even at older ages. Keeping and using a paid-up life policy solves the problem neatly.

According to James E. Rogers, CFP, CLU. CH.F.C., a specialist in retirement planning, there are some important advantages for consideration of an annuity:

- A life annuity is the only investment where the annuitant can spend the principal and still be absolutely certain that she or he will not outlive it.
- An annuity is a worry free investment. The average rate of return within an annuity may be known in advance—unlike a typical stock market type of investment.
- An annuity is a *peace of mind* kind of investment; the very sort of investment desired by most retired people.
- There is no absolute best investment for anybody. An annuity is no exception. However, if it is a generally accepted sound investment principle, that one should never invest beyond ones sleep point, or never invest to the point one's stomach starts to churn, then an annuity will appeal to the conservative investor.

Several *authors* like to compare an annuity to a Registered Retirement Income Fund (RRIF). Rarely, if ever, do they make a fair and reasonable comparison. One such author, Graydon Watters, wrote; "I start the comparison for the RRIF at age 66 when it provides a minimum payment of $4,649." He compares this to an annuity payment, which according to the author, pays $9,600 per annum. He proceeds. "At age 70, the RRIF provides $7,281, per annum. By age 75, it pays $14,021. In fact, it overtakes the fixed-term annuity in the 71st year. By age 80, you receive $18,097 in the RRIF; by age 85 you receive $23,339; by age 90 your payment is $30,086 and by age 95 your payout is $32,781." Why would anyone ever follow this advice?

This is a totally unfair and unreasonable comparison for several reasons and it resembles a calculation done by Dr. Riley Moynes several years ago. First of all there should never be such a comparison made in *any way*. These are two separate kinds of plans with entirely different purposes. Annuities and RRIFs are not mutually exclusive. They are on the same team. Second, why would you start an annuity at age 66, for $9,600, if you only need or want $4,649 per annum, as illustrated for the RRIF in the above example? Any comparison, if one must be done, should be made on the basis of equal payments from both plans. Keeping an extra $5,000 per annum invested in a tax sheltered plan is going to result in a larger accumulation, naturally. *That's a no brainer.*

Third, you do not need to start either plan until after age 69. If you do not need $9,600 but you do need some money, you could simply withdraw an amount such as $4,649 from your RRSP at any time you want it. The author of this example should know that the older you are when you begin an annuity, the higher the payment. Similarly, the minimum required withdrawal from a RRIF would be higher as well. Consequently, the examples made by both Moynes and Watters, would not be nearly as dramatic, if they made them at age 69.

Fourth, this entire analysis begs the question. The real purpose of a RRIF is not to postpone income until you are age 85 or age 95, nor is it to save money for the benefit of your heirs. It *is* to provide a flexibility of withdrawals when you are younger. *Flexibility is the key word.* You may want larger amounts when you are younger, but not necessarily every year. Most people at age 65 are somewhat more active than the majority of people at age 85. Why would anyone want to take less income when they are young enough to really enjoy it? Why do you want more income at an age when you might not be able to tie your own shoe laces? Are you trying to preserve this part of your estate for your heirs? Are you trying to use the RRIF, as an insurance policy? Do you want to provide a larger sum at age 85, in order to offset the possible costs of becoming too feeble, or too ill to manage on your own? After both you and your spouse die, do you know that the balance in your RRIF will be taxed in your estate, before it passes to your heirs? The question is, should you spend it and enjoy it, or give half of the remainder to the government?

As you know, an annuity has a different purpose. It should be the cornerstone of most retirement plans, because it is the only vehicle in the financial world that guarantees periodic payments to annuitants for as long as they live. A comparison of payment amounts between RRIFs, LRIFs and annuities is pointless, but if an author must do one, he should attempt it on an apples to apples basis.

In many situations it may be prudent to have both, that is, a RRIF to provide flexibility funding and an annuity to establish a foundation that you cannot outlive. Another approach may be to start with a RRIF that you can change to an annuity, at an older age. Of course, you can do this free of charge only with a life insurance product. Consequently, some authors will not advise you of this alternative, because they do not sell or promote the product, directly or indirectly. Another reason may be that they do not understand it.

As I have stated elsewhere in this book, annuities are not new, and when the banks get the right to sell them, they will present them as the greatest innovation of the century.

There are many other uses of an annuity, some of which I will attempt to describe at this time. I have had some experience with them. Not all annuities arise from registered funds such as RRSPs or Group Pension plans. In practise, there are many uses of annuities for non-registered funds. There are basically two kinds of non-registered annuities: (a) a prescribed annuity, and (b) a non-prescribed annuity. The differences mainly involve taxation, although a non-prescribed annuity is generally more flexible as you may purchase it on either an immediate or a deferred payment basis.

Other advantages of a non-prescribed annuity, compared to a prescribed annuity are:

- It may be commuted to a lump sum payment
- It may be assigned as collateral for a loan
- Payments may be indexed
- Ownership may be by an individual or by a corporation; whereas, only an individual may own a prescribed annuity

Regarding taxation: On a *non-prescribed annuity* your taxes occur on what we refer to as an accrual basis. That means that the tax department treats payments for tax purposes, in the early years mainly as income from interest. Later after the annuity has made a significant number of payments, the installments qualify proportionately more as non-taxable capital.

Conversely, your tax on a *prescribed annuity* remains for the duration of the contract, on a basis of a level blend of taxable interest income and non-taxable capital. There are situations in which this tax treatment is clearly beneficial.

One use of a *non-prescribed annuity* in recent years, has been the settlement of claims for damages for *personal injury* and even for death. Instead of a lump sum payment, the insurance company may provide an annuity contract designed to make periodic payments for a specified period or for the life of the claimant. This annuity may be, and usually is, designed specifically to meet the claimant's special requirements. Its use, in this type of situation, allows the claimant to receive a larger total tax-free payment while at the same time permitting the casualty company to pay out a lower lump sum. It is a win/win situation.

Another use of a non-prescribed annuity is for *alimony* settlements. The recipient of alimony payments may want a guarantee, that he or she will receive them, even if the payor dies or becomes insolvent.

There are advantages to the payor also, such as:

- Payments are tax deductible if the plan is properly structured
- If the payee predeceases the payor, payments may revert to the payor for the remainder of the guarantee period
- There may be a tax deduction of interest on a loan taken to purchase the non-prescribed annuity

Still other advantages may accrue to the benefit of the payee, such as:

- Payments may be indexed
- Payments may be commuted to a lump sum payment

Alternatively, you could use *a prescribed annuity* which, while it forfeits the flexibility described above, could provide an offsetting tax benefit, as taxes would be payable only on the interest income portion of the payment.

From the payor's viewpoint, the lump sum required to make this settlement via an annuity could be significantly lower.

Charitable Gifting

A strategic use of annuities for charitable gifting is finding some favor, currently, with people who have significant non-registered funds. The income from this asset is fully taxable. If the owner makes a donation to the charity at death, her estate will receive a tax credit. However, there is a better solution. The would-be donor can transfer these funds to the charity, in trust, on an irrevocable basis. The trust purchases *an interest income annuity* that provides an income for the donor, until death. The donor receives a tax receipt immediately for the principal amount destined for donation at her death. She may use this credit in the year of its receipt or spread it over future years. The tax department considers income from this source to be a return of capital, and therefore, not subject to tax.

There is still another approach in which the charitable organization makes the annuity payments directly. As I have no experience with one, I am not going to attempt to outline the advantages or the disadvantages. If it appears to be an appropriate approach, it would be wise to consult a tax accountant.

There are many other creative uses of annuities. A favorite of mine is one that we used to call a back-to-back annuity, now more appropriately referred to as pension maximization. This involves combining the maximum annuity payment until death, with a life insurance policy for the benefit of the survivor(s). For those who live past life expectancy the result would be most satisfying. Conversely, dying at a younger age does not create a financial loss to the survivors. This technique preserves the principal for the benefit of the heirs while permitting the annuitant to enjoy an income that he or she cannot outlive.

There are other ways to use an annuity, which, unfortunately I have not as yet experienced.

Some are:

• The financing and funding of lottery payments

Often they advertise these as optional payments of a monthly sum for life. Alternatively, you may elect a much lower lump sum.

Most of us have received such offers in the mail, but many people do not realize that the vehicle in use is the annuity.

• Salaries for athletes

We hear of the settlement of a huge amount such as ten million dollars. If the owner paid this amount in one lump sum, how much would the athlete retain after taxes?

• Additional compensation for corporate executives

In place of a raise, which the government would tax at the highest level, an employer may establish a deferred compensation arrangement.

As you can see, the imaginative use of an annuity can be of great benefit when it is used in estate and tax planning. To overlook its potential would be a serious loss.

Dinosaurs no longer roam the land,
but annuities are alive and vibrant.

Myth: Government Authorized Agencies

In 1963, Norman Dacey wrote a book entitled *What's Wrong with Your Life Insurance*. I do not have a copy of that book. Perhaps it's out of print, as it should be because, in 1989, this book reprinted under a new copyright in the author's own name. There is very little material in the new edition of any great importance. The author does not refer to this book as a revised edition or an updated version, so it is obviously a rehash of the original.

Agreed, this is nitpicking on my part, but with a purpose, as you shall see shortly. On the copyright page—the one just before the Contents page—writer Dacey gives grateful acknowledgment for permission to use material that purports to illustrate his points. All of this material is from the period 1956 to 1958—forty or more years ago. An amazing number of changes have occurred in every industry that has survived since that era. It was a time when a loaf of bread cost 20 cents. Elvis Presley sang *Heartbreak Hotel*, and *Don't Be Cruel*. Yul Brenner won an Oscar as Best Actor, for his role in *The King and I*. During the following years, the life insurance industry responded with alacrity, imagination, and leadership, but not so according to Mr. Dacey.

The 1989 edition does have a FOREWORD by Michael Pertschuk, a member of the Federal Trade Commission from 1977 to 1984, which gives this book an aura of greater authority, and borrowed respectability. The Federal Trade Commission is an agency of the United States government that speaks with authority, accurately or otherwise.

If we can believe that the words in this foreword are those of Mr. Pertschuk, there are some interesting anomalies. For instance consider this passage, "Twenty-six years ago the author of this book produced a work bearing the same title in which he catalogued the life insurance industry's improprieties of those days. In an era when costly endowment and retirement income policies were being sold in the face of long-term inflation which would rob them of their value, he pioneered the concept of 'buy term insurance and invest the difference.' The publicity given by the book to undesirable practices helped to force the grudging elimination of many of them."

Isn't that a mouthful? Taking these points in reverse, let's analyze them starting with the last sentence:

(a) *His efforts helped eliminate many undesirable practices*. If so, this recent version should delineate them as we proceed. It will not. If I were successful in correcting an error or an injustice, I would want to take full credit for it; specifically and precisely. (Dacey does not do so, even after this grandiose introduction.)

(b) Mr. Pertschuk claims Dacey pioneered the concept of *buy term and invest the difference;* twenty-six years ago in 1963. No kidding? That's very interesting. I joined the life insurance business May 13, 1955, eight years before Dacey's book, and that was the most common topic at that time. One company advocated the concept quite openly and it advertised, in a variety of ways, just how *low* their term rates were. Other companies were less obvious, as they quietly offered even lower rates. *The agents knew!*

So, did Mr. Dacey pioneer this concept? No! No! A.L. Williams took credit for that, twenty-five years later. Didn't you know A.L. Williams created that concept and popularized it? How dare you claim it Mr. Dacey?

(c) The statement that *costly endowment and retirement income policies were being sold in the face of long-term inflation thereby robbing them of value* is an interesting one for several reasons:

First, in this book the author confuses time periods magically and mysteriously. He states that companies sold endowments in the face of inflation. Actually, endowments were popular during the prior period; an era of relatively level inflation. The reason was that they paid a higher return than what the banks and other financial institutions would or could match. Second, they were guaranteed endowments. *Watch for the return attack of the guaranteed endowment, only this time the banks will spearhead it.* This revival will be introduced as an innovative development by the banking industry. Behold, *the guaranteed savings plan.* It is fully insured against premature death.

Your deposit, and the rate of interest paid on it can be guaranteed for up to twenty-five years. Sounds good to me! Inflation killed the popularity of endowments, rather than any of the arguments made by Dacey, Milton or McLeod. For mathematical proof of the nonsense statements against endowments refer to *No Salesman Will Call?*.

NB. With proof of purchase of this book, the author will send you a copy of No Salesman Will Call?; for $15.00 Canadian (GST and shipping included.)

Whenever I read the books of these three authors, or of several other even lesser scholars, I wonder if there is a secret school for writers of garbage and trash about the life insurance industry. Also, I wonder how these authors would like to have some of the passages in their books read on national TV, while they sit there on stage in full view. I insist on selecting the passages.

It has been said that there are very few writers of nonsense, perhaps only one, but he moves around a lot. Perhaps he ghost writes for the others who cannot think for themselves. Actually, this entire clique of writers searches through the ruins of the decrepit minds of similar minded authors for little scraps of information on which they can build a foul framework.

There does not appear to be a central source of putrid misinformation, but rather it seems that *they* share *their* dubious facts freely within the brotherhood. All of the authors previously critiqued, demonstrated a sufficient amount of originality to prove that they only copied the idiotic ideas of the others, before adding their own ingenious mathematical *proofs*. It was not too easy to disprove some of these marvelous examples. Given the precise set of assumptions, displayed by these devotees of the nefarious art of statistical mis-analysis, the conclusions appeared to be most plausible. The trick was to discover the trick, the deception, the sleight of hand, or the legerdemain. When you uncover the method of their chicanery, it is not that difficult to expose the misleading information. Doing so gave me great pleasure and it tempts me to continue here, in kind. However, I promised to avoid mathematical examples in this book, if possible.

There is one final thought on the invoking of the Federal Trade

Commission report in order to discredit the industry. This body was examining the insurance industry, broadly. It isolated *some* practices, of *some* companies, that according to their reasoning, should, either be changed, or modified, or stopped. This was supposedly an internal report to the industry for the benefit of all concerned, including the public. Of course, the report fell into the hands of people, such as the authors mentioned here, and many others who could use it to benefit personally. Naturally, those insiders privy to the report, who could gain by the negative aspects leaked some parts of it. Before I leave this preoccupation with a totally outdated Federal Trade Commission report, let me point out a few matters of importance that illustrate key points. First, the leaking of the report was similar to someone intercepting and publishing a letter from you to your brother in which you chastise him for messing around and ignoring his family.

Second, the report referenced specific practices and occurrences, but the critics generalized it. Third, even though this is an outdated report, and many of the problem areas alluded to have disappeared, the negative critics continue to use segments to suit their purposes. They do this on one side of the ledger, while claiming credit on the opposite page for bringing about changes to the benefit of the public. Frequently, authors take statements from the report out of context, magnify them for effect, and use them to draw conclusions that support their preconceived premises.

Finally, you may be sure, neither the report nor the authors claiming victories over the industry had any substantive impact on changes. The industry is sensitive to the needs and wants of the public, and it always has been so. The buyers of our products, cause the companies to change. We cause the products to change; we dictate what products will survive and which ones will disappear; we determine which companies will prosper and which ones will suffer, fail or change. We have the power to determine the fate of every aspect of the industry.

I have long suspected that some companies have commissioned certain authors to write this trash. Otherwise why would some authors expound with such outlandish misinterpretations of fact? To reason otherwise, is an agreement that these writers are seriously deprived of knowledge and rudimentary comprehension. The other possibility is that for whatever private, personal reasons, these authors developed a colossal hate for the life insurance industry. Frankly, I think it may be somewhat more crass than ignorance or emotion. It may be as simple as this. *These distributors of hate literature, bad news purveyors all, being smarter and more clever than we credit them, understand intuitively, that the public wants to hear and read bad things about the life insurance industry*. I suspect, that in the absence of a sponsor; they just knew that negativism sells. Positive, value laden concepts do not warrant much attention from the buying public, and to most people they sound like sales pitches. Be assured of this; the other authors are making a sales pitch. It is: *buy term and invest the difference*.

It amazes me even now that in our industry, individual companies or the various industry associations do not do more to counteract the ignorance of authors and journalists. Some writers continue to spew forth volumes of inaccurate or misleading information about the industry and its products. On the other handour leaders, whoever they are, continue to remain aloof while ignoring the antics of those who, to them, amount to little more than a few mosquitoes on an elephant's rump. So far as our people at the top concern themselves, it's the job of the advisors. The gigantic field force can deliver the message to the public. They can counteract this nonsense, one on one, face to face, person by person. The officials may be right, but perhaps *they* take too lightly the power of the word—the written word. It is especially disturbing when some companies attempt to ride the waves of popular opinion. It is equally alarming when they get the support of significant numbers of advisors who find it easier to ride the tide than to determine, to know, and to do—what is right. Nothing is more disturbing to me than the discovery, after the death of a life insurance agent, that he has inadequately provided for his family. It is unfortunate when this happens to the family of any breadwinner. It is extremely disconcerting when it happens to the family of a life insurance agent, simply because he bought term insurance that did not survive his death. Buy term and invest the difference is hollow solace to a surviving spouse when *the difference is not enough*.

Before you say or think, at least, that I am *on the payroll* of some company or industry organization, let me assure you that I am not. I wish I were. I would like direct compensation from a company, as opposed to an indirect, irregular stipend from book sales. However, if it happens, *this I promise;* I will state categorically that I am being paid by a company or an organization to write as I do. Secondly, I promise I will not write anything that I do not believe fervently, as I do now.

It would be foolhardy to believe that I am so naive as to think that the industry is perfect, or that the life insurance companies in it are without blemish, and without closet skeletons. You do me wrong who believe that I am not aware of the ignorance, the arrogance, and the malfeasance, of some agents who ply our trade. As I have written elsewhere, the agents in our business are no better than ministers of the gospel, politicians, lawyers, doctors, accountants, teachers or presidents of oil companies. (If you like—you may substitute mining companies.) Furthermore, you could substitute farmers, if you insist, but since I came from an agrarian background, you might find me aggressively defensive of my rural kinship.

Of course, there are some practices in our industry, by some companies and by some advisors, that I find disconcerting and offensive. None, however, are practised by all companies, nor by all advisors, universally. Would it be right, therefore, to castigate the many because of the misdemeanors of the few. Nevertheless, that is what some authors, these writers of fiction, do in the guise of fact, and on the pretense of public enlightenment. They fail, for the most part, to be specific and name names, but rather they imply, by clever innuendo, that what they say is accurate and universal. With over 2300 companies operating in North America, and many thousands of agents, it is probable that you could find a company and an agent guilty of whatever misdemeanor you might choose.

If you know of a specific infraction, you should report it. In our industry there are organizations just waiting to pounce on the individuals or the companies who stray from the specified guidelines. Unfortunately, that may be the more serious offense against the public, that is, that these organizations exist to maintain the status quo or to vouchsafe the best interests of the insurance companies. But that's a different story, one not germane to my task in this book.

Back to Dacey. Who is he? I still do not know. When I read the rest of his book, I discovered that he is now living in England. I love it. An American living in England writing books, that is, one book revised, about our industry in North America; to make money so he can continue to live in England. Apparently, he was in the business as an agent for two years, 1931–1933. Thus, he qualifies as a statistic—a less than successful two year visitor to the web. Perhaps we can trace the seeds of his hatred to this period. When he did this revision, he must have been about eighty years old.

What else do we not know about this alienated author? Did he graduate from high school? After leaving the life insurance business, did he sell stocks like Milton? Who is this guy? (Actually, he admits later in his book that he was a mutual fund salesman.) If he had credentials, or qualifications to write and expound on these matters, why would he avoid displaying them? You know I would shout it right up front. Check it out—I did it. I write from knowledge and experience. I have earned the right to display my credentials.

Also while we are on the subject of me, be assured that I have no problem with term life insurance. As I have explained and in agreement with most other knowledgeable life insurance advisors, I do not adhere to the philosophy of buy term *and* invest the difference.

Let me finish this nonsense with two statements.

One: In my opinion most advocates of the concept, buy term and invest the difference, are not knowledgeable life insurance advisors. Mutual funds are okay in my books, but buying term insurance in order to make any investment is ridiculous. *Buy whatever life insurance is right for you, but never make that determination on any basis of term plus an investment.*

Two: When authors make outrageous claims about salespeople selling you the wrong life insurance for the wrong reasons, they insult your intelligence. For every agent who sells the wrong product or service, there are dozens of advisors waiting to point out the error and to correct it. A licensed advisor is accountable for his advice, and that is an important factor in any consideration. Unfortunately, authors of some books have no obligation to meet any performance standards. Perhaps licensed sales people who use this dubious material, as a third party reference, should be taken to task by *the authorities*. That might be a good recommendation if we could assume that these so called authorities *know enough to make an intelligent determination.*

Nearly all of the writers that I have critiqued have been most contemptuous of life insurance advisors, but Dacey and McLeod are the most vociferous. They take an example of one agent and project an illicit practice on a screen large enough to encompass all of the agents and advisors everywhere. One cherished example that these peripatetic *thinkers* love to quote, is that of the various studies done which rank life insurance people compared to other professions. Dacey, above all others, is exuberant in his elation that life agents rank below lawyers and used car salespeople on these surveys, for honesty, for integrity, for reliability and so on; as a group.

The real significance, however, is the fact that these authors report on only a small segment of the study. All of the surveys have indicated, that while we, as a group, must look up to see bottom, individually we rank at the top of the list with doctors and ministers.

Why don't these deep thinkers deliver the entire report—all of the facts? Why do they not interpret the surveys correctly and honestly, and report them fairly and accurately?

We, in the life insurance business accept it that surveys of our clients, friends, and neighbors, indicate that our profession is not held in the highest esteem. We are trying to do something about that.

Nevertheless, we can and we do take solace in the fact that all of these surveys show considerable respect for individual advisors. This public dichotomy of thought demonstrates a love hate relationship. Our clients, while expressing a general distaste for us, as a group, have a very high opinion of their own advisor. Why do these writers not report the facts on the complete survey? That's obvious! To do so does not serve their nefarious purpose of discrediting us. However, it illuminates something more sinister about their biases. These writers and the books they write cannot be trusted, in any way, on anything.

Dacey, similarly to several other authors relies too heavily on reports from government agencies. Some of them were not officially authorized. All of them were biased. The fact that an agency is a creation of the government does not make it more responsible. Reports such as those quoted by Dacey make broad band sweeping statements which may apply in only specific situations. Outdated reports are dangerous. They never go away, because some overzealous type continually refers back to them.

Giving too much credence to a report because an obscure government agency made a statement could mislead the reader seriously.

It's impossible to teach anything to someone
who already knows the answer.
~ Philipidese
Roman Empire—Greek Slave

Myth: What's Wrong With Your Life Insurance—part one

By this continuing review of Norman Dacey's book, I will be able to address most of the ridiculous arguments made by various authors, who write with a similar bent. Perhaps they base some of their thoughts on concepts written by Mr. Dacey. Also, a large number of agents use segments of his book to justify their own biases. Buyers of life insurance and related products should be aware of the fact and of the fiction. Everyone has a right to know the facts.

The author of this rather myopic book illustrates his lack of understanding of life insurance, immediately, when he makes the claim on page 2, that the early industry *invented* a new policy to save itself. Dacey says: "First, by requiring level premiums, the new policy eliminated the problem of those constantly increasing premiums that induced healthy policyholders to lapse their *annual renewable term policies* later in life."

Chronologically, Mr. Dacey is confused. The innovative insurance people did not start off with a concept of YRT (Yearly Renewable Term). They did increase the premium regularly to offset increasing costs, and provide for the increasing *probability* of death, as clients grew older. Each year the insured client received a surprise-me offer, which he or she could accept or reject.

Initially, there was no actuarial science nor any group of mathematicians making such calculations. The pioneer risk-takers were gamblers in a sense. Probably they had some understanding of the odds of winning or losing on the cast of the die, referred to as the law of probability. It is possible that those early adventurers had some mathematical skills, but they did not have the statistical evidence with which to create a mortality table. Understanding the laws of mathematical probability alone, did not provide a precise science on which to base a premium. We know for a certainty that insurance came first and that actuarial science evolved slowly over a period of time.

In spite of this, Mr. Dacey provides an example of annually

renewable term (YRT), on page 3. It illustrates the annual incremental premium increases to age 75, that we required as people grow older. Dacey claims that the concept of whole life grew out of that table of rates or one like it. Frankly, the table on page 3 illustrates a rather *recent* or current version of a series of premiums for YRT, from $2.13 per $1000 at age 30, increasing to $78.45 at age 75. [That means that at age 75 an annual premium for $100,000 would be $7,845.00.]

Dacey correctly points out that healthy people do not keep their policies very long. That leaves those who are not-so-healthy, and that is bad for the company. What the author ignores, however, is the fact that very few of those in poor health could afford to keep their coverage. He also fails to acknowledge how much money in total you would have paid between age 30 and age 75. The total deposit required for those 45 years would be $8,415.30 for a $10,000 policy or $84,153.00 for a $100,000 policy based on Dacey's illustrated rates.

My clients, on the other hand, could buy a $100,000 policy for $629.00, per annum, fully paid up at age 65. Their total premium would be $22,015, rather than $85,053.00. So much for the concept of *you can invest the difference*. However, that's not the end of it: If you still need insurance at age 75, Dacey's premium continues to increase, and there never will be a cash value nor a paid up benefit. On the other hand, if you discovered that you did not need life insurance, you could cash our policy for $66,300 at age sixty-five. If you did not take the cash, the cashable value of the policy would continue to increase every year even though you did not make additional deposits. Mr. Dacey may have a great imagination, but his respect for chronological order is in disarray. To intermingle or juxtapose modern day tables and concepts with the beginnings of insurance is irresponsible.

In the beginning, as all good stories start, most would-be life insurance people were aware that the average age of a natural death was about age 38. (In some parts of the world, the averages may have been even younger.) Those calculating premiums may have known how to calculate the probability of an accidental death, but even the best calculation in those early days, would constitute a wild guess by today's standards.

In the absence of an exact historical description of the initial attempts to calculate premiums, we can assume that establishing a premium, was a mathematical estimate, at best. Naturally, they guessed a little higher each year as their clients aged. Dacey claims that *whole life* grew out of the need to have a product that the clients would keep and for which they would continue to pay. He states that whole life was *created* for this purpose. NOT SO!

First, let me assure you that every company would be very happy selling YRT, just as we sell auto insurance policies. Later in his book, on page 136, Mr. Dacey says, would you buy an automobile or a fire insurance policy that charges a level guaranteed premium? My answer is: indeed I would. I do not like annually increasing premiums, at the apparent whim of the companies. Furthermore, if I do not have an accident, I would like to have my premiums returned. YRT, with its increasing premium is a very profitable product for the companies because relatively few people die when they are young, and they will not or cannot keep it when they grow old.

Evidently, the underwriters realized that their estimation of cost was too high and, consequently, the reserves grew too quickly. In other words, the profits were higher than an investor might reasonably expect. Competition forced the companies to look for products that were more palatable and more salable. They began offering longer term premiums—level guaranteed premiums for five, ten or twenty years. The premiums for these plans were higher initially than for YRT, but over a period of several years, the total premiums charged were lower. As a buyer of the product, you would be elated to know that your insurance premium would not increase. Furthermore, your death benefit would be paid even if you lived past your life expectancy. People were living longer; some lived past age 65.

In the early years, term to age 65 was the equivalent of *coverage for life*. Eventually, as people lived longer, the need for life insurance past age 65 became evident. Meanwhile, the companies began to offer two longer terms with level premiums. The second one had a slightly higher premium than those offered by competitors. When they did not require the extra amount deposited, they refunded it. Doing this made the net cost lower than that for competitors' plans. In time, this refund of extra premium became known as a *dividend*.

Dacey points out, correctly, that this *dividend* was akin to asking the buyer to share in the risks with the company. What Dacey ignores is that the *reward* for taking this risk provided a substantially lower net cost of insurance. Dacey, and the other invest the difference sycophants, are great at exposing negative features, while ignoring positive benefits. Buyers of our product one hundred and fifty years ago were neither ignorant nor naive. Life insurance was created for, and purchased by, business people. Why do writers, like Dacey, insist on making them appear helpless and hapless, when in fact, they were clever, astute investors. They did not spend money recklessly on a whim, rather than on *benefits*. Nevertheless, Dacey would have you believe that they were willing dupes.

Sometime in the distant past, some enterprising mathematically inclined employee discovered that they could make a further refund. Consider it a reward, if you will, for keeping the policy until maturity, or some specific date in the future. A significant number of factors combined to cause the evolution of modern day life insurance products, in order to meet the changing needs of the public.

Some of these factors were:

- Increasing longevity
- Better mortality records
- Precise calculations of the law of probability
- The use of compounding interest (it is not a new concept)

One thing you may be sure of, competition was the fuel that drove the companies to use these factors, in order to create products with new and better benefits. Nevertheless, the products created were reflections of a need. They were provided as an answer to a trend or perhaps sometimes, in anticipation of a trend. To assume, however, as Dacey is prone to do, that the sinister minds of the life insurance executives dream up iniquitous schemes, to create needs in the collective public mind, is preposterous. Mr. Dacey, you do them too much credit.

Most products, if not all, and nearly all usable ideas and concepts come from advisors trying to meet the requirements of their clients; not the reverse as Mr. Dacey would have it.

The concepts of coverage until death and of cash values if you did not die grew out of the public's need for it and from the companies' desire for a competitive edge. The endowment, which Mr. Dacey abhors, was merely an extension of the earlier refunds. It developed from the application of compound interest to the unused premiums. Compounding interest, when it was applied to the reserve for level annual premiums, led to the concept of a guaranteed cash value at a specific future date. Meanwhile, that specified amount, that is, the endowment or face value was available immediately at death.

No company employee dreamt up these concepts and products to *save the industry,* as Mr. Dacey claims emphatically. Both the concepts and the products evolved from financial mixtures brewing in the pot of the day. In those days, interest rates at the bank were lower than the rates being applied on the accruing cash values of a life policy. When Mr. Dacey entered the life business in 1931, and lasted until 1933, he should have noticed that the return on an endowment was higher than that available from a bank; *and it was guaranteed.* In fact, that was still true in 1955, when I joined the business, and for several years thereafter. Mr. Dacey forgets that mutual funds did not enjoy center court before the 1970s.

Dacey and the others like to point out imagined frailties or misdemeanors while often overlooking real ones. For example: In the early days, most, if not all policies paid cash values only at maturity. If you did not keep your plan to *maturity*, you forfeited the benefit. In the United States it is a statutory requirement that all policies contain standard non-forfeiture provisions. In Canadian common-law provinces, no such statutory requirement exists, but permanent life policies normally contain equivalent provisions. Now *that*, Mr. Dacey, was a significant event. But it obviously was not worthy of his prodigious mental acumen. Actually, Mr. Dacey does cast aspersions on the companies in this regard between pages 300 and 309. On page 301, he claims that *the non-forfeiture option involves the termination of a policy along with the protection afforded by it. This is called surrender.*

What utter nonsense! Just the opposite is correct. Non-forfeiture provisions provide for the continuation of the policy even if you do not continue paying premiums.

The three basic provisions are:

- Automatic premium loan
- Extended term coverage
- Reduced paid-up life insurance option

Mr. Dacey laments the life insurance companies' involvement in the banking industry. Excuse me, Mr. Dacey; it seems to me it is the other way around. But no, Dacey is adamant that cash value on a life insurance policy and all of the variations involving cash values constitutes a banking function. His insistence that having a cash value inside the policy is the same as a saving account at the bank allows him to disparage the policy for not having a first year return. He states; *few life policies have any refundable value in the first year or so*. Unfortunately Mr. Dacey never understood the real purpose of cash values in a life policy.

Dacey et al., claim that cash value plans are made up of two elements: (a) the cost of *pure* term insurance, and (b) a savings feature. Usually they suggest that the so called saving's feature receives a very poor rate of interest. The most common rate quoted is 3%. There is a modicum of truth in this, in that older plans guaranteed 2½% to 3% interest. Some interest sensitive plans have a minimum guarantee of 4%. However, these plans are usually tied, with a formula, to one or more outside indices, such as the TSE300, or the S&P500, which determines the actual and minimum interest to be applied.

Most of these authors claim that a declared dividend is merely a return of an overcharged premium. Significantly, however, they neglect to explain how annually declared dividends, on older policies, can exceed the total premium payable each year.

Regarding their insistence that a cash value is nothing but forced savings, it is obvious that these authors do not understand its actual purpose. Saving for investment is not the purpose of the cash value, unless one refers to an extra voluntary deposit, paid in addition to the basic or minimum required premium. They also overlook, conveniently, that this extra premium causes the policy to become paid up in fewer years.

The facts are that the premium on a permanent plan is made up of two basic elements:

(a) the cost of insurance—an increasing expense as proven by all renewable plans, and

(b) a reserve—an additional amount which allows:

- Premiums to remain level
- Death benefits or face values to be paid at age 100
- Policies to become paid in full sometime prior to age 100

The cash value is a VALUE ADDED BENEFIT which:

- Helps to avoid accidental lapses
- Provides for a reduced paid up policy
- Allows for extended term coverage
- Provides a cash return which may be equal to or greater than all of deposits.

There is another way of looking at the cash value, according to Peter Maddocks of CAIFA. It represents the amount a company is willing to pay in order to get off the risk.

Let's think about the following.

Guaranteed vs. Dacey Double Talk

For those, like Dacey, who advocate that you have a decreasing need for life insurance and that you will not need it when you are older, ask them for a guarantee. Ask them if they will guarantee to provide you with the required death benefit, at their own expense, if their advice is wrong. Those of us who advocate life insurance until death do guarantee the return of your deposits, with interest, if you decide you do not need coverage later in life.

Keep this in mind:

- If *they* are wrong—you pay!
- If *we* are wrong—we pay! (How? We refund your deposits.)

The modern concept of whole life never took shape until later in the 1800s. In 1955, when I started, most people geared their policies to age 65. They recognized the need for life insurance until at least age 65. They often felt that, thereafter, the need would be reduced somewhat. A very common attitude among my clients was that if they did not need coverage any longer, they wanted a return in cash.

At age 30, the cost of a term to age 65 policy for $10,000 was $78.20 annually. The cost for whole life payable to age 65 was $157.50. Thus, for an extra $79.30 for 35 years you could have a fully paid up $10,000 policy. Furthermore, for the total extra premium of $2,775.50, your cash value would be $6,630—*guaranteed.* At the same time, you could have purchased a $10,000 pay for life policy for only $95.10, annually, or just $16.90 more than a level term plan to age 65 at $78.20. This whole life plan would have provided $4,020 in cash or a fully paid life policy of $7,970, at age 65.

Dacey and his ilk are quick to point out that the events that occurred in the past forty years made those early policies totally inadequate. Inflation, high interest rates, and an increasing need for life insurance, made those original $10,000 policies totally insignificant and inappropriate. One should remember that forty years ago most people were not apt to buy $100,000 policies.

While I agree with Dacey that those policies gradually became inadequate, we should keep in mind that *inflation never happened all at once.* Furthermore, the insurance companies never caused inflation nor rapidly increasing taxation. Mr. Dacey's solution of investing the difference in premium in mutual funds, would not have made up the difference.

Should insurance companies have anticipated this continuous growth caused by inflation? Maybe, but generally as I have already shown, insurance companies react to the changing needs of clients rather than anticipate them. Also, for a number of years we solved this problem by selling additional policies; and the average size grew as our clients' incomes increased. This worked very well until about 1986. (The significance of this date will become apparent in the next section.) To meet the increasing need for higher amounts of death benefit, we sold and the public bought term insurance as additions to their basic policies. It was considered temporary coverage for what appeared to be a short term need.

During this period, many people began to realize that they were successfully creating a significant estate that could cause a significant tax problem. This was true, especially as our governments found ingenious ways to tax estates, to death, at death. They also realized that death may not occur at or before age 65. Consequently, the need for proceeds at death remains until—when? Until death, obviously! The purpose of this estate insurance is to provide liquidity for taxes and for other costs of dying. We call it estate preservation.

What is Dacey's solution? He advocates; save enough outside your life insurance to provide for these needs from your own investments. To follow this advice successfully would be to become self-insured. Behold, *we have come full circle.* Our predecessors created insurance to avoid the necessity of self-insurance. Ironic isn't it? The Dacey's of our world advocate a declining need for life insurance on the one hand, but they admit, on the other, that you may need to use your savings to *self-insure*. However, the more successful you are with your self-insurance fund, the more taxes you will have to pay. To quote a line from one of my own books: "A savings program is a poor excuse for a properly drawn life insurance contract."

In this section, Norman Dacey resorted to archaic reports to prove a premise, but he failed in all respects, other than to prove that he is terribly biased. Being an agency of the government does not guarantee any degree of accuracy. Quoting them with reckless abandon is irresponsible.

> By the way, do you know what the real problem is with investing the difference?

The difference is not enough.

Myth: ***What's Wrong With Your Life Insurance*****—part two**

A crayfish propels itself backward through the silt and muck to see what it can stir up at the creek bottom. Whenever this small crustacean reaches a section where it fails to find anything of interest, it simply changes directions. Characteristically, it reverses its path to go over the same area just examined. Sometimes it continues this process ad nauseam until it exhausts any further potential of gathering a tidbit.

Norman Dacey, in his book, portrays the tendencies of a crayfish thrashing around until he stirs up something that appears to have some usable value. Then he hangs on with the tenacity of a bulldog. You may be curious, thus, as to why I write so much about an author of such little consequence, one for whose writing I have such an abhorrence. Fair enough!

In my opinion, Norman Dacey is a fairly good writer, in that his material is very readable. He has done some research. His concepts and conclusions are quotable. He poses as an expert. He claims that the life insurance industry cringes, when someone as knowledgeable as *he* exposes any of its weaknesses.

He is right, but we do not cringe nearly as much as we should. Concerned we are, but not enough apparently, to do anything about these writers who have such a prodigious lack of knowledge. Dacey and his fellow alumni prove that about themselves by what they write. They are graduates of the classical school of ignorance. It is that terrible dearth of knowledge that concerns me most. Dacey actually brags about it. Who needs the greater skill, the worker with a crowbar who tears down an old dilapidated barn or the carpenter who, with hammer and saw, builds a home from a pile of lumber and some bags of cement? That's a no brainer—right? It is *always* easier to rip something asunder than it is to create it from the foundation with bricks and mortar. So what, you may persist? Surely my previous book made this point in its fashion. Again, I agree! However, Dacey's is the embodiment of the material from all the other writers. Dacey's commentary provides a frame work for all of the truly ignorant arguments made in all the other books of negativism. Dacey has captured the essence of all of the stupidity railed against the life insurance business.

Some say, that's fine but nobody cares. Then I must ask—why do so many bookstores display this book on their shelves? It would not be there very long if it did not sell. If Dacey told the truth, his book has sold over 400,000 copies. If that is a factual number, it means that he has misled too many people. Why do our libraries house a book so filled with misinformation? It would go into the *bin* if no one read it. Space is limited. Unfortunately, Dacey's book is quotable. Those who need a third party reference; an appeal to authority; or the power of the written word, in order to persuade a trusting client to buy their products, can turn to this source of negative froth to shore up an otherwise crumbling argument.

Why do some clients, having read such a book, readily accept the conclusions drawn by the author even though he does not display his credentials? Their own advisor, in most cases, is demonstrably more knowledgeable. Before examining any more of Dacey's irritating examples and conclusions, it may be interesting to find out more about Mr. Dacey. However, modest fellow that he is, we can learn very little about him except through a process of deduction from the things he writes.

Later in his book, Dacey states that you should get impartial advice or preferably *unbiased* advice. He recommends getting your unbiased advice from an accountant, a lawyer, a banker, or, if necessary, someone on a fee for service basis. Well okay, but the first three are neither impartial nor unbiased, but far worse they are generally not knowledgeable about our products. Consequently, we can only classify their advice as biased opinion. A fee based consultant may be a good choice if he or she has the credentials (knowledge and experience). It fascinates me that someone as obviously biased as Dacey, *advises* you to find unbiased advice.

Dacey claims that it is against the law for a licensed agent to charge a fee. He is wrong! The only requirement is that we advise our clients in advance and let them know when the clock is running. Most clients do not require a fee based analysis of their situation. If they were willing to pay for it, it would cost more in some cases than its value to them. You do not need to look for unbiased advice. What you do need is up front knowledge of the *special bias* of an author, or of your advisor? Dacey admits, on page 370 of his book, that he was a mutual fund salesman, for fifty years, until he retired in 1980. If he admitted this at the beginning of his book, we could have understood some of the ridiculous conclusions made by him. However, he wanted us to believe that he was a knowledgeable life insurance agent for a significant period of time. If a writer can keep his biases hidden for 370 pages, he can paint a shady picture with subtle nuances.

Dacey makes a huge issue of the Armstrong investigation in 1905. He claims they uncovered a "fantastic host of evil practices." He continues that, "I shall not repeat them here. They are history—ancient history." Be that as it may, throughout his book, he harped back to that investigation of 1905. Similarly, he leapt on tidbits from the unauthorized investigation made by the Federal Trade Commission in 1979. He repeatedly took material out of context to prove his unverifiable points of view.

One of Dacey's *charms* is his ability to misinterpret figures unmercifully. He fairly gloats over some purportedly negative industry figures. For example: According to this charming wit, *in 1986 over $1.3 trillion of new life insurance was purchased, while $19 billion was paid out in death benefits, and $49 billion in cash surrender values.* Dacey claims that he took these figures from The 1987 Life Insurance Fact Book, published by the American Council of Life Insurance. The source of these figures is not of much importance, but it is most disconcerting to see what a mind such as Dacey's can do with this information.

Dacey's figures suggest, that in 1986 one out of every nine ordinary life policies in force, was lapsed or surrendered, for a total of $490 billion. His conclusion was that this happened because policyholders did not want, or they did not need the coverage any longer. In my opinion, his flying leap at a substantive conclusion amounted to little more than a guess. Anyway, it would account for approximately 1% of the total insurance in force.

This author's fascination with meaningless mathematics continues with the following amazing tidbits. It would be reasonable to ignore this analysis by Mr. Dacey, except that what he does with is it dangerously misleading. He takes simple statements or factual figures and turns them into a cleverly misleading analysis.

According to Dacey's accounts;

- The number of policies sold in 1986 was 16,811,000. The total number in force at the end of 1986 was 159,331,000
- The number of policies that went off the books in 1986 was 16,084,000
- The number of death claims was 1,358,200
- The number of matured endowments was 109,456

Therefore, adding the number of death claims to the number of matured endowments, that is 1,358,200 + 109,456 you get a total of 1,467,656. The policy shrinkage from this calculation is readily understood. Now by subtracting the total above, from the total policies canceled, 16,084,000, you get a net result of 14,616,344. The author then claimed that this net figure represented 87% of the total *new* sales made during 1986. Impressive right? Not so; it is insignificant. The mathematics may be accurate but the application of them is pointless. A comparison of this calculation of 14,616,344 surrenders, to the number of policies sold during the year—16,811,000, is of no significance whatsoever. It is irresponsible of Mr. Dacey to paint pictures of doom from it. A more useful bit of information might be that of the 159,331,000 policies in force during 1986, 14,616,344 were lapsed or surrendered for various reasons. In other words about 9% of the total number of policies in force went off the books—9% Mr. Dacey not 87%.

It is even more significant, according to Dacey's calculations, that people bought 910 billion, 944 million dollars of new death benefit, in 1986. During the same time frame, according to Dacey, an amount of $489 billion, 761 million was lapsed or surrendered. He claimed that represented 54% of the total *new* sales made during the year. So what? As a percentage of the total life insurance in force—3 trillion, 247 billion, 289 million, the net lapse figure as a percentage, is only 15%. Dacey concludes that huge numbers of clients found their plans to be *wrong* for them and, therefore, they canceled their policies. He makes a big deal of his figures, of 87% and 54%, which are not only misleading and insignificant, but they are outright dishonest misrepresentations. *Of course they do serve Dacey's purpose to discredit the industry.*

Dacey ignores some very important and significant factors that occurred in those years around 1986.

- Inflation was out of control.
- Interest rates were excessively high.
- Life companies had created a variety of new interest sensitive policies.
- The cash values in old style policies were at an all time high.
- Mutual funds emerged as the best answer to offset inflation.
- Life insurance companies developed their own mutual fund style investment programs, called segregated funds.
- Companies allowed their clients to exchange the old policies for a new type.

In so doing the company kept the cash value of the old plans and often they substantially increased the total death benefits; a fact to which Dacey's figures bear witness.

- Mutual fund salespeople found ready sums of money available from old policies.
- Many clients found it beneficial to move the cash values into high interest savings' accounts in banks or savings and loan companies.
- Real estate in some cities became very attractive investments as property values rocketed upwards.

Cash values from old policies provided down payments that were readily available.

- Finally, a proliferation of books advocating the concept, buy term and invest the difference, sprang into being.

It was a popular theme and authors of all types marched to the pipers tune. Dacey is right about one thing. It was a trying period for the life insurance companies.

Since that period, the companies have reacted quickly to meet the demands of a rapidly changing financial scene. Some companies made serious errors in judgment about the new products they offered. Furthermore, they were sometimes careless about the illustrations they generated.

In 1989, Dacey charged forth again with this revised edition to gloat over the errors of the industry. In his new version, he left in all of the idiocies of the first edition and added many more based on the proliferation of new industry products. That Dacey is chronologically incompetent and that his misuse of facts is of no concern to him, matters not—to him nor to his followers. It matters to me!

To argue that Dacey is not seriously lacking in knowledge would be a statement to the effect that the methods, assumptions and conclusions are those of a scoundrel. Whatever! His clever twisting of figures and his analogies based on illogical premises puts him in a class by himself. Like so many of the other authors, Dacey proves masterful at making trivial tidbits of insignificance grow into gigantic monstrosities. He does this even to the point of suggesting that the companies were the cause of poverty in North America—the richest continent on the globe.

Following are some Dacey dipsticks:

Page 83. “How many policies…were bought simply to get an obnoxiously aggressive salesman out the front door?” (That would not matter, because that client would decline the policy.)

Page 84 “…and it gets worse every year.” (No comment required.)

Page 85. “Are not these cold indisputable facts the refutation of all the industry’s pretentious to high purpose?” (To which cold *indisputable* facts does he refer? There were none in this book.)

Page 89. *Commissions*

Oh yes, every author on financial matters attacks the commission system. Similarly to the classic statement by Churchill on Democracy,

I have found the commission system to be the very worst system, except for all the rest. I covered this topic extensively in *No Salesman Will Call?,* so I will not repeat those arguments here. However, I will say this. If you must consider the commission system, you should do so in relation to alternative systems of compensation. Dacey would suggest that we should work for humanitarian wages—free. He, on the other hand, sold mutual funds on a *commission basis.*

Let's consider the following:

(a) *Fee based system:*

For the well to do, to the very wealthy, a fee based system makes sense. For most people, however, this kind of expenditure would not be justifiable. Very few advisors could afford to work on a fee for services only.

(b) *Salaried Agents:*

Who pays the salary? If a single company pays it, whose products do you think the salaried agent will sell?

(c) *No Salesperson will call:*

(Good one, old chap, that.) Where will you get your advice? Books? The internet? Seminars? It is quite possible to learn enough to do it yourself, if you want to study, and then keep studying to stay current. When you make a mistake, however, who are you going to blame? *If you need any advice, be sure that your source is accountable for his or her input.*

(d) *Direct writing companies:*

While these companies may not have a field force, they advertise extensively on TV. Have you ever priced the cost of one such ad? These companies could feed a large number of agents from their advertising budgets. But no salesperson will call, because they overprice and undervalue the product they offer. When all is written and published, the commission system is still the least expensive system, that works; or it would not exist.

Another of Norman Dacey's techniques is to attack such matters as, surpluses, reserves, and company solvency. What kind of responsible critic would rant and rave about the possible insolvency's of some companies in case of catastrophic reversals, and then ridicule them unmercifully, for maintaining reserves for unforeseen contingencies. Make up your mind Mr. Dacey—you cannot have it both ways.

He uses the terms surplus and reserve interchangeably. However, a surplus is what remains after the company establishes reserves for all future expenses, such as commissions, salaries, and policy obligations. The debate on the proper use of this remainder or surplus, is a subject which neither of us qualifies to consider. However, I do know the difference between a reserve and a surplus.

On page 121, Mr. Dacey makes another amazing observation:

These policies are on the books just long enough for agents to collect their big first-year commissions. The company shrugs off the loss, charging it to surplus. Now, Mr. Dacey knows this is a massive falsification of fact. His statement is irresponsible. There is no question in my mind that Dacey knows about commission chargebacks. He knows that in case of a lapse, during the first two or sometimes three years, there would be a reversal of commissions. During the first six months the companies charge back 100% of the remuneration paid. There is a declining scale thereafter.

For example: If a policy lapses in the twelfth month, 24/36ths or 2/3rds of the commission reverts to the company. Anyway, is it not inappropriate for a commissioned mutual fund salesperson to criticize the method of compensation of other salespeople?

Between pages 122 and 135, author Dacey makes several wild statements about mutual companies. A book, such as his, would be considered incomplete if it did not try to explain the differences between a stockholder's company, and a shareholder's company. It seems as though most financial authors, claim that a company without stockholders should be able to pay more to the clients. They lament that it does not. Why should this be so? According to the author, it is *because stock companies have to pay high amounts to shareholders.* What idiotic nonsense! Dacey knows very well, or he should know at least, that stockholders receive about 9/10 of 1% of the divisible surplus as a stock dividend on the participating policies. That does not provide a significant excess for any mutual company to waste.

Dacey attacked some products that were good in their time, like endowment policies, but they are no longer being sold. Other products also served a need or a purpose that is no longer apparent. Some products created by over zealous staff members were mistakes, and they disappeared for lack of sales. Many others, that Dacey described in detail, have changed so much since 1989, that his arguments are not even applicable. Even his method of ridicule cannot be used effectively today! Finally, since he revised it, nearly ten years ago, the new products available make his book totally outdated. *So why is it still on the bookstore shelves?*

There remain some generalized statements that we cannot leave unchallenged, such as the favored taxation of life insurance. Dacey claims, page 149; it's a *tax subsidy the cost of which...is incalculable. The cost of this tax subsidy on our economy may well be disastrous*. (In addition to the other expletives I have applied to Mr. Dacey—let me add, melodramatic.) This so called tax benefit *is a benefit to the buying public*, not the insurance companies. The fact that the public benefits from this tax sheltering, is not a question, and it should be of no concern to anyone. Nevertheless, several authors would like to have it *taken away* because it negates some of their arguments and makes it impossible for them to compete. Understand carefully; they are trying to destroy a valuable benefit for their own purposes. Instead of trying to wreck that which is good and valuable, in order to be competitive, why do these masters of negativity not create something of equal value, in their chosen areas of the financial world? Creative innovation is not the forte of a mad bull in a china shop, nor of writers of negative drama.

On pages 157 and 158, Dacey lauds the marauding efforts of a life insurance company referred to by him as MILICO. In this author's estimation, they are wonderful because they attack all cash value policies and replace them with term life. He claims that their results are remarkable. Actually he is right! Their success has been amazing, especially since most other companies offer the same term product, but on a less expensive basis.

If you really believed in the concept of buy term and invest the difference, wouldn't you, as a salesperson, want to provide your clients with the best, or at least, the lowest premium available?

The success of this company was not because of a reincarnation of a very old concept. It was because of the method used for distribution,that is multi-level marketing, with multi-levels of compensation. I am an advocate of multi-level marketing, but not when the compensation system causes them to overprice the product. That is exactly why they cannot offer their plan, as inexpensively as other agents can sell a similar program. *Mr. Dacey, please tell the whole story, not just the part that works for you.*

One of the most preposterous statements made by this author is: *Inflation has made life insurance almost worthless*. Actually, inflation, and the devaluation of our dollar, has made life insurance VITAL. A realization that inflation is a fact of life, even though hopefully it is under control, means that there is a need for increasing life insurance. In the past, we met the growing need for life insurance with additional sales; periodic increases in total coverage. This led to individuals owning several different policies. Upstart advocates of buy term and invest the cash values, thereby, found a fertile field; a gold mine resource, of readily available funds. Today we offer policies that tend to grow as required. Some, for example, can increase as dictated by the cost of living index.

There follows yet another amazing statement, from one who refers to himself as a financial advisor. It is; *I will begin by reminding you once more that there is no such thing as a permanent need for life insurance nor is there such a thing as permanent life insurance*. Would you deny, Mr. Dacey; that death is permanent?

One thing I must compliment the author of these words on is his consistent bulldog tenacity. He has made one statement throughout the book, without any explanation of the value of his fundamental belief. Dacey continually advocates, that by investing outside your life insurance policy you can acquire enough wealth to become *self-insured*. However, he makes no attempt to consider the many values of life insurance, other than if you die prematurely:

- He ignores the evidence that the total premium paid for term insurance, during the period of accumulation, would be greater than the total premium paid for a fully paid up policy.
- He ignores the fact that the difference in premium invested elsewhere will not accomplish the required amount to be self-insured.
- He ignores the information that many people need an immediate source of cash to pay taxes and other expenses, at the time of death.
- He ignores the fact that if you collapse a registered plan to pay taxes; it causes even more taxes.
- He ignores the possible use of life insurance to leverage an annuity.
- He ignores the fact that you may use some of the policy's internal values, or reserve values, to augment your retirement income.
- He ignores the evidence that cash values within a policy may provide many other living benefits.
- He ignores the tragic fact that most term policies, *by design*, will not be in force when you die. The tragedy is that you will have paid for a benefit you will never receive.

Perhaps, I am mistaken. Perhaps, Dacey and his horde of followers do not merely ignore these things. Perhaps, they really do not understand them.

****

Myth of Increasing Mortality Charges

That is not all. There is much more ignorance, or woefully willful misleading information in this book. On page 286 Dacey states that *companies selling universal life have a contractual right to significantly increase the mortality charge*. He goes on to say that *the potential effect on mortality of AIDS alone is enough—that mortality charges will have to be increased*. What Mr. Dacey avoids explaining is that most, if not all, of the policies issued have a maximum guaranteed rate in the policy, beyond which mortality charges cannot be increased. Meanwhile, the policyholder benefits from the lower current charges by 10% to 20%. Anyway, it would be a simple matter to find fully guaranteed policies. The total lower mortality charges give some policies a slight competitive edge—to the benefit of the policyholder. Mr. Dacey takes several statements of some officials out of context, to misrepresent the positions being taken regarding AIDS, and other possibly unknown causes for an increase in mortality. They are saying, quite correctly; that mortality costs in the future may have to be increased substantially. That is, for *new policies* sold in the future, the cost of the death benefit may be higher. Mr. Dacey is saying that companies can increase the cost of your policies without limit. In my experience that is not so. I have yet to review a policy that does not guarantee an upper maximum. The current saving on mortality costs is about 20%. If no such guarantee existed, then I would agree that you should change to a policy with the maximum clearly stated. It does warrant checking your policy. It does not deserve the scare tactics used by Mr. Dacey.

****

Myth of the Dastardly Dividend

No book berating life insurance would ever command respect without an attack on the so-called dividend. Dacey claims that the industry denies that there is an overcharge for the right to participate in the divisible surplus, or in a sharing of the profits. On the one hand, he unleashes his vitriolic criticism of companies keeping and misusing these profits. Then he denies the fact that companies do share these profits. All authors attacking this feature, which the industry chose to reference as a dividend, ignore the fact that it is optional. In other words, in most cases, the buyer could buy a policy with or without this dividend option. That is; a client could purchase a plan on a participating or on a non-participating basis.

Dacey claims that the extra charge, or the overcharge, is between 8% and 13%. We can examine this using a fairly common rate for a conventional whole life policy, paid in full at age 65 (guaranteed). The non-par rate for a male age 35 per $1000 is $16.08. An 8% increase would provide a rate per thousand of $17.36; and a 13% increase would create a rate of $18.98. Those amounts would hardly justify the vehement damnation made by these self-appointed critics.

Using the rates from an actual rate book, the extra or optional amount charged is closer to 33%. The non-par rate is $16.08. The optional par rate is $21.35.

The question would be; can we justify paying the extra premium of $5.27 per thousand? On a $100,000 policy, that extra charge of $527.00 projected an annual return as follows:

In the		
5th year	$ 408.00	You can see that some time after the fifth year
10th year	$ 750.00	but before the 10th year, the amount declared
20th year	$1,613.00	annually was greater than the extra premium
25th year	$2,678.00	charged.

The accumulation is projected @ 7.5%;
if left on deposit, it would amount to: Total extra premium paid was:

after	5 years	$ 1,400	after	5 years	$ 2,635.00
	10 years	$ 5,500		10 years	$ 5,270.00
	20 years	$27,900		20 years	$10,540.00
@ age 65		$87,300		to age 65	$15,810.00

and @ 10%

after 5 years	$ 1,500	Of course in recent years, the interest paid
10 years	$ 6,000	for amounts on deposit became taxable. No
20 years	$ 34,100	attempt will be made to consider the effects
@ age 65	$121,400	of taxes at this point.

There are several dividend options, one of which is; left on deposit to accumulate. This refers to the option of leaving the declared dividend on deposit to be increased using compound interest. An alternative option is the declared tax free dividend that a client could use to reduce the annual premium. Doing so would cause the need to pay premiums to disappear before the twenty-fifth year.

After the interest paid on proceeds from *the left on deposit option* became taxable, the popular choice became paid-up additions. Using the declared dividend to buy paid-up additions causes the policy death benefit to increase as follows; projected @ 7.5%:

after	5 years by	$ 6,200
	10 years by	$18,100
	20 years by	$53,400
	@ 65 by	$98,300

This means that an initial death benefit of $100,000 would increase to $198,300 by age 65. These are not Dacey conjectures. They are real projections from an actual rate book. Projections are of no value, as he would point out, without actual results. Well, a review of several policies sold by members of my agency, 20 to 30 years ago, proves that the company actually outperformed their projections. In fact, most of the referenced policies nearly doubled in death value in less than 20 years.

Conversely, if our clients had purchased the non-par policy, as was their option to do, at $1,608.00 per annum they would have a fully paid policy of only $100,000 at age 65, rather than $198,300 as projected above.

Of course, you might wonder what would have happened if they had used the extra premium to buy additional insurance coverage—and be assured some clients did that. The $21.35 per thousand would have purchased $132,770 worth of initial coverage, i.e., $32,770 more coverage initially. Where that amount was of significance to the client, that is what he should have done. However, considering the effects of inflation which one is better at age 65—$132,770 or $198,300? Rhetorical! Rhetorical! Rhetorical!

We could have provided the extra initial coverage with an inexpensive term rider. The term rider disappears, gradually, as the paid-up additional coverage increases. Again, you may see that Mr. Dacey and the others do not tell the whole story.

A discussion of dividends, from participating policies, would be totally useless in view of current day products; except that large numbers of conventional whole life policies remain in effect. We should not allow the Dacey's, of the day, to mislead the owners of these policies causing them to give up something of considerable value.

There is one criticism of consequence; these *old* policies are not too significant in relation to current needs caused by inflation. Many older policies are much smaller, but the premium is relevant. Continuous railing against the benefits offered by policies from 30 years ago is an insufferable injustice to the companies and the agents who sold those old policies. If we were selling them today, the *authors* would have a valid argument, but their continuous railing in the light of currently available products, is merely evidence of fossilized thinking.

****

Myth of Life Insurance As a Saving Vehicle

On page 315, Mr. Dacey states, *most men leave too little life insurance*. He claims the reason is that they buy savings type policies. At the same time, he overlooks the fact that the majority of people do not die young. He complains about the small average amount of death benefit being paid out, but ignores the fact that term life is not in force unless you die young. Dacey refers throughout his book to the reserve in a cash value plan as a bank account. He compares it to a savings account at the bank. According to him, the policy is simply a life insurance policy plus a separate bank account. He cannot resist the concept of borrowing your own money. Earlier in the book, he admits that the money, in the reserve, is no more *your money* than the cash value in a bond, or in an automobile, or in a home, or in any other investment. Of course, that is the purpose of his method. He confuses old style plans with current plans; and outdated concepts with modern day approaches. By doing this, he can infer that the policies sold today have some of the inadequacies of policies sold fifty years ago. The unfortunate thing is that some people accept his addled thinking and judgment without critical analysis.

These comparisons are no more accurate than a comparison of a personal computer from 1979 with a high powered computer of today. A personal IBM computer cost me over $22,000.00 twenty years ago.

Programs to run it, averaged around $5,000 each. Today a fully loaded, high powered computer, costs about $2,200.00. Does Mr. Dacey rail against the companies that dumped those white elephants on us?

Myth of Term Insurance Plus Mutual Funds

Finally after 336 pages of ranting and raving against life insurance, Mr. Dacey admits that he is actually promoting mutual funds. As I have said, I have no animosity toward nor about mutual funds. That is not the topic of this discussion. I do object, as I have always objected, to the idea of buying term insurance in order to buy a mutual fund, or any other investment.

To make his premise of buy term plus a mutual fund work, Mr. Dacey recommends decreasing term. He claims that a premium for a $100,000, decreasing term plan, for twenty-five years, would be $352.00, for a male non-smoker age 40. (Page 337) At the same time he admits that *no mutual fund is a substitute for life insurance* (page 339). The next several pages illustrate, that by using the difference in premium between $2,000 and $352.00, or $1,648 annually, to buy a carefully selected mutual fund, you would become fully self-insured over a 25 year period. Once again Dacey compares one plan from the past with a different one from today. Reducing term 25 years ago cost considerably more than the rate illustrated in his examples.

The first error in Mr. Dacey's calculations is that the difference between his decreasing term and a current universal type policy is $1,648. The plan I would choose is only $8.03 annually per thousand, leaving a difference to invest of only $451.00 per annum. That difference would not allow Mr. Dacey's tables to appear so impressive. At 8.5% interest, my choice of policy becomes paid in full in only 14 years. Why would you settle for disappearing insurance, that costs $352.00 for 25 years, when you could have a $100,000 policy for $803.00 per annum, paid in full after 14 years. Remember, your own words Mr. Dacey; *No mutual fund is a substitute for life insurance.*

If we use the total $2,000, for comparison purposes, our life plan becomes paid in full @ 8.5% in just four years. Continuing to pay two thousand dollars annually would cause the death benefit to increase to $282,082 at age 65. How is that as an answer to Dacey's earlier statement that too many people die with too little life insurance in force. How can an author make this lament in one chapter, and then afterwards use a declining term illustration?

Mr. Dacey's non-life-insurance solution to an insurance problem would require tax sheltering. If, then, you required the money so invested to pay for things caused by death, such as taxes, you would be taxed in full on the cash retrieved.

Not a pretty picture Mr. Dacey.

What's wrong with your life insurance? If it is not in some type of term plan, Dacey would have you believe that it is all wrong for you and for everybody. Dacey and so many authors beat on this theme with monotonous regularity. His book falls far short of providing proof of anything other than the author's lack of knowledge. My hope is that my information in refutation of his arguments was equal to the task.

Why do so many writers promote this unreasonable approach? After reading a very large number, approximately sixty, I can draw only three conclusions for a plausible explanation:

- Some of them have a serious lack of knowledge.
- Some of them think that by deprecating one product, they can support a competing product.
- Some of them believe that this approach is what the public wants to hear.

Which one is the correct answer? *All of the above!*

The real reason they write as they do is to sell books.

Myth: Charitable Gifting

Myth? Surely not! People give millions of dollars to their favorite charities every year. The appeals have become so clever and sophisticated that many of us give much more than we actually planned to donate, if we planned to do so at all.

Frequently, in our office, we get three calls on the same day from just one soliciting group. We have a rotary telephone system with three lines. The ones I enjoy the most are when the same solicitor makes all three calls. On other occasions we get a call for both of our listed companies—for the same charity on the same day. Additionally, every few months the phone rings at home about 8:00 a.m., just as I am toweling off after my shower. Sometimes it is someone soliciting accidental death and dismemberment insurance, but at other times it is for some obscure fund raising association. If you add to these telephone calls, direct mail, door to door solicitors, and television appeals, you know that there must be a lot of money collected in the course of a year.

Many of the solicitors present their appeals very well. They design some to make you feel guilty if you are not doing your share. The better presenters make their appeals sound like a great opportunity to do something for the youth of our communities, or the underprivileged in our society, or the starving children of some far away country.

When someone comes knocking on my door, in person, soliciting for a well-known charity such as the heart fund or cancer fund or multiple sclerosis, I can usually find some money for them. I feel sorry for the solicitor. It is a tough job. I have done it.

On one occasion a gentleman calling on homes for the heart fund came to our door which, unfortunately, was partially open. Our Bouvier, a very large black dog, beat me to the door and scared the solicitor so badly that I thought he might have a heart attack. I gave generously in the hope that the caller would recover quickly from his ordeal.

How then, with all this seemingly continuous effort, can I refer to it as the *myth of charitable gifting*? If this process did not work, it would not be continued year after year would it? Well, yes it would be, because paid solicitors make many of the telephone calls.

Now please understand that I have no objection to people being paid for the work they do. On the other hand, I am from the old school of volunteers. The old approach was to work for the charity of your choice and to contribute as much as possible to it as well. Admittedly, solicitation of this type was and is very difficult and thankless. Furthermore, according to my information, the net result to the charity is much greater than we ever achieved using the *old* system. So be it, but I have a limited budget and when I give $100 to one of my favorite charities I want them to receive $100, not $30 or $40.

Many of my associates have developed a front line defense against telephone solicitation. They simply ask for written material, from the charity in question, to be sent to them in the mail. They want full disclosure. They want to make sure first of all that the charity is legitimate.

Also, they want time to review whether or not it fits their charitable gifting objectives. They want to take time to decide the amount of their donation. Furthermore, they want to know exactly how much of each dollar will reach the charity. Most of my associates want at least 90% to go to the end user, not 30% or 40%. Usually I do most donations in a way to guarantee that 100% reaches the charity.

It surprises, or even shocks, some people to learn that sometimes as little as 30% reaches the intended recipient. The soliciting group determines the split based on the popularity of the charity. Obviously, it is easier to solicit for a well-known onc; therefore a lower split is in order.

How about using television appeals? How much does air time cost? How about the actors; do they work without remuneration? In paid commercials, the answer is obviously *no*.

However, there are some telethons wherein the entertainers contribute their time freely. There are some instances where outstanding performers have put on charity concerts and raised millions of dollars. Some entertainers have made tapes or albums for sale, with the net proceeds for charity. No doubt everyone can think of many other examples of worthy contributive efforts similar to these.

Having said all this, you would expect, perhaps, that I would admit that charitable gifting is a fact of life, not a myth. But alas, I cannot do so! The myth lies in the fact that the huge sums we hear about represent only a small percentage of the money needed. Furthermore, these highly publicized money raising programs do not belong under the auspices of charitable gifting.

The myth arises from the ashes and perpetuates itself on the wings of success stories such as a Jerry Lewis telethon, or the Light Up A Child's Life campaign. Some programs surpass the fondest dreams of the organizers—each year bigger and better than the one preceding it.

When we contribute a little bit, $10 or $25, or whatever, we may feel that we have done our part; and indeed we have, if it makes us feel all warm and tingly. And that perpetuates the myth. We think everyone else is doing his or her best as well.

However, people, who supposedly know, have stated that on average the people in the work force contribute less than $100 each, per annum. Those who give considerably more than $100 annually know, therefore, that some others have contributed nothing. Please understand this. *It is not my intent nor my purpose here to question anyone's charitable instincts, nor the amount given by anyone whether it is zero or one million.* It is not my purpose to admonish anyone to make any contribution whatsoever. That is a very personal matter, and as such, what someone gives or whether or not he does donate, is none of my business. That part I leave to the professionals who are so good at making some of us feel guilty about our good fortune. That is not my task.

On the other hand I remain steadfast in my conceptualization of the myth of charitable gifting. If every employed person in Canada gave $100, we would raise over one billion dollars each year. According to the information I have, we do not do anything near that amount. We are misled by the great success of a few high-profile successful campaigns. The myth persists for the many others that continue to struggle for amounts far below their reasonable goals.

My objective is to show those who would like to accomplish more with the limited funds available, a way to do so which is relatively painless, but highly effective at the same time. Of course, I refer to charitable gifting through the use of life insurance. This is not my way of blind-siding the reader, as it were, with a sneaky attack from ambush, using the camouflage of the myth—for two reasons:

First: I write this material for those people only, who would like to know more about it, so as to be able to do more with less. Second: those of my associates who have attempted to support their favorite charities, will tell you that while the vehicle exists in a near perfect state, the results of their efforts have been frustrating. For the few amongst them who have succeeded, the rest of us have great admiration. For the many of us who have tried, and will try again, we know that on the whole our efforts merely prove the myth.

For some readers, if you got this far, the story is over but for those who would like to know more, this is the beginning. Charities, churches, universities, and all institutions that rely on donations need two kinds of funding. (a) current or short term; and (b) long term.

In the short run, all charities and fund raising institutions need money currently, on an on-going basis, to pay for immediate requirements and day to day operations. Some internal fund raisers have expressed concerns that a successful appeal to long term needs, may detract from, or deplete substantially, funds which are now available for current needs. What good would our gift do for them if our funding for future needs of the institution, was at the expense of current needs? They may not survive to receive our largesse. Unquestionably, this is a reasonable concern and therefore we must work with *additional* funds that may be available beyond those slated for current gifting. That's the real beauty of the life insurance approach. We can provide relatively large gifts in the future with small outlays today.

In order to demonstrate the uses and benefits of this approach as effectively as possible, I intend to direct my comments to charitable gifting through life insurance for universities. While I have worked on other appeals, such as for churches, I know best the university one, as I have had more experience in this area. There are many similarities with every institution, but there are also subtle differences that make a comprehensive study for each one too onerous a task for one chapter within one book. Even within a university complex we could be selective and specific. We could select one or more separate areas, such as: for student scholarships; or for funding research projects. Of course each and every donor could specify his or her preference for the use of the funds when they become available. That's for individual consideration; and as such, it is not my concern in this outline. For my purposes here I will illustrate only the general benefits of providing such a gift rather than any benefits from personalized refinements.

Before proceeding with the case for life insurance, it would be appropriate to recognize some of the other ways of providing *planned gifts* to the institution of your choice. Planned gifting, as opposed to periodic small gifts, is an opportunity for an individual to make a significant difference. Planned gifting takes into account your personal and family needs, and you can design it to fit your financial situation. Each program can be and should be structured to maximize tax advantages. Your planned gift may be:

- A *current gift*, such as cash, securities, real property or art
- It may be a *future gift* made by a will or by life insurance
- It may be a *life income* gift of an annuity
- A *remainder trust*
- *A residual interest*

Donations of cash may be a one time donation or a pledge with several installments.

Securities, publicly traded stocks, bonds, and mutual fund shares, can provide tax benefits such as a reduction in taxable capital gains.

Property such as real estate, private shares, jewelry, collections, antiques or art may generate a tax receipt for the fair market value of the donation.

Using a *charitable gift annuity* may have a great benefit for some people. You may gift a substantial sum of money to the institution to buy an annuity. The annuity, thereafter, provides an income for life usually on a completely tax free basis. The remainder of the gift is immediately available to the institution at your death.

Similarly with a *charitable remainder trust*, you may contribute cash, securities, mutual funds or real estate to a trust fund and receive an income for life, or for a specified period of time. Thereafter, the institution receives the assets from the trust.

Another option is a gift of *residual interest*. With this approach you gift or transfer an asset, such as art, or a cottage, or your home, to a trustee giving the institution a *residual interest* in the property so transferred. You may continue to enjoy this property until your death while receiving an immediate tax benefit.

*N.B. Specialists at the chosen institution may be able to provide excellent advice regarding the tax benefits, or you may wish to c*onsult *your accountant.*

For those who have the right situation, one or more of the above options can be very valuable. Not everyone will be able to benefit from these approaches, but everyone can provide a significant donation and make an incredible difference using the miracle of paper and ink called life insurance.

What are the pros and cons? On the part of charitable institutions there are both negative and positive concerns about the use of life insurance products.

ON THE NEGATIVE SIDE:

- Annual receipts must be produced by the institution
- Donors must be insurable
- A policy may lapse leaving the intended recipient with nothing
- Current funding is required but some funds may be diverted to the life policy
- Proceeds from life insurance usually require waiting many years
- Inflation may reduce the principle if you use a fixed value policy

ON THE POSITIVE SIDE:

- A larger gift can be provided at a lower cost to the donor
- Premiums are tax deductible—via tax credits
- Cash values of existing policies may be tax deductible
- There is a large range of insurance options available to the donor
- When the policy is completely funded it cannot be canceled
- Reduced paid up or extended term coverage options are available if the donor does not continue payments
- Some policies permit a cash release for current needs, while maintaining the full death benefit
- Using modern day products the ultimate benefit to the institution may be considerably higher than the initial amount
- One hundred percent of the proceeds are immediately available to the charity on death
- Estate administration costs are avoided

ADDITIONAL ADVANTAGES TO THE DONOR:

- You can make a substantial gift on the installment plan
- The minimum value of your gift to the charity is guaranteed so long as the premiums are paid
- You get a current income tax credit
- Your gift is self-completing in case of death or disability, whereas if you die or become disabled your contributions may stop or be interrupted
- Your estate assets remain intact for the benefit of your heirs
- Your gift to the charity is assured of privacy and is protected from disgruntled heirs, since the proceeds pass outside the estate
- You are not locked-in since you can stop future appreciation of the gift by discontinuing premiums

In setting up a charitable gift of life insurance the charity should be both the owner and the beneficiary, otherwise the recipient may not receive immediate tax relief. The donor should make the premium payments directly to an insurance company to remove collection responsibilities from the charity.

If the donor would like to designate the proceeds gifted, for a specific project or use, she should have a separate agreement with the charity. Term insurance is not an appropriate product unless the donor can guarantee that he will die before the policy expires. Permanent plans permit you to pay your policy in full within ten years. Thereafter, any premiums deposited would result in higher cashable values and death proceeds. At death, the charity would receive the initial face amount, or death benefit, plus the cash values. Interest sensitive or variable return options on policies, known generically as universal life, may cause the ultimate gift to be several times greater than the initial amount purchased.

Universities and Graduate Gifting

You may want to stop reading this article at this point because what follows is a sales pitch. Notwithstanding the fact that I have stated that your charitable gifting habits are none of my business, I do reserve the right to make one exception—universities and their graduates. It is my sincere conviction that all those who have benefited, or who are benefiting, or who will enjoy the benefits of a university education, have an obligation to give back something to the institution from which they have gained so much.

Since I came from an agrarian background, I tend to think in farm yard logic rather than with sophisticated rhetoric. Thereby, an allegory of an acorn and a shade tree seems appropriate. Is it too much to ask of everyone who has ever enjoyed the shade of an oak tree to plant one acorn. That's what I ask of university grads—just plant an acorn and nurture it to grow into a mighty oak.

Too often those of us relaxing in the shade of a marvelous tree take it for granted and even consider it our right to enjoy it. If, however, we cause trees to be cut down without causing more trees to be planted, we will use up this precious resource all too soon.

Similarly, too many people take an education, or the right to an education, for granted. We hear many statements about the value of an educated youth to our nation. We refer to them as a great resource. We consider their education to be an investment in the future.

In principle, all of these arguments are correct, but there is more, so much more, on an individual basis. Think back in memory to those mind stretching years in university. Think back to the experience that *is* university, rather than of bricks and mortar, marble halls and lecture rooms, or labs and stacks of books. That experience cannot be bought and you cannot pay for it. That experience could not have been enjoyed by you, nor by me, except for the efforts of those who preceded us.

Relaxing in the shade of a tree, or sharing the privilege of the experience that is university, was and is possible only because of the acorns that were planted by someone before us. That should be our common objective, as graduates of our respective universities, to perpetuate this magnificent experience. Not all of us can plant a forest, but we can plant an acorn and together we can grow a forest.

Consider this; what would happen if every graduate pledged a $100,000 life insurance policy at age 30? An annual premium of $600, or $50.00 per month, payable for up to 35 years to age 65 would provide an amazing legacy. At 8% interest earnings, the policy would be paid in full in just 13 years. ($600 per annum for 35 years = $18,000) If you paid premiums until age 65 @ 8%, the death benefit at age 80 would be over $275,000. Just imagine, for only $600 per annum for 35 years, each graduate could provide a gift of a lifetime of about $275,000. If one thousand graduates started this program every year, eventually we could donate over $275,000,000 every year—*that's $275 million*. What a forest! What a legacy!

However, one thousand graduates per annum is only a small percentage of the total. What if everyone contributed something in this way? For example, $25.00 per month provides for a $50,000 initial death benefit. While I have no accurate figure on the total number graduating each year, the figure would be impressive. The total amount generated in this way could be awesome.

Together, we could provide a resource that would eliminate future financial needs for all institutions of higher learning.

There is an obligation. There is an opportunity.

Myth: I Don't Need A Will

Contemplation of death is not a popular pastime for most people. One of the most compelling reasons for not making a will is that it causes us to think about the consequences of our own demise. It never fails to amaze me, that a very large number of the people I meet professionally, do not have wills. Some authorities have estimated that approximately 1 of 3 Canadians has a valid will at the time of death. Nearly two thirds of the total population allows the government to make important decisions for them. Why? Why? Why?

There are many excuses for not preparing a will, ranging from;

- We don't really need one—our estate is too small
- It's too expensive
- We just haven't thought about it yet
- We are too young to worry about that
- We haven't got around to it yet
- We know we should—but…

Many people do not realize it, but everyone actually has a will; provided by the Province in which she or he lives. If you die intestate, not having made a valid will of your own, your estate is subject to the Provincial law of intestate succession. This law may be modified somewhat by a claim from a surviving spouse under the Provincial family property law. Otherwise, if you have no will, the Province has already made your decisions for you.

The incredible thing is that the government's plan would not be satisfactory for most people, if they understood the terms of the statute. In any case, it is doubtful if the statutory plan provided would effectively meet the individual needs of various family members. In many situations, it would not provide a proper disposition to minimize the impact of taxation at death, except for relatively simple estates. For example, in all Provinces, if only your spouse survives you, your spouse receives the entire estate. If your spouse does not survive you, your children share the proceeds equally, after probate fees, and after taxes. What if there are no children and no surviving spouse?

There is some uniformity in the laws of intestacy between the provinces, but there are enough differences that you should avoid generalizations. You may find that the formula in your province is not a satisfactory solution. Seven of the ten Provinces in Canada, reserve a p*referential* share which is payable to the surviving spouse. A preferential share is a sum of money that passes to your spouse before the law distributes the remainder of your estate to your family. The law provides a preferential share of $50,000 in Manitoba, Nova Scotia, and Prince Edward Island. The amount is $40,000 in Alberta, $65,000 in British Columbia, $100,000 in Saskatchewan, and $200,000 in Ontario. In the other Provinces there is no preferential share. Therefore, in those three Provinces, your family shares in the full estate according to formula.

The remainder of your estate, after the preferential share, is referred to as a distributive share. The law of intestate succession in your Province of domicile distributes your remaining estate according to a formula. This formula varies from Province to Province depending on whether you have only one child or if there are two or more children. Furthermore, a distributive share may allow for the *issue* of a predeceased child.

In Alberta, after the preferential share of $40,000, the distributive formula allows 50% for the surviving spouse, and 50% for your child or the issue of a predeceased child in equal shares per stirpes. If there are two or more children, the formula allows only one-third for the spouse. The issue of the deceased share the remaining two-thirds equally per stirpes. There are some subtle differences to this formula in some of the other Provinces. If you want to know about the specific formula for your own Province, I recommend that you check on it with a lawyer.

It is possible that an estate that passes totally to a spouse could be sufficient to sustain the family. If, however, you allow it to be split according to the laws of intestacy, it could be quite inadequate. There are many more questions to be answered depending on specific circumstances. In view of these questions, a generalized formula could rarely hope to achieve the most effective disposition of any estate.

Some of the questions you may want to review are:

- What happens if there are no children and your spouse does not survive you?
- Could you be sharing your assets with your spouse's relatives?
- What about a situation where one child has special needs—should she have special consideration?
- Do you have a specific property or asset that you want left to only one person?
- Does the statutory formula achieve the best split for taxation purposes or could you devise a better plan?
- Are you too young to have a will? If you are 18 years old and have any assets, bank account, RRSP, equipment, automobile, etc., do you have a preference who receives any or all of your valuables?
- Should you own life insurance? If you have life insurance, have you named a beneficiary other than your estate? Do you have sufficient assets to pay your final expenses? Your parents paid your way into this world; why should they be burdened with the costs of your exit?
- Should young married couples have wills? Young people have told me that it's simple. We leave everything to each other; the survivor gets it all. Okay, but what if there is no survivor? Will your deaths be simultaneous or could one spouse survive a short time longer? If there is no evidence, such as a witness that one spouse lived beyond the other's death, the law may deem that the younger person survived and that his or her estate would receive everything. What happens then? Perhaps you should check it out for your Province? Would all of the property pass, according to the laws of intestacy, to the deemed survivor's parents, brothers and sisters, while excluding yours? If you care, you should check into it.
- Should a recluse, a peripetetic vagabond, a derelict, or an itinerant wanderer have a will? A cursory consideration would suggest that there is no reason for anyone in this category to have a will. However, what if this person inherits

> from someone else? What if one of them gets hit by a drunk driver and there is a substantial settlement? Who should share in this estate?

A will allows you to name the executor(s), trustee(s) and guardian(s). If you have children, these may be very important considerations. Who do you want to look after your children if you die? Who should be the guardian? In most situations, perhaps all, the court has the final say, but it would strongly favor your recommendation. What about a trustee? Should this be someone other than the guardian?

Consider this: if the guardian is also the trustee, she can make all the decisions regarding the expenditure of funds. She also bears the total responsibility for the use of your funds, and the liability for the preservation of your assets. If a third party is the trustee, he shoulders the liability and the guardian can shift some of the responsibility to him as well.

For example: If the trustee is Uncle Joe and young Jamie is putting pressure on you, the guardian, to buy him a car at age sixteen with arguments such as, "After all it is my money," you do not have to disagree. Let Uncle Joe say no. He does not have to live with Jamie every day.

Should you appoint an executor or an executrix? If no valid will exists, the court will appoint an administrator. If no one applies for the responsibility, the public trustee may step in and assume the duties. Such an event will normally slow down the process of estate settlement and it will not reduce expenses.

If you agree that your estate requires an executor/executrix who should you appoint? Your first consideration should be to learn what his or her duties will be. Is your choice physically close enough to effectively carry out her responsibilities? Should you appoint your lawyer as co-executor or should you allow your appointee to select her own legal assistance?

Most people need professional advice in matters pertaining to probate, filing the estate's tax forms and for other possible requirements. Generally, the executor instructs the lawyer and the lawyer advises the executor.

The following information is not an exhaustive study in the duties of an executor or an executrix. Rather, in general, the duty of the one appointed is to see that the instructions in the will are carried out within the laws of your province. Does the estate require probate? Should some assets pass outside probate? Your executor will have certain duties and obligations in this regard. He will need to inventory all assets, and debts, and determine who are the beneficiaries.

He must acquire legal title to the assets and accept responsibility for them, until he can transfer them to the beneficiaries. This could mean making decisions about investments or even running a business. Does she have the necessary skills, abilities and the time to devote to it? She must pay any debts owed and collect whatever is due to the estate. She must take the necessary steps to provide for the survivors immediately after death. There is more, but the foregoing should give you some basic insight into the duties and obligations.

How about liabilities? Can the executor become liable for losses to the estate? Definitely! If he commits a breach of trust or knowingly permits a co-executor to do so a liability may arise. How about paying out assets to the wrong beneficiary or some other misuse of estate funds? Does the appointment of someone by will, as an executor, require him to act in this capacity? No! He can reject the appointment. Do the fees payable to the executor offset the responsibility and the liability? Probably not!

Why would anyone want to act in this capacity? For some lawyers and some accountants it may be a source of income, in which capacity they are qualified and highly proficient. For others, such as parents or children, the justification may be to make sure that everything is done promptly, efficiently, and according to your wishes.

Should you discuss this appointment with your choice of executrix in advance? There are different schools of thought on this matter. Some people feel that if they announce their choice of who is best for the duties today, it might complicate matters if they want to make a change in the future.

It's a private decision between spouses and if it gets out that you have appointed Aunt Mary as the guardian of your precious wards, will the other possible choices feel slighted? Perhaps at one time I thought this way, but now I think a different approach is better in most cases. In my opinion, the pendulum swings heavily in favor of telling everyone what you would like to do. Would Aunt Mary want this added responsibility? Does she understand what the law expects of her? How about Aunt Mary's husband; would he like to be saddled with three more kids? How about your choice of executrix; would she want the added responsibility? Have you made it clear what the duties, responsibilities and liabilities will be?

How much life insurance do you have? If you approached me about either of these duties, that would be my first question. Looking after your children is enough responsibility, without adding a financial burden.

Are wills too expensive, compared to the costs of dying without a will? If you think about it, that question is redundant. There are several types of wills that cost very little. You could make a simple written or holographic will. You could purchase a wills kit. These kits, prepared by lawyers, should be quite effective as a guide. However, in my opinion, you should still submit your self-designed will to a lawyer to validate it. As the complexity of your estate increases, the value of a capable lawyer becomes more apparent. The expenditure of a few hundred dollars now may save your estate thousands of dollars later. It is wise to get professional advice.

It is imperative that you do not consider anything in this article as legal advice. The purpose of everything written on these pages is to illustrate the importance of having a properly drawn, valid will.

Another thing that I notice is that many people do not review their wills often enough. Any change in personal or family circumstances may justify a review of your will. My advice, throughout this book remains consistent. Take your advice regarding life insurance or investments from someone who can be held responsible for it. Similarly, have your will drawn by someone legally responsible.

Remember, you will not be present when they read your will. Your will is your final statement of how you want your assets distributed. It is your only way to suggest a competent executor of your choice. It is a way for you to divide specific assets amongst chosen heirs. It is your final instruction about how your children will be raised and by whom. It is your last chance to establish trust funds and/or make bequests to charities. Wills and the planning of a will should not be left to amateurs.

One codicil: In most cases, you should not make a disposition of RRSP assets, or of life insurance policies, or annuity proceeds, via your will. These should have a named beneficiary to avoid probate and probate costs wherever possible. You should also take care that your will does not cause other assets to become subject to it, such as jointly owned property and/or buy-sell agreements.

In some situations, you may want to have a specific life insurance policy, or a specified amount of a given policy, payable to your estate in order to pay all just and reasonable debts. This may be a preferable way to provide liquidity, rather than to cause other assets to be redeemed at an inappropriate time. Remember Murphy's law: You never die at the right time. On the other hand, you could instruct your executor to pay all your just and reasonable debts from your insurance proceeds which pass outside the estate. Be cautious. Consult a lawyer.

If you are not convinced by now of the value of a properly drawn valid will, perhaps you should read the following:

Is this your will?

I, John Doe, whether of sound mind or not, do hereby agree that in the case of my death the following terms shall apply to the assets of my estate.

I forego my right to appoint an executor or an executrix being fully aware that the provincial government where I live must appoint an administrator/administratrix. To the best of my knowledge the Provincial Government will appoint my spouse, generally speaking, providing that my spouse survives me.

Furthermore, I forego my rights to a say in the distribution of any of my property specifically, or generally, even though my spouse may make divisions and distributions of my property with which I might otherwise disagree.

Also, I recognize that all assets, property and businesses not held jointly with my spouse may be frozen until such time as an administrator may be appointed. Decisions regarding my business will be suspended and no contracts may be made during this time regardless of their potential value to my heirs. Likewise, no one will be permitted to make any decisions nor take any action regarding my investments, including my stock portfolio, even though its value may be shrinking rapidly. In such a situation, my spouse should move with alacrity to press the judicial system to make an appointment, assuming that he or she is physically and/or mentally sound and able to do so. Otherwise, it is to be expected that someone who cares would be encouraged to assume this vital service.

Since the beneficiary designation of my entire life insurance program is payable to my estate, there should be sufficient liquid assets there to pay all of my just and reasonable debts including funeral expenses and any other costs that may have been caused by my death. Of course the funeral director will be expected to exhibit reasonable patience while waiting until the required legal procedure can be completed. Otherwise, considering the substance of my estate, it is my expectation that the bank will loan my estate a reasonable sum in order to pay the hospital, the doctors, the undertaker, and even to provide food and necessities for my children providing, of course, that my estate is not in litigation.

Hence, I furthermore state and declare that I am satisfied with the provision that my spouse will receive a preferential share of $40,000 and will, thereafter, receive a distributive share of one-third of the remainder of my estate while my surviving children will share equally in the other two-thirds. This must be a fair and reasonable disposition since it is the proposal of my Provincial Government. In the unlikely circumstance that my spouse should not survive my demise, then we, in common, do hereby and forthwith instruct the court to appoint an administrator (of any gender), with all due haste. Furthermore, we recommend that the Province selects trustees and guardians for our three minor children. Our relatives may not agree among themselves as to the best choice of an appointment. If that is the case let the court decide. That way we do not need to be involved.

Being of sound minds and bodies, or otherwise, my spouse and I acknowledge that the public trustee may assume control of our assets, liquid or otherwise. This government agency has our permission to invest our liquid assets in a safe secure program, even though the return may be exceedingly low. As for our lucrative businesses, we authorize the public trustee to appoint someone to run them safely until the youngest of our children reaches age 18 or even in such instance as she or he may decide in his or her sole discretion to sell the businesses to the highest bidder, notwithstanding the fact of continued profitability of said businesses, from which our issue would otherwise benefit.

Finally, we state emphatically that we are thankful for the statutory will provided for us, by the Province, through the laws of intestate succession, even though the cost to our estate may be considerably more than for a properly drawn and otherwise valid will.

Would you sign this will? **If you do not have a valid will, you have already signed it. Are you happy about that? If not, perhaps you should consult a lawyer immediately to make the appropriate changes.**

N'est-ce pas?

Myth: Group Life Insurance Is Enough

Please cancel my life insurance policy. I don't need it any more because now I have group insurance.

Over the years, I have received several letters or telephone calls with a message similar to the one above. Sometimes it reads: I renewed my mortgage with an institution offering life insurance. *It is less expensive than my plan through your office. Please cancel my coverage and send the cash to me.*

If you have ever written such a letter or made a similar comment to your advisor, we have failed you somewhere. If you are an insurance advisor and you have received a communication such as this, ask yourself and your client why and how you messed up. Perhaps we have never discussed it. Perhaps we have never even thought about it. In fact, why would we consider it? It is not a viable alternative. We assume that most people understand the frailties of group life insurance. Obviously, we should not make such an assumption. You know how some people read the word *assume*, do you not?

Unfortunately, even some sales people do not understand this product's weaknesses. Several years ago, a relatively new sales representative attempted to replace the insurance program one of my clients had established. This involved an insurance policy covering the entire family:

$100,000 on the father; $50,000 on the mother; and
$25,000 on each of three children.

The agent proposed her group plan as a better deal because it was less expensive. Life insurance was part of the group package. Our client had no option. Take the entire package or no sale. The family wanted extended health and dental coverage, and if life insurance was a part of that package, so be it. After a thorough review we resolved the situation to everyone's satisfaction, by cancelling a five year renewable and convertible term rider instead of the basic contract.

Now let's examine the opening statement. *I don't need it now that I have group insurance.* Is that comment ever correct? Probably it is not. To make that determination there are several factors that one should consider.

- What was the original purpose of your life insurance?
- Has the objective or reason for it changed?
- What did you design your plan to accomplish?
- Will group coverage achieve the actual goals and cover the real needs?

Consider the second comment. *It is less expensive.* Well, if you are part of a large group plan that may appear to be so. Group insurance may have seemed inexpensive, before the revenue department declared the premium to be a taxable benefit on any amount of life insurance over $25,000. Many of my clients have company perks wherein the entire package is being paid for in full. Some even have additional optional coverage paid for by their employers. Even after part of the premium became taxable, it was clearly less expensive than paying the entire cost for the benefit.

On the other hand, if you pay your own premium, any saving may be more illusionary than factual. If you are comparing it to a ten year renewable and convertible term plan, the group premium may be slightly lower. That would be so especially if you are a male who is older than the average of your group. Remember, however, if you have a fairly stable group of employees, your premiums will increase as the group ages. To keep the premium low, you need an increasing number of younger people. For one male over the age of fifty, it requires several young people to offset his cost.

How about *group creditor insurance*, such as that available from loaning institutions for mortgages or whatever? Keep in mind that usually you are paying a level premium for declining coverage. You may be paying a premium equivalent to what we would require for a $100,000 policy. While you continue to pay for full coverage, in case of death, you get only the actual reduced amount outstanding at the time of death. With some plans your premium may reduce after each reduction in debt of $1000.

If both you and your spouse are insured, only one pay-out applies in case of a common disaster. Conversely, individual plans pay the full face amount for both deaths regardless of the debt remaining. Why would you pay for something you will not get? Anyway, our individual plans may cost less. Ah yes, some will say, but the premium increases after every ten years. That is true, but if you do not want the extra coverage you may reduce it and receive a corresponding reduction in cost. The choice is yours.

In addition, there are some other serious drawbacks to so-called mortgage insurance, known to the industry as creditor insurance. Some things you should know about this product are:

- It is not portable. Therefore, you cannot transfer it to the mortgage on a new home or to a new lending institution.
- It is not renewable. When your loan is finished, so is your coverage. If you renew your mortgage, a corresponding renewal of death benefit is not automatic.
- It is not convertible. This disappearing coverage *cannot* be converted to any other plan, at anytime.

For a full disclosure about this product and its usage, refer to No Salesman Will Call?, page 50.

Some of these factors do not apply to *regular* group insurance. However, everyone should be made aware of some aspects of group life insurance. Generally, the common occurrences to be concerned with about group plans are as follows:

- The insuring company reviews the cost of coverage annually. An insurance company may increase the premium because of its experience with a client's firm, or even because of their claims experience from risk pooling.
- As the people in a group grow older, the premiums increase in anticipation of more deathes.
- A life insurnace company may cancel the group plan for any reason. Of course, your firm may acquire a new plan from another company. However, there are some situations where getting new coverage may be a problem. What happens

when the rules of what consitutes a valid group have been changed? A more common difficulty arises if one company cancels a client's group coverage because of bad claims.

- The firm you work for may cancel the plan. This may not be a popular move but they have the right to do it. The plan may permit you to convert to an individual policy if your company discontinues your program, provided that you were insured under the same plan continuously for at least five years.
- At age 65, life coverage automatically reduces to fifty percent.
- At age 70, all group coverage ceases.
- Upon retirement, group coverage usually stops. There are some exceptions. Your employer may allow you to continue in the group until age 70.
- If you become disabled what happens to your coverage? Will your employer continue to make payments or allow you to pay the premium? After six months of total disability, some group plans do allow for continuance of your life insurance with no further premiums.
- If your employment terminates, your coverage ceases, but your contract may allow you to convert to an individual plan. Rules for conversion may vary from one company to the next, but usually they read somewhat similarly to the following:

  * any regular plan then being issued by the insurance company. You may want to check out the definition of *any regular plan.*
  * one year convertible term insurance if you are not yet age 65
  * term to age 65

It should be clear from the above that with group insurnace you are not in control of your insurance program.

Group insurance is a good idea, especially for extended health and dental coverage. However, you should not rely on this coverage for your basic life insurance program. Many people see group health and dental not much more than an exchange of premiums. In other words, it is obvious that the group company tries to recover the amount paid out, plus a small profit. However we should keep in mind that there is a risk of much larger claims in any given year. Also group premiums may be charged as an expense for tax purposes.

Relying on group life insurance caused a serious problem for an acquaintance of mine. He had a superior group plan with a life coverage of $200,000. He resigned from his company to go into his own business. He moved from Ontario to Alberta. He worked fifteen to eighteen hours a day to get his new company going. After a few months, he discovered that he needed life insurnace to cover the line of credit for which he had applied. On the surface, he appeared to be a great candidate for coverage. However, his application was rejected. He had become uninsurable without his knowledge. He could not qualify even for creditor insurance. Of course, you may point out that this was not the fault of group insurance. It was his own carelessness. He should have made sure that he had coverage before he left his group plan. Fair enough, but in my opinion, the real culprit was too much reliance on group life insurance. Group life, like any term insurance, is relatively inexpensive because most people do not die while it is in effect.

Group disability income is another concern. There are two separate parts available:

(a) Weekly indemnity. This coverage is designed to be equal, at least, to the coverage provided by UIC (now,employment insurance). (Many people are not aware that their employment insurance premium also qualifies them for a disability income for up to one hundred and twenty days, after a two week waiting period.)

(b) The second part of group disability income is referred to as long term disability (LTD). It may dovetail with weekly indemnity (WI), or it may stand on its own. The period of coverage may be for two years, or for five years, or to age 65. The benefit usually is for a percentage of income to a specified maximum. Often people with higher incomes are inadequately insured.The definition of what constitutes being totally disabled should be reviewed carefully. Sometimes it states that you are covered for two years if you cannot perform the important duties of your own occupation. Thereafter, you must be unable to do any occupation for which you are qualified, or for which you may become qualified. That could mean that even though you could not do parts of your regular job, you may be required to accept one with lower responsibilities.

Another matter for careful consideration is any *offsets* to monthly payments. For example; amounts received from other insurance plans, government or private; or for all compensation from a legal settlement following an accident; are some things that may reduce or eliminate any income from your group plan. For a full review of disability income I recommend reading Dr. John Paterson's book, *RUSSIAN ROULETTE Gambling with Disability.* In it John illustrates several potential problems that could seriously affect your coverage.

Everyone should be careful about canceling individual life contracts because of group insurance. If an advisor assists you to change plans, he or she must make full disclosure regarding your current plan as well as about the one to which you are changing. Your advisor must explain the benefits of your current plan and the relevant inadequacies of any new plan. There is no such requirement for group life insurance. To the best of my knowledge, the question is never asked on any application for group insurance. The question that should be asked is *will this group plan replace any individual coverage?* Perhaps supervision of this type of replacement would be too onerous a task. In that case, the group company should be required, at least, to disclose the above information before a contract goes into effect. There should be a notification or a disclaimer statement that points out that group life insurance should not be used as an alternative to a proper individual program.

Group insurance may be a great benefit to many families, but it should never form the cornerstone of a financial program.

Myth: When Writers are Right!

In most of my books, I have done some bashing of journalists and writers for some of the shoddy inaccurate information that they have been disseminating. It is cause for concern that they expound their particular biases with a degree of pugnacity, even though they are based on inadequate or inappropriate information. When I discover their fallacious reasoning, I feel that it is my right to lash back at them with equal vehemence. This is fair in every way. These writers have the power of the pen to retaliate if they think their case has not been treated fairly. They are not neophyphitic nymphs who need skirt-sheltering from the big bad insurance agent. Furthermore, some of their own associates have taken pot shots at them for some of their careless media reporting.

No Salesman Will Call? (Page 238) reprinted an article, with permission, from the Alberta Report, a weekly news magazine with national readership. Ted Byfield was the author. In this article Ted deplored the state of modern journalism and he was deeply concerned by the "Awesome gullibility of the modern media." His point was neatly illuminated by Christine Hoff Sommers in her book *Who Stole Feminism?*

Ms. Sommers detailed three case studies to illustrate her points:

• Gloria Steinem wrote the following in her book *Revolution From Within:* "In this country alone about 150,000 females die of anorexia each year." The story of how this figure is used and interpreted or misinterpreted, as the case may be, is quite fascinating. However, Ms. Sommers challenged this quoted figure and traced it back to the supposed source, *The American Anorexia and Bulimia Association.* The association president denied the death figure and stated that an association newsletter had reported, in 1985, that 150,000 to 200,000 American women *suffer* from anorexia—not die from it.

• Ms. Sarah Buel, a founder of the domestic violence advocacy fund at Harvard, prepared a paper for the family violence professionals.

In it she quoted her source as saying *there were more birth defects caused by family violence than by all other known causes.* Her source, the March of Dimes Association, however, had not said that. Its report was that *more women were screened each year for evidence of birth defects than were screened for evidence of wife beating.* Again, what happens as this authoritative misquote unfolds is truly fascinating.

• Perhaps the most entertaining case study was the one called *Super Bowl Sunday—the Abuse Bowl.* Someone from a women's group announced that the super bowl game drives men into such a macho frenzy that they beat their wives. Reports to police, they claimed, were up 40% during the game. The story grew and took on an aura of shame and fear. This prompted one group, known as FAIR, to warn women via the media: *Don't remain at home with him during the game.* The *New York Times* took up the cudgel. *Good Morning America* took the bait. *The Boston Globe* did a report from the perspective of women's shelters. A major TV network ran an anti-wife beating commercial, during the game. This one was blown away by Ken Pringle of the *Washington Post* who followed up after the big game and reported on the report's gross inaccuracy.

It is no secret to most of us that journalists, writers, authors and storytellers are prone to embellishment, on occasion, to add interest to an otherwise drab report. Their task is to fill a space with interesting news; to entice people to read and to return to read again. By their nature, these people have fertile imaginative minds. Usually they can see a humorous twist or a heart-rending approach to a dull or mundane report that will catch attention of readers. Fair enough, some entertaining material in the report is great, so long as the integrity of the facts is not compromised. Even a misinterpretation of facts is tolerable provided that the writer makes it clear that he or someone else has drawn this conclusion based on the known facts.

On occasion, I have read some articles by writers who interpret certain things in such a way so as to cause a reaction. Link Byfield, editor of a large western weekly, the *Alberta Report,* is a master, in my opinion, at writing about controversial subjects to stir the pot and generate further dialogue. In his writing, I detect a tongue-in-cheek approach, quite often. What he says may be his real opinion or it may be a goad to bring out the *best* in those who like to answer editorials. Nevertheless, I have never caught Mr. Byfield misquoting someone else nor embellishing the facts. His opinions are clearly stated as such and you may accept them or rail against them. My suspicion is that Mr. Byfield has respect for those who dare to challenge him. To date, I have never been tempted to challenge his opinions, but if I catch him in a flagrant misinterpretation of facts, or worse, if he misquotes the source, I will not hesitate; you may be sure.

In spite of these challenges to other writers, I hope that I do not come across as one who denies someone else the right to his or her own opinion or the right to draw conclusions that differ from my own. My purpose has been, and it remains, to encourage people to look at the facts—to make conclusions based on knowledge rather than an opinion; especially popular opinion.

Believe it or not, I have found some journalists, in addition to the people mentioned above, who do write entertaining articles while staying within a factual structure. It would be negligent to avoid giving them their credit. It is true that I agree with what they say, and with the conclusions they draw. However, let me stress that it is not of any vital importance to me if their conclusions differ from mine, if their *truths* are correct. *How's that for pounding a point with a club?*

Jonathan Chevreau, Personal Finance Section of the *Financial Post,* Friday, July 24, 1998, wrote an article entitled "Beware of potential half-truths." That title caught my attention because I have always despised half-truths. *A half-truth like a half-brick is more dangerous than a full brick or the full truth because either may be cast much farther.*

Reading Mr. Chevreau's report on the "zero commission" brouhaha about the misleading advertising by a Canadian trust company and the rebuttal by a dynamic fund company was very entertaining. He claims that these ads *provided a highly instructive glimpse into mutual fund sales practices. Half-truths in the hands of sharp marketers can be effective sales instruments.* Mr. Chevreau claims that the Investment Funds Institute of Canada "blessed" the offending advertisements as being within the mutual fund industry's communications guidelines.

Mr. Chevreau then drew a conclusion. I like it—you may not agree, as is your right. His conclusion was: *If the mutual fund industry's sanctioned advertising only presents one side of the story, what's happening in the trenches? What's taking place every day in thousands of private encounters between fund sales reps and the people who buy mutual funds?*

Mr. Chevreau continues, with a case in point, about a colleague of his whose mother was accorded a full-service treatment by a brokerage firm owned by one of the big five banks.

- This colleague's Mom is in her fifties.
- She has a small RRSP.
- She plans to retire in three years.
- Half of her RRSP was invested in a defensive short-term income fund; an in-house product sold by the banks no-load unit.
- This *Mom* had completed a *Know Your Client* information form in order to select a portfolio that fit her needs.
- There was no face-to-face consultation with any *full-service* broker.
- The representative decided that *Mom's* proprietary fund had not been performing well.
- The rep proposed that *Mom* buy Fidelity Canadian Asset Allocation Fund for the Canadian content of the RRSP, and Templeton Growth Fund for the 20% foreign content.
- The rep never informed *Mom* that this change involved partial-exposure to the stock market: asset allocation being a mixture of stocks, bonds and cash.
- Remember, *Mom* was a novice investor who had never bought stocks nor equity mutual funds in her life.
- Now, she was talked into buying into the market near all-time highs.
- The rep said straight out, this was a no-load fund; thus *Mom* would not be assessed a sales charge.
- It was not conveyed that there was an annual trailer fee.
- The rep stressed the performance of these funds over the previous three years and left the impression that she could expect double-digit returns in the future.

- *Mom* was not aware of the usual advertising fine print that declares that *past performance is no guarantee of future results.*
- The rep never discussed that the performance of the past three years arose because of a singular extended bull market.

Mr. Chevreau summarized:

- The rep used two half-truths to generate a sale that immediately generated a 5% commission for herself and a 1% annual trailer fee.
- Half-truth is perhaps too generous: she called a rear-load fund a no-load fund.
- The rep, according to Chevreau, implied *Mom* was taking no risk to get a sure 23% return over the next year.
- Mr. Chevreau and his colleague concluded that *Mom* was led to see the new fund as a sort of guaranteed investment certificate that pays four times more than the GICs sold by the same bank through its deposit unit.
- The rear-load fund has a seven year period during which a sales charge will be assessed on any withdrawals.
- Remember, *Mom* may need to draw on some of these funds within three years.

Mr. Chevreau should be commended, in my opinion, for presenting this story so forcefully. Perhaps it can keep some people from making a similar potentially serious decision error.

Another insightful article under Personal Finance was the one published in the *Financial Post* August 13, 1998, written by Jonathan Kirshblum. His article was entitled "Investors find comfort in segregated funds."

He stated:

- A concern among many older investors is how to participate in the potential continued growth of the stock markets, while not putting their investment principal at risk.
- Segregated funds are an investment vehicle well suited to investors seeking principal protection and growth potential for the benefit of others.
- Until recently, they have been offered exclusively by life insurance companies.

- Now some mutual fund companies have joined forces with life companies in order to offer their own funds in the segregated market.
- Segregated funds look and act like mutual funds, but they also have several unique advantages:

(a) They guarantee up to 100% of the principal investment at maturity (usually after ten years).

(b) They guarantee up to 100% of the principal in case of death (called death benefit guarantee).

(c) They offer potential for creditor protection.

(d) The investor can name a beneficiary, thus avoiding the estate associated probate and legal fees.

- Recently, several insurance companies have added benefits that have made segregated funds even more attractive. One of the new features is called the freeze option. It provides investors a method to lock-in investment gains as the market value in their portfolio rises.

The author of this article does a reasonably good job of explaining this feature, which is new for some companies. He explains the death benefit aspect rather well. However, he does overlook the fact that at least one company has had a superior concept for many years now. This company is a leader in the industry. Since I have known them, they have offered three guarantees:

(a) the death benefit of up to 100% of the initial deposit or market value whichever is higher;

(b) the 100% of principal guarantee after 10 years;

(c) an additional automatic guarantee of the entire growth of the investment up to a point ten years prior to maturity—a date that is set by the investor.

Furthermore, the investor may change the date for his or her benefit. This company has always permitted the investor the right to change his or her maturity date that effectively locks in the gain. Therefore, the author's concept that this is something new with segregated funds is not entirely accurate. In his defence, however, the author does not appear to be posing as an expert.

Mr. Kirshblum continues his article with a very interesting insight:

- Another consideration is the annual management fee.
- Some seg funds now invest in brand name mutual funds and, therefore, they have higher management fees than the underlying fund.
- Many *traditional seg funds* have lower management fees than other mutual funds that invest in the same asset class.

Mr. Kirshblum does not make the purpose of the increased management fee totally clear to the reader. The reason for the extra charge is the cost of extending the guarantees and benefits to the non-seg fund, that is to the name brand mutual fund. Beyond these few points, Mr. Kirshblum has provided a tolerably accurate educational article. His explanation should help to clarify some of the half-truths of some of this associates who preceded him.

Although I am not a movie buff, I do watch the occasional one late at night. It helps me relax my mind and allows me to fall asleep. Recently, I awoke with the TV blaring, in the middle of a story that I would not have watched if I had been awake. Before I could rouse myself enough to turn if off, I was caught up in the dialogue, briefly.

It seems that this metropolis newspaper, called *The Sun,* was 90,000 papers into a run when an enterprising reporter discovered a major error. The caption on a picture of two youths, as they were arrested by an overzealous police crew, was *Caught In The Act*. In a rare spate of conscience, the night editor raced to the pressman shouting, *stop the press, stop the press.* However, it seems that this editor did not have the authority to *stop the press*. His relentless efforts got him physically beaten and bloodied by the managing editor—a woman whose strength and tenacity belied her physique.

The night editor shouted at her, "The headlines are wrong—it should read: They Are Innocent!"

"So what?," replied the managing editor.

"So what?," challenged the night editor. "We'll be misleading thousands of people."

"That doesn't matter," retorted the managing editor. "The public knows what to expect of us—we are *The Sun*." And then came the coup de grace; "We can run the correct version tomorrow."

Throughout this book self-serving reporting of facts and misinterpretations of those facts have been challenged. They are sufficient to provide justification to the cynicism of many people. It is my fervent desire that this collection of essays and the exposé of some of the more common misconceptions will be helpful, in some way. In this book we have travelled from the early attempts at providing insurance against potential losses to the present. This journey took us through some turbulent times in history. Many businesses began only to falter and disappear. The insurance industry and the companies in it were not immune to the rigours of an ever changing world.

The history of the industry would provide a mirror image of the events of those years. When disasters fell on their clients the companies suffered similarly. Some companies failed to survive the losses caused by calamitous events. However, for the most part, the cautious nature of the industry and the monetary reserve that has been kept since near the beginning, has sustained most of them during the bad times. As we know the industry continues to prosper.

During my many years of service to this business and to my clients I have observed that the industry continues to change as is required. It reflects the needs of the public. In spite of all the changes there remains a constant basis in product and in purpose. From the start people bought insurance of all types to provide an offset to an unexpected loss. In so doing the attempt was to avoid self- insuring. *So what has changed?* The vehicle has changed but the purpose for the product has not changed. The method of delivery has changed, but the end result is the same.

One of the greatest pleasures in my life so far was writing this book. My hope is that others will enjoy reading it equally. The truth is that I wrote it for me, but the final joy is the sharing of it with other people. These are the concepts that I have been sharing with my clients during the past forty years. Now they are yours.

Finally, it is my hope that the readers of this book will be fully equipped in the future to identify the Legends, the Lies and the Myths—and consequently to know the truth.

Experience Is The Best Teacher

Who has not heard that old adage? No one would deny its popularity. It is a very useful expression, actually. If someone makes a serious mistake, you may assuage his or her embarrassment with a simple pronouncement. "Oh well, experience is the best teacher." If another guy brags about his recent success, but you know full well that he has had many failures along the way, you can re-instill a note of reality. "Right, experience is the best teacher."

We use this marvelous phrase in many ways to explain many things with a variety of results. Its usefulness is limited only by one's imagination and resourcefulness. So far as it concerns me, it needs no modification, no limiting adjectives, and certainly no revision. But that's too much to ask. Many people have observed that the school of hard knocks is not such a great academy to attend if you wish to avoid some bumps and bruises. A bloodied nose is serious enough but it could be, just as easily, a broken nose. Clearly the school of hard knocks can damage your pride all the way to the psyche. It can wrack your emotions with wild abandon. It can wreak havoc on your wallet and leave you tattered and torn, physically, emotionally, and financially.

Those of us who have attended this infamous institution, and survived it, like to brag about it a little. "Yeah, I got my undergraduate degree at university, my masters degree from the school of hard knocks, and a Ph.D., from the street." Those who deal with people every day will recognize *the street*.

Some of us, perhaps most of us, go back on a regular basis to take refresher courses. Hopefully, we do not learn the same lesson over and over again. If one bloody nose does not teach you to duck next time around, you may have a problem. The new lesson comes just as you congratulate yourself on your knowledge garnered from your previous experience. The thought dances through your brain, "Ha, I saw that coming from a mile away," just before the lights go out, that is, your lights go out. Later you awaken with a mild concussion from ducking your head into a door jam while attempting to avoid the blow to the nose.

At least now you have learned two lessons and you did not make the same mistake twice. That is not your style. There are so many new lessons that we can learn on the street, in the school of hard knocks, that there is no time to mess with a repeat of the old ones. Once around the circuit with each mistake is enough for a great mind like yours.

Well, just about the time you think you have the process under control, so you can avoid serious injuries, emotional, physical, or financial, some wag, a professional speaker or an author of great books on inspiration, drops another insightful bromide on you. “Experience may be a great teacher, but you should learn from other people’s mistakes.”

Of course! Let other people get the experience and make the mistakes.You can observe those who are foolish enough to try something new, see the folly of their efforts, and avoid the humiliating feeling of defeat. You can read everything on the topic, learn about all the pitfalls and how to avoid them. You can study about the proper methods to accomplish your goals. You can listen to polished speakers, or at least, those who have been there and done that. Why should you make mistakes, if you can learn from the experience of others?

That sounds so erudite! It is glib and learned, clever and intellectually appealing. But, what if you want to try something beyond the level of the available knowledge? If Edison had not failed 999 times to make a light bulb, would we still read from the light of a flickering kerosene lamp?

Of course, Edison denied that he failed so many times. His explanation was poetry, pure and simple. He saw his efforts as something quite different from failure. He claimed that he succeeded in inventing 999 ways that a light bulb would not work.

Let’s apply this other-peoples-mistakes philosophy to hockey. Would you study a book about stick handling by Eddie Shack? No, definitely not, but if you could skate like Shack, stick handling would not be so important. However, to learn about handling the puck, you could read a book by Wayne Gretzky. You could watch films showing Bobby Orr, Mario Lemeaux, and Wayne working their magic. Astute as you are, you would learn a great deal, but even so, you still would not be able to do it. You would not be nearly as adept at it as those who practised, practised and practised. The knowledge in your mind will not translate to action in your arms and legs until you practise.

You cannot learn to skate reading about it. You cannot learn to stick handle watching the great players. You cannot learn to play basketball by watching Magic Johnson or Michael Jordan in action. You cannot learn to golf like Tiger Woods sitting in front of your TV. In fact, we may never excel in anything unless we try and fail. Somebody really clever, like Vince Lombardi, said: "It's not how often we fall that matters. It's how often we get up that counts." Learning to skate, without learning to fall would be foolish. Great skaters fall. Great hitters in baseball strike out at the plate. Great golfers make dumb shots.

Cowboys have a great line, "There's never been a bronc (a bucking horse) that can't be rode. There's never been a cowboy that can't be throwed." Well, cowboys never learned to ride sitting in the stands, and before they learned to stay on they got *throwed* many times. You may query am I trying to say that a cowboy cannot learn from another's mistakes? Not at all! There is a school for would-be cowboys. The instructor can show you how to wrap the rope around your hand. He can show you how to grip it using your powerful arm muscles. He can show you how to dig in with your spurs and balance against the upward thrust of a ton of thrashing fury. He can warn you against the twists and turns and leaps and kicks and how to *flow with the go*. You can watch all the great riders and study their techniques. You can learn to recognize the mistakes they made that caused their ignominious dismounts. You can observe every positive successful ride, but know this, the first time you get up there and the chute opens, you are going to get *throwed*. Moreover, before you learn to ride, you will get *throwed* and *throwed* and *throwed*.

It matters not what you do in life, you cannot master it from the sidelines. You must take action. You cannot learn to balance a bicycle standing still. It must be in motion. Eventually, when you have learned to balance a moving bike, you may be able to maintain your balance after you stop, for a brief moment at least.

Everyone says that no writer can write a great book without a good editor. That may be so, but I wonder who edited Shakespeare's material. I also wonder who first made that comment—probably an editor, right? Apparently Samuel Clements, known as Mark Twain, published *Huck Finn* himself because he did not like what the editors tried to do to his first book—*Tom Sawyer*. Nevertheless, an editor can be vital to the success of most authors. There is no question in my mind that a writer can learn from the experiences of others. However, a writer must write if he or she wants to develop the skills of writing. The trick is to learn the techniques while retaining ones own uniqueness, in spite of the editors.

Frequently, I have heard outstanding speakers claim that by reading and studying the best books on a topic you can become an expert on any subject. Perhaps to a point, you could talk like an expert and sound knowledgeable if the material you studied was based on real experience. With an outstanding delivery you may convince the majority that you are an expert. But, you can read about it and talk about it forever and you still will not be able to skate and stick handle, until you practise, practise, practise. Consider something else, when you get your knowledge from books you are borrowing the credentials of the authors. Have you studied authorities with experience or have they simply usurped the knowledge for which you search from someone else? You could find yourself delivering someone else's opinion, whose knowledge based on experience is no greater than your own. You may be advancing a viewpoint or a theory that is not accurate and you may do so much better than the original proponent of the concept.

Warren Buffett is reputedly the greatest investor in America. He speaks with authority, and when he does everybody listens. He is a legend in the investment world. However, an analyst studied Mr. Buffett's portfolio and made the following statement. *If you removed the best fifteen transactions from the hundreds of investments Warren has made, the result would be mediocrity.*

The point is that Warren Buffett has become an enormously wealthy guru and he has carried a large number of people up that trail using a system of trial and error. Mr. Buffet achieved his success and his knowledge from making his own mistakes. By learning what not to do, he is now an expert on what to do. Can you and I learn from the knowledge and insights of Mr. Buffett? Of course we can. If you follow his advice assiduously will you be right every time? No! Definitely not! You may study every word written by Mr. Buffett, or about the Buffett method—known as Buffettology. However you could never learn the precision, the timing, nor the instincts of a Warren Buffett except by doing it for yourself. You have to make your own mistakes to become the guru.

You and I can learn from the mistakes and the experiences of others if, and only if, we are trying our best. If you struggle in the school of hard knocks and you gain new insights from the experience of others at the appropriate time, your growth and development can be accelerated. Learning from others while getting first hand experience reduces the steepness of the learning curve appreciably.

Experience is the best teacher, is a truism that we cannot deny. You cannot learn effectively from someone else until you discover what it is that you do not know. Combining the efforts of the student with the experience of the mentor often results in the student surpassing the skills of the teacher. There are two kinds of experience, yours and that of others. You can learn from both but you will learn best and most from combining both sources of information simultaneously. It *is* like riding and balancing a bicycle. You can do it more effectively if you are in motion.

Can you really explain to a fish what it is like to walk on land? One day on land is worth a thousand years of talking about it, and one day running a business has exactly the same kind of value.

~Warren Buffett

Warren Buffett Speaks... by Janet Lowe.

In A Vacuum You Cannot Hear

Have you ever tried to make a stubborn mule listen?

How often have we heard this inane bromide, *you were given two ears and only one mouth so that means you should listen twice as much as you talk.*

Besides being tired, overused, and trite, this statement is anatomically incorrect and biologically ridiculous. You cannot *listen* with your ears. Ears, by design, receive vibrations and transmit signals. We learned *that* in high school, but it would seem that we did not listen.

The statement that we have two ears so we would *listen* twice as much as we speak is cute. And I agree, the message to the listener is clear. If we want to learn from someone we need to *listen* to what she says.

Hearing the spoken word is not *listening* any more than seeing the written word is reading. You do not need to see words with your eyes in order to read. There are many other ways to *read* words. One of the best is by *feeling*—feeling symbols with your finger tips. If you had eighteen fingers and four thumbs, could you *read* better? Maybe you could if they would help you hold the book steadier. Can you read better with two eyes than you can with only one? Probably! Slightly! That is not to say that two eyes are not better than one. Of course two eyes are marginally better, but people with only one eye can adapt very well—and one good ear is likewise quite enough.

Ears are for hearing—not listening. If we were expected to hear better our ears should have been ten times as long and mounted on swivels, like a mule's ears.

Now, surely you would not argue that you can hear better than a mule. A mule can hear a pin drop in a stack of hay. A mule can point one ear forward and the other one backward, simultaneously. A mule can point both ears forward, upward, outward, or lay them flat back along its neck.

You cannot even be there if you do not want a mule to hear you.

It does not take a genius to make a mule hear what you say. If you move your lips, while reading in the presence of a mule, be very careful about the context of your material. Mules are very sensitive. You can hurt their feelings very easily and you will know when you have done that. *It makes them very stubborn*. Have you ever tried to make a stubborn mule listen?

How about that notorious conundrum, *if a tree falls in the forest and there is no one present to hear it fall, does it make a noise?* Or, *if your spouse is not with you, in the forest when the tree falls, does he or she win the argument anyway?*

It saddens me slightly to dispel the inaccuracies suggested in these statements, and to destroy the playful humor involved. Nevertheless, it serves my purpose here to do so. *Anyway, I suspect that most people will not listen to my arguments*. Have you ever tried to understand a foreign language—a language of which you know not one word? You try to listen to the words being spoken but you cannot do it. What you *hear* is a garble of meaningless noise no more intelligible than the burbling and the gurgling of a baby. That is an apt analogy because babies make all of the sounds necessary and basic to the development of speech, in any language. The inability to pronounce some syllables properly, later in life, comes from the lack of a need to use them. Most people could learn to make these difficult sounds again if they desired to do so. But, they would have to learn to listen.

As already stated, h*earing is not listening*. You can hear the babble of a foreign language without being able to discern even one separate word. Before you can understand the spoken word you must be able to separate the syllables of each word. It is a great feeling of accomplishment when you are able, at long last, to recognize individual words, and then phrases, or a series of words, portraying one thought. Only then can you begin to understand the meanings of the words and phrases and ultimately to comprehend the language.

You hear a new language and to make anything meaningful from it, you must learn to *listen* to the music of the words. You must *listen* to the nuance and the rhythm. *Your ears cannot do that.* Your ears can accept a cacophony of stimuli and they can isolate, or *zero in* on, specific vibrations as directed by your brain. However, your ears cannot separate, select, nor reject, any specific vibrations without the aid of your brain. When the tree falls in the forest, it sets up a flow of vibrations that the particles in the atmosphere carry to your ears. The stimuli flow outwardly in a similar way to the concentric ripples caused by a pebble dropped into a pond. These ripples or vibrations from the cracking twigs and limbs, and from the quake of the earth caused by the crash of the mighty trunk as it lands and then erupts into the space above it, and settles again to its final place of rest, albeit more gently this time, create a continuous noise pulsing outwardly and meaninglessly for any and all to hear.

Vibrations, like the rhythm of a wave, are silent until they crash on the waiting ear of a would-be listener. Our ears are receptors of vibrations and transmitters of signals. Without any attempt at modification or editing our ears translate this concussion of noise into signals that are appropriate for interpretation by our brains. There, they may be accepted or rejected, understood or questioned, catalogued or reacted upon.

Only meaningless noise results from the waves of vibrations striking the outer ear and stimulating the auditory nerves. Then that tiny drummer in the inner ear translates them into signals for the brain to interpret. These vibrations become sounds that you may interpret, evaluate, and use. Then they become meaningful *if* we wish to *listen*.

Everyone knows that the speed of light far exceeds the speed of sound. If you were watching from a distance as the tree falls in the forest, you could see the breaking twigs and the eruption of roots well before the *sound* could travel the air waves to your ears. However, if everything between the tree and yourself were in a vacuum, you would see the tree fall but you would never hear it. You cannot *hear* in a vacuum.

If you want to listen to someone's words, he or she cannot merely command, as did Antony, "Friends, Romans, countrymen, lend me your ears." Julius Ceasar; Act III, Scene II.

Of course, we understand from that command that Antony wanted his audience to listen with their minds alert. However, his *countrymen* could have sat there attentively without hearing a word that he spoke, if they did not listen. They could have *shut off* that switch between their ears and their minds.

We can all do it, that is, shut-off or tune out. To listen we must focus our attention on the speaker's words. We can hear much faster than any speaker can talk. We can process the information and react to it, positively or negatively, before the speaker finishes the vocalization of his or her thought. We can receive and process thousands of bits of information in very short periods of time. However, non-pertinent external vibrations, or worse, our internal personalized thoughts, can distract us.

It is my experience that a good listener:

- Looks directly at the speaker;
  Paying attention is more than staring at physical features.
- Focuses on the speakers thoughts;
  You should not be lulled by the lilt of the words.
- Asks questions;
  In a group write your questions down to be asked later.
- Takes notes selectively;
  One useful idea is more valuable than a page of scribbles.
- Does not interrupt the speaker's thoughts;
  Wait for your turn to speak.
- Controls emotions;
  Too much reaction gives the speaker to much control.
- Is responsive;
  Provide appropriate feedback to the speaker.

Even though you anticipate, and you are sure you know what the speaker will say, it's impolite to interrupt. Furthermore, the speaker may have a need to say it aloud if only to see how it sounds that way. If you allow yourself to daydream or tune out or if you only fake attention, you are wasting your time. If you become too emotionally involved you may fail to grasp the intent of the speaker.

Taking notes obsessively, as we did in college, is a form of tuning out.By writing the speaker's words down without processing the thought behind them, we avoid responsive listening.

Listening is so much more than *hearing* the speaker's words. In order to *listen,* your mind must be present. To listen, you must process the speaker's thought, grasp his or her meaning, internalize it, and catalogue it for future use. You may accept these words or challenge and question them, but you need to actively process them. Questioning the speaker's thinking is a process based on a need to get clarification. Also, questioning may be a way of expressing doubt as to the veracity, accuracy, or value, of the information. Listening critically is not necessarily the same as being critical of the speaker's thinking. In fact, it is a valid approach to fully grasping the intent of the message. It depends on your attitude.

Give me one good ear to hear, and an alert attentive mind, and I will tell you the secret to making a stubborn mule listen.

You gotta get his attention.

Quick Reference Glossary of Terms

The jargon and industry expressions used by financial advisors, authors, writers, and journalists, can be confusing. Sometimes, even sales people use certain terms or phrases in a slightly different context with a very different meaning. The definitions of the following terms and phrases reflect their meanings or usages as they apply in this book.

Accident and sickness: Otherwise known as disability insurance, it is intended to replace earned income in the event that the insured is unable to pursue a livelihood due to a sickness or an accident. In other words, it provides an income when the insured person is unable to work.

Accidental Death Insurance: refers to an additional amount of money payable by an insurer in the event the person whose life is insured dies by accidental means. Some people are confused by this optional extra benefit and sometimes believe that the basic policy does not cover death by accident. This benefit is sometimes referred to as double indemnity. In other words, if death occurs by accidental means as opposed to natural causes, the company pays double the basic value or applied for amount.

Actuary: An actuary is someone who calculates risks and projects insurance premium requirements for various classes of risks. Moreover, actuaries are mathematicians who are involved in most of the financial matters of a company. They are especially concerned with matters of profitability, financial reserves, company stability, reports to the board of directors and shareholders, annual reports and government reports. They are not "odds-makers" as other writers refer to them facetiously.

Advisor: Financial advisor, tax advisor, investment advisor refers in this text to those who offer information or advice for fees or otherwise. There is an expectation that an advisor offers more than merely sales advice.

After Tax: This phrase refers to taxable investments which are adjusted for the effects of taxation.

Agent: Many authors use the dictionary definition as: one who acts on behalf of another person or a company. Some writers have claimed that the agent acts solely for the company. In practice the insurance agent is the intermediary or catalyst between the two parties. He or she represents one or more companies and their products to the client and presents the risk to the company. Contrary to most dire warnings, any conflict of interest is more imaginary than real.

Annuitant: a person receiving the annuity or the one who has the right to receive these payments.

Annuity: a periodic contractual payment of money usually of a fixed or specified amount during the holder's lifetime. The minimum number of payments may be guaranteed. There are several options available.

Application: the form which provides information to the company about the client; his or her health; the amount of insurance and the type of plan; investment options; and the statement of health and habits, is known as the application. It is a legal document and forms part of the contract.

Asset Allocation: is the designation of the deposit(s) into various types of investments or risk categories. It takes into account an individual's age, needs, goals and level of risk tolerance.

Attribution rules: These rules were made to prevent income splitting. Even though certain income may be directed to a person in a lower tax bracket, the income will still be taxed in the hands of the person from whom it was diverted.

Average: When applied to stocks, it is an indication of market performance. Examples are: The Dow Jones industrial average; The Standard and Poors index (S&P 500); The Toronto Stock Exchange (TSE300 or TSE35). These indexes provide a measure of the state of the stock market or of the economy based on the performance of stocks.

Back-end load: refers to a redemption charge which applies to mutual funds or segregated funds which may apply for between four to ten years. This charge reduces annually until at the end of the period specified there is no further charge. Some people refer to a back-end load fund as a no-load fund. Knowledgeable people disagree with this definition, of course.

Basis point: A basis point is 1/100 of a percentage point. It is used to express bond yields and also the management and administration charges for mutual/segregated funds.

Bear market: a market condition in which the representative stocks are declining in value.

Beneficiary: is a person, other than the insured, to whom the insurance money is made payable in the contract or by declaration. A beneficiary declaration may be: one's estate, an individual, a company or an institution.

Broker: see life insurance broker and stock broker.

Bull Market: As opposed to a bear market, this refers to a market whose index has been rising in value.

Capital Gain: the profit resulting from the sale of capital investments. It results from the sale of real estate, stocks, bonds or other capital assets where the sale price is higher than the purchase price.

Capital loss: any loss that results from the sale of a capital asset at a price below the purchase price.

Certificate of deposit (CD): a deposit with a specified maturity date.
Commission: compensation paid for the selling of a service or product. It is usually expressed as a percentage of the deposit.
Compound Interest: When interest is paid on the initial deposit or principal as well as on any accumulated of previously earned interest, the result is referred to a compound interest. Usually, the interest paid on the accrued interest is at the same rate as is applicable to principal. However, sometimes the interest earned is reinvested at the current rate. Obviously this is advantageous to the investor during periods of increasing rates, but disadvantageous during periods of declining rates.
Consumer Price Index (CPI): This is a statistical measure of the increase in the cost of living for consumers.
Contract: In insurance law, a contract refers to a policy, a certificate, an interim receipt, a renewal receipt, or writing evidencing the contract, and a binding oral agreement. When we use the term, it means a contract of life insurance.
Convertible: This could be the condition attached to a security, such as a bond or a debenture, or to a preferred share. In the case of the preferred share, the usual meaning is that the share may be exchanged for common shares depending upon the conversion privilege
Convertible Term Insurance: means that a term life insurance policy may be changed to other plans as described in that section of the policy contract. A policy may be convertible to a different kind of term insurance or any so-called permanent plans (as described under Permanent, Whole Life, Interest Sensitive, Variable and/or Universal).

Declaration: an instrument signed by the insured with respect to insurability, or an endorsement on the policy, or any alteration or revocation of beneficiary designation.
Decreasing Term: any type of term insurance which reduces monthly or annually while the premium remains constant.
Deferred Annuity: as opposed to an immediate annuity, refers to payments which begin at a later date.
Deferred Profit Sharing Plan (DPSP): refers to a plan that allows a company to share profits with employees who are not shareholders.
Defined Benefit Plan: a pension program in which the retirement benefits are determined by a formula based on salary and years of service.
Disability Insurance: insurance undertaken by an insurer as part of a contract whereby the insurer agrees to pay a sum of money in the event that the insured person becomes disabled as a result of bodily injury or disease. (See also Accident and Sickness)
Diversification: a spreading of risk by buying a variety of stocks in different companies or industries and/or countries. It is achieved with mutual/segregated

funds by selecting several different funds in a given family of funds or alternately by a selection of several different funds.

Dividend: the most common meaning of the word in the financial world is the portion of a company's profit which is paid out to common and preferred shareholders. It may be in the form of cash or additional stock. In life insurance jargon, a dividend is a participation in the divisible surplus of a company's reserve. This is an amount determined by the chief actuary.

Dollar Cost Averaging: a process of buying securities at regular intervals with specific and equal dollar amounts. This approach allows the buyer to buy units or stocks during both upward and downward trends.

Earned Income: refers basically to the total income from employment, self-employment, pensions, and alimony.

Equities: shares in a company that represent ownership. Both common and preferred shares are equity stock.

Estate: All of the assets owned by an individual at the time of death form part of the estate. Certain assets such as life insurance and jointly owned property with a named beneficiary will pass outside the estate for probate purposes.

Face Value: the death benefit as it appears on the face of the policy. With bonds or debentures, it also means the amount due at maturity.

Family Insurance: insurance whereby the insured and one or more persons related to the insured, by blood, marriage or adoption, are insured under a single contract.

Fixed Income Funds: mutual funds or segregated funds that invest in combinations of mortgages, bonds, or preferred stocks. Fixed Term usually refers to an annuity with a stipulated period such as to age 90.

Fraternal Society: means a society, order or association incorporated for the purpose of making contracts for life or accident and sickness insurance in accordance with its constitution, by-laws and rules. The products offered are for members only and not for profit.

Front-end load: refers to the amount charged by a company to cover sales commissions and management overrides. These are in the 4% to 5% range.

GIC: A Guaranteed Investment Certificate represents a deposit issued by a financial institution for a specified period at a guaranteed rate of interest.

Growth Stock: refers to the stock of companies whose earnings are expected to grow faster than the average of similar businesses.

Guaranteed Income Funds: offered by mutual funds and segregated funds that invest in term deposits and guaranteed income certificates.

Holographic Will: a will prepared in an individuals own handwriting and signed by that individual. It may not be valid in some areas.

Income Splitting: the practice of diverting taxable income from an individual in a higher tax bracket to one in a lower tax bracket.

Incontestable clause: Every life insurance policy contains a clause which allows the company to reconsider the policy if pertinent information comes to their attention that should have been disclosed to the company at the time of application. After two years, this clause is no longer in effect except in the case of fraud. Fraud is a deliberate attempt to mislead the company by knowingly withholding information which would affect the issuance of a policy.

Institutional Investors: large investors such as insurance companies, pension funds, trust companies and mutual funds.

Instrument: as applied in insurance law, section 171 of the act, includes a will which may be used to make a beneficiary designation.

Insurance: as provided in the act, Section 1, provides that insurance means the undertaking by one person to indemnify another person against loss. As per Section 171, insurance means life insurance.

Insured: means the person who makes a contract with an insurer, except in the case of group insurance where it relates to the designation of beneficiaries and to the rights and status of beneficiaries.

Insurer: means the person who undertakes or agrees or offers to undertake a contract.

Inter-vivos trust: a living trust created during one's lifetime to minimize probate expenses by passing assets directly to beneficiaries.

Intestate: a reference to someone who dies without leaving a valid will.

Joint and last survivor: is a type of annuity which provides an income until both the annuitant and his or her spouse dies.

Leverage: the concept of leveraging is based on the use of borrowed money, preferably at a low rate of interest, to be invested in order to obtain a higher rate of return.

Life Income Fund (LIF): A LIF provides an alternative method of payment to a life annuity for funds from a locked-in annuity. Under a LIF there is a maximum as well as a minimum amount that can be withdrawn each year until age 80. The benefit of a LIF is flexibility of investments and withdrawals.

Locked-in Retirement Account (LIRA): is an account which is set up to receive locked-in funds from a registered pension plan.

Locked-in RRSP: Pension legislation requires that funds transferred from a pension plan be made to a locked-in RRSP.

Life Broker: a life insurance advisor who sells for multiple companies.

Management Fee: the sum paid to the investment manager for services such as management and administration of the fund. This fee is usually a percentage of the total fund.
Maturity: Loans, bonds and debentures each have a maturity date at which time proceeds become payable in full. With segregated funds, the significance of the maturity date is as it applies to the guarantees.
Money Market: a term which usually applies to short term fixed interest instruments such as government bonds, treasury bills and commercial paper.
Money Market Fund: mutual funds and/or segregated funds which invest in fixed income and short term securities.
Money Purchase Plan: a type of pension plan wherein employees purchase retirement benefits which are based on contributions.
Mutual Funds: any pooled group of assets providing diversification and professional management.

No-Load Fund: any mutual fund or segregated fund where there are no sales charges or redemption charges levied for buying or selling.

Power of Attorney: an instrument which gives signing authority for your assets to a spouse or another trusted person in case of any incapacitation which leaves you unable to manage your own affairs.
Prescribed Annuity: provides a guaranteed income in which regular payments of principal and interest are made to an annuitant.
Principal: the amount of the deposit to a fund or contract.
Prospectus: a legal document which describes the fund or security. It contains information regarding the funds investment objectives, management fees and other pertinent details.
Pure term: an actuarial calculation of the actual costs of death, at each specific age, before adjustments are made for related costs for reserves, expenses and profits. No such product is available for sale.

Registered Education Savings Plan (RESP): a savings plan designed to make provision for post-secondary education. The benefit of this savings plan is that it earns tax-sheltered income which is taxable in the hands of the recipient.
Registered Pension Plan (RPP) is a private pension plan established for employees for retirement purposes.
Registered Retirement Income Fund (RRIF): an alternative investment vehicle to an annuity which can be used for maturing RRSPs. The most significant benefit of a RRIF is its flexibility: (a) in variety of investment options; (b) in variable withdrawal amounts. A minimum withdrawal is required annually to age 90, but there is no restriction on the maximum that may be withdrawn.
Registered Retirement Savings Plan (RRSP): a government approved

savings program that permits tax-deferred savings for retirement purposes. The significant benefit is that deposits are tax deductible and earnings are sheltered within the plan. All withdrawals are taxable as income.

Reverse Mortgage: a serious financial commitment that is intended to provide an income. It carries an obligation for life. Most strategies currently involve a re-mortgaging of a residence and the purchase of an annuity. It should not be considered until all other solutions are reviewed.

Risk: the possibility that an investment will not achieve its expected return. A generally accepted concept is that the higher the reward expected, the greater the risk involved.

Self-Directed RRSP: one in which the plan holder directs all investment transactions. It may include stocks, bonds, residential mortgages or other types of investments approved by the government.

Speculation: refers to investment in speculative or high risk stocks or other non-proven investment vehicles.

Spousal RRSP: contributions are those made by a taxpayer to an RRSP held by his or her spouse, usually in a lower tax bracket. This contribution forms part of the tax payers total RRSP limit.

Stock Broker: refers to someone who sells stocks, bonds, mutual funds, GIC,s and other investment vehicles.

Suicide Clause: during the first two years after a policy is issued, suicide is excluded. Thereafter, the policy will pay even in the event of suicide.

Tax Shelter: any investment that has government approval to defer taxes to a later date. The advantage is that earnings may accrue within the plan tax free until they are withdrawn.

Taxable Income: one's total earnings from all sources, including employment income, interest on investments, and realized or deemed realized capital gains.

Term Deposit: a similar instrument to a guaranteed investment certificate (GIC). It is an interest paying investment to which the investor commits funds for a specified period of time at a guaranteed interest rate.

Term Insurance: or temporary insurance. The dictionary meaning of term is a period of time having definite limits; the time during which anything lasts. Usually the type of plan is defined by its name or description.

Example: One Year Term; 10 Year Term; Term to age 65.

- *Renewable Term* means you have an option to renew the insurance at a new rate for an extension of time equal to the original period, i.e., term 5 would renew for an additional five years.
- *Convertible Term* is a second option. If your plan has this feature, you may change it to any of the companies non-term plans without evidence of good health. Some plans allow this conversion or change to be made to Term 100. In most of the plans offered today,

these features, renewability and convertibility, are not optional. Most term plans become progressively more expensive as the clients' age increases. Very few term plans have cash values, paid up values, or other non-forfeiture benefits. Consequently, if you do not pay the premium within thirty days after the premium due date, the policy will lapse. A statement of continued good health is required for reinstatement.

NB. When you re-apply for new coverage to maintain the lowest rate available and/or when you re-instate a lapsed policy, the **suicide** and **incontestable** restrictions start over.

Term to age 100: in its purest form has no cash values nor paid up values. The payor simply pays the premium until death or to age 100 whichever is longer. Can you imagine paying this premium for sixty years (to age 100) and then living one year longer? Most plans, therefore, have a built in feature that at age 100, the policy is paid-in-full. Some of these plans also have a reduced paid up benefit starting at age 75. To complicate matters, some plans also have cash values after a certain date.

Reducing Term: or in the jargon of the industry, disappearing term, is not as popular currently as it was thirty years ago. The most common usage today is for mortgage insurance.

Other forms of term insurance:

- *Group life* is one of the features of group insurance along with accidental death and dismemberment, family coverage, disability income, extended health, and dental.
- *Creditor Insurance* is a form of group life. It mirrors the exact amount of debt, i.e., it is reducing term. It is non-renewable, non-convertible, and not portable.
- *Mass-Marketed Insurance* is a form of group life, but it is only available to individuals within a group, i.e., engineer's group. It usually has automatic renewal provisions. It may be either convertible or non-convertible. It may carry on past age 65 at a significant reduction in death benefit.
- *Accidental Death and Dismemberment*: This benefit may be offered as a rider or as a separate policy. Exactly as it sounds, it pays on claims from accidents only. There are many exclusions therefore, and it should not be considered as a substitute for life insurance. If you need it for accidental death, you probably should have coverage that pays out for any death.

Testamentary Trust: a trust established by a will. In the will, the testator may specify that certain assets are to be held in trust for a person or for several people. The will would also name a trustee to manage the trust.

Trust: A trust is an instrument that places ownership of property in the name of a person or a company, known as the trustee, to be held and managed for the benefit of another person or for two or more people.

Units: Mutual funds and segregated funds sell *units* in the fund. Each unit represents a portion or share of the total fund value. The number of units multiplied by the unit value determines the dollar value of the investment.

Universal Life: or variable interest sensitive plans are currently in vogue. The original meaning of universal life has been obscured somewhat until the current plans resemble the early concept in name only. The current version is really a hybrid or combination of term insurance and whole life. The basic guarantees of whole life are included without the restriction of minimal guaranteed earnings. The reserve may be tied to any of several indexes, at the option of the owner. This allows for the potential of a higher return than would be available on a basic whole life plan. One benefit of note is that the tax free death benefit increases by the amount of the cash value.

Vesting: applies to the ownership rights in your pension plan including the employer's contribution. This occurs automatically after a certain number of years of service.

Whole Life: (also referred to as **permanent insurance**.) In its purest sense, means life insurance for one's lifetime. In that sense, term to age 100 qualifies as whole life. Most people, however, think of whole life as plans which include non-forfeiture values such as cash value, loan value, and paid up value.
Variations of whole life are: premiums payable to age 100 or prior death; whole life payable to age 65; 20 pay whole life; or whole life paid at age 65.

Yearly Renewable Term (YRT)**:** any policy on which the premium increases each year.

Sources Of Information

- Brandes, Charles H. ~ *Value Investing Today*
- Buffett, Mary and
  Clark, David ~ *Buffettology*
- Byfield, Ted ~ *The Alberta Report*
- Clason, George S. ~ *The Richest Man In Babylon*
- Cohen, Bruce ~ *The Money Advisor*
- Cunningham, Timothy and
  Mansfield, Clay ~ *Pay Yourself First*
- Dacey, Norman ~ *What's Wrong With Your Life Insurance*
- Gadsden. Stephen ~ *Life Cycle Investing*
- KPMG ~ *Tax Planning For You and Your Family*
- Lowe, Janet ~ *Warren Buffett Speaks*
- Lynch, Peter ~ *One Up On Wall Street*
- Manery, Lyle ~ *No Salesman Will Call?*
- Paterson, John ~ *Russian Roulette Gambling with Disability*
- Pedoe, Arthur and
  Rudd, D.S. ~ *Life Insurance and Annuities In Canada*
- Reddin, W.J. ~ *Successful Spending Saving and Investing*
- Savage, John ~ *The Easy Sale*
- Tyrwhitt Janice ~ *Small Things Grow Great*
- Vaz-Oxlade, Gail ~ *The Retirement Answer Book*

- Fire Insurance and Marine Insurance
  from
  The Insurance Institute of Canada
- Personal Finanacial Planners Manual
  from
  The canadian Institute of Chartered Accountants
- The Canadian Institute of Chartered Life Underwriters
  and
  CharteredFinancial Consultants
- The MDRT Annuity Sales manual

ABOUT THE AUTHOR

Lyle Manery, B.A., CLU, CH.F.C.

- **Life Insurance Career began in Head Office May 13, 1956, as Editor of Company Publications**
- **Graduate, University of Western Ontario ~ Major in Psychology**
- **Graduate, Purdue University ~ Life Insurance Marketing Institute**
- **Chartered Life Underwriter (CLU)**
- **Chartered Financial Consultant (CH.F.C.)**
- **Life Member Million Dollar Round Table**
- **Top of the Table - qualified twice**
- **Experience: * Head Office**
  - *** Sales Management**
  - *** Branch Management**
  - *** Regional Supt. of General Insurance Agencies**
  - *** Managing General Agent**

- **AUTHOR**
  - *** Eclectic Mushrooms for the Wealthy Network Marketer**
  - *** No Salesman Will Call?**
  - *** Network Marketing SUCCESS for everyone**
  - *** Legends Lies Myths - Financial Planning**

- **SPEAKER**
  - *** Available for Keynotes and Sales Training Seminars**
  - *** Member of Canadian Association of Professional Speakers (CAPS), Calgary Chapter**